AF805271

Explaining and Illustrating the *Laozi*

OXFORD CHINESE THOUGHT

Series Editors
Eric L. Hutton and Justin Tiwald

Explaining and Illustrating the *Laozi*
The Earliest Commentaries on the Daodejing
Edited by Eirik Lang Harris and Eric L. Hutton

Xiong Shili's *Treatise on Reality and Function*
Edited and translated by John Makeham

The *Daode jing* Commentary of Cheng Xuanying
Daoism, Buddhism, and the Laozi *in the Tang Dynasty*
Translated by Friederike Assandri

Treatise on Awakening Mahāyāna Faith
Edited and translated by John Jorgensen, Dan Lusthaus,
John Makeham, and Mark Strange

Zhu Xi
Selected Writings
Edited by Philip J. Ivanhoe

Explaining and Illustrating the *Laozi*

The Earliest Commentaries on the Daodejing

Edited by
EIRIK LANG HARRIS
ERIC L. HUTTON

OXFORD
UNIVERSITY PRESS

OXFORD
UNIVERSITY PRESS

Oxford University Press is a department of the University of Oxford.
It furthers the University's objective of excellence in research, scholarship,
and education by publishing worldwide. Oxford is a registered trade mark of
Oxford University Press in the UK and in certain other countries.

Published in the United States of America by Oxford University Press
546 Fifth Avenue, New York, NY 10036, United States of America

Library of Congress Cataloging-in-Publication Data
Names: Harris, Eirik Lang editor | Hutton, Eric L. editor |
Laozi. Dao de jing. English
Title: Explaining and illustrating the *Laozi*: the earliest commentaries
on the *Daodejing* / edited by Eirik Lang Harris and Eric L. Hutton.
Description: 1. | New York, NY, United States of America :
Oxford University Press, [2026] | Series: Oxford Chinese thought |
Includes bibliographical references and index.
Identifiers: LCCN 2026010908 (print) | LCCN 2026010909 (ebook) |
ISBN 9780197514917 paperback | ISBN 9780197514900 hardback |
ISBN 9780197514948 | ISBN 9780197514931 epub
Subjects: LCSH: Laozi. Dao de jing
Classification: LCC BL1900.L35 E9713 2026 (print) | LCC BL1900.L35 (ebook)
LC record available at https://lccn.loc.gov/2026010908
LC ebook record available at https://lccn.loc.gov/2026010909

DOI: 10.1093/9780197514948.001.0001

Paperback printed by Marquis Book Printing, Canada
Hardback printed by Lightning Source, Inc., United States of America

The manufacturer's authorized representative in the EU for product safety is
Oxford University Press España S.A. of El Parque Empresarial San Fernando de Henares,
Avenida de Castilla, 2 – 28830 Madrid (www.oup.es/en or product.safety@oup.com).
OUP España S.A. also acts as importer into Spain of products made by the manufacturer.

MIX
Paper | Supporting responsible forestry
FSC
www.fsc.org
FSC® C103567

Contents

Series Editors' Foreword

Eric L. Hutton and Justin Tiwald

Chinese writings from pre-modern times constitute a vast body of texts stretching back over 2,500 years. This corpus is one of the richest in human history, measured in terms of the variety and depth of the philosophical and religious views it contains. While Western studies of China have been growing, however, many riches from the Chinese tradition have remained untranslated or have been given only partial translations, sometimes scattered across multiple publication venues. This situation obviously poses a problem for those who want to learn about Chinese thought but lack the ability to read Chinese. Moreover, it also poses a problem even for scholars who specialize in Chinese thought and can read Chinese, because it is not easy to read across all the time periods and genres in the Chinese corpus. Not only did the Chinese language change over time, but in some genres particular vocabularies are developed and familiarity with certain earlier texts—sometimes quite a large number of texts—is presumed. For this reason, scholars who focus on one tradition of Chinese thought from a given era cannot simply pick up and immediately understand texts from a different tradition of thought in another era. The lack of translations is thus an impediment even to specialists who can read Chinese but wish to learn about aspects of Chinese thought outside their normal purview. Furthermore, scholars are often hampered in their teaching by the lack of translations that they can assign to students, which then becomes a barrier to promoting greater understanding of Chinese history and culture among the general public.

By offering English translations of Chinese texts with philosophical and religious significance, Oxford Chinese Thought aims to remedy these problems and make available to the general public, university students, and scholars a treasure trove of materials that has previously been largely inaccessible. The series focuses on works that are historically important or stand to make significant contributions to contemporary discussions, and the translations seek to strike a reasonable balance between the interests of specialists and the needs of general readers and students with no skills in Chinese. Translators for the series are leading scholars and experts in the traditions and texts that they render, and the volumes are meant to be suitable for classroom use while meeting the highest standards of scholarship.

We are pleased to add the present volume to the list of titles in our series, and hope that it will help foster in readers a heightened appreciation for the wealth of insights to be found among Chinese texts, as well as inspire them with a desire to explore Chinese thought further. We look forward to presenting readers with more gems from the Chinese tradition, such as this one.

Acknowledgments

This book started from a long-standing fascination with the "Jie Lao" and "Yu Lao" shared by Eirik Lang Harris and Eric L. Hutton. The two of us also regularly teach the *Han Feizi* at our respective institutions, and we had lamented to each other the lack of a student-friendly translation of those two chapters that we could present to our classes alongside other important pieces of the *Han Feizi* and other commentaries to the *Laozi*. As an undergraduate, Hutton had done a translation of the "Jie Lao" for a class project, and later revised it during graduate school, but then let it languish in a filing cabinet for many years. However, at one point, he had shown a copy to Harris, who liked it better than other translations of the text that he had seen, and Harris suggested trying to publish it in a volume that could serve the needs of our students. Thus was this project born.

The translation here is a vastly revised, improved, and expanded descendant of Hutton's early work. Over the years, it has benefited from the suggestions of many readers, too many to all be named individually here. However, he would like to thank especially the other contributors to this volume for their helpful comments, along with P. J. Ivanhoe, Michael Puett, Nalei Chen, Joonho Lee, Colin Lewis, Drew Ruble, the anonymous reviewers for Oxford University Press, and the students in Hutton's and Harris's classes who served as test audiences for earlier versions of the translation.

Hutton's work on this project was supported in part by a Charles H. Monson Award and a Sterling M. McMurrin Award from the

Department of Philosophy at the University of Utah, for which he expresses his gratitude.

The help of Nalei Chen, who served as Hutton's research assistant, is likewise gratefully acknowledged here. In addition, Harris expresses his appreciation for the funding he received from the endowment of the Department of Philosophy at Colorado State University in support of this book.

We would also like to thank Vergil Sun Tik Wong for his assistance in the preparation of the Chinese text that will accompany this volume on OUP's website, and we thank Justin Tiwald for providing financial support for Vergil's work.

Finally, we thank David Prout for his diligent work on composing the index.

About the Companion Website

www.oup.com/us/laozicommentaries

Oxford has created a website to accompany *Explaining and Illustrating the* Laozi. Material that cannot be made available in a book, namely the complete Chinese text on which these translations are based, is provided here. The reader is encouraged to consult this resource in conjunction with the chapters.

About the Contributors

Alan K. L. Chan is Provost and Kwan Im Thong Hood Cho Temple Chair Professor of Inter-Religious Studies and Harmony at Singapore Management University (SMU). Previously, he served as Provost and J.S. Lee Professor of Chinese Culture at the Chinese University of Hong Kong. His research focuses on classical Confucian and Daoist philosophy.

Eirik Lang Harris, an associate professor of philosophy at Colorado State University, focuses much of his research on examining differing conceptions of normativity in classical Chinese ethical and political thought, with a particular interest in understudied political realists. He is the author of *The Shenzi Fragments: A Philosophical Analysis and Translation* (Columbia, 2016) and *Meritocracy in Early Chinese Political Thought* (Cambridge, 2026), and co-editor of *Adventures in Chinese Realism: Classic Philosophy Applied to Contemporary Issues* (SUNY Press, 2022).

Eric L. Hutton is Professor of Philosophy at the University of Utah. His research primarily concerns early Chinese thought, especially Confucianism. He also has strong interests both in ancient Greek philosophy—most specifically, the moral and political views of Plato and Aristotle—and in contemporary moral theory, especially virtue ethics. His major publications include *Xunzi: The Complete Text* (Princeton University Press, 2014) and the *Dao Companion to the Philosophy of Xunzi* (Springer, 2016).

Yuet Keung Lo is Adjunct Professor at the Institute of Chinese Studies of the Universiti Tunku Abdul Rahman in Malaysia and Numata Visiting Professor of Buddhist Studies at Leiden University. Many of his publications concern hermeneutical traditions in China, such as his book 文内文外—中國思想史中的經典詮釋 *Intratextual and Extratextual: Interpretations of Classics in Chinese Intellectual History* (National Taiwan University Press, 2010), another volume co-edited with Alan Chan, *Interpretation and Literature in Early Medieval China* (State University of New York Press, 2010), as well as numerous articles discussing Confucian and Buddhist commentaries on various Chinese texts.

Introduction

Eirik Lang Harris and Eric L. Hutton

The *Laozi* 老子, or *Daodejing* 道德經, as it is also known, is one of the most popular and influential texts to have been passed down from ancient China to present times. However, the text is also famously difficult to understand, and thus from very early on, people have been producing commentaries on it. Among the commentaries that have survived to the present, the "Jie Lao" 解老 ("Explaining the *Laozi*") and "Yu Lao" 喻老 ("Illustrating the *Laozi*") have a strong claim to be the most ancient, and hence to represent in the greatest detail how at least one reader who was fairly close in time to the initial formation of the *Laozi* construed its meaning. For this reason, the "Jie Lao" and "Yu Lao" should be of interest to anyone who is concerned to learn about how the *Laozi* was received in its own cultural and historical context. However, in providing commentary on the *Laozi*, the "Jie Lao" and "Yu Lao" articulate a set of ideas that are worth considering in their own right, independently of their relation to the *Laozi*, and hence these works also merit attention for their philosophical content.

For these and other reasons (to be discussed further below), the "Jie Lao" and "Yu Lao" are worthy of study, but previous English-language scholarship on these texts has done little to make them readily accessible to those outside the relatively small circle of specialists in Chinese thought. The present volume seeks to open these works up to a much broader audience, by providing annotated translations aimed at students and general readers, along with a

Eirik Lang Harris and Eric L. Hutton, *Introduction* In: *Explaining and Illustrating the* Laozi. Edited by: Eirik Lang Harris and Eric L. Hutton, Oxford University Press.
DOI: 10.1093/9780197514948.003.0001

handful of essays that will help readers to appreciate the place of the "Jie Lao" and "Yu Lao" within a number of different contexts of which they are part. Since the accompanying essays treat such issues at length, this introduction will focus on reviewing historical background information that is useful to know in approaching the commentaries, as well as highlighting some of the important ideas to note when reading them.

Before proceeding any further, though, a caution is in order. Although the "Jie Lao" and "Yu Lao" may be the earliest commentaries on the *Laozi*, they are not well suited to serve as a person's very first exposure to the *Laozi*, since—among other factors—they do not comment on the whole of the received version of the *Laozi*. For that reason, we recommend that readers who are wholly new to the *Laozi* first read one of the many complete translations of the received version that are available,[1] and then read the translations of the "Jie Lao" and "Yu Lao" here alongside that translation, for comparison.

I. The Origins of the "Jie Lao" and "Yu Lao"

The "Jie Lao" and "Yu Lao" have been transmitted to us as two chapters in a larger text, the *Han Feizi* 韓非子. That text is in turn named after a person, Han Feizi, whose thought it claims to record, and whom ancient sources report to have died in 233 BCE (his year of birth is unknown). It is in large part on the basis of this attribution to Han Feizi that the "Jie Lao" and "Yu Lao" are dated to

[1] There are literally hundreds of renderings of the *Daodejing* into English alone. Among those that we especially recommend to readers as good complements to this book are the translations by P. J. Ivanhoe (2003), D. C. Lau (1963), Richard Lynn (2004), and Arthur Waley (1963). For a recent attempt to give a comprehensive listing of all published translations of the *Daodejing*, see Tadd (2022), which lists a total of 2052 translations across 97 languages at the time that bibliography was compiled. The section there on English-language works presents a total count of 603 publications, of which 342 are categorized as direct translations from Chinese to English (Tadd 2022, 56).

the third century BCE and hence have come to be regarded as the earliest extant commentaries on the *Laozi*.

However, that attribution is also potentially problematic. In particular, the ideas put forward in the "Jie Lao" and "Yu Lao" have seemed to many readers to be quite different from and even at odds with the views found in the other chapters that are typically regarded as most likely to be genuine works of Han Feizi. In turn, this ostensible mismatch between the "Jie Lao" and "Yu Lao" and the rest of the *Han Feizi* has prompted a number of different reactions from scholars. Some have argued that the dissonance is merely apparent and have advocated for interpreting the *Han Feizi* in such a way as to render the "Jie Lao" and "Yu Lao" compatible with the rest of the text. Others have suggested that the "Jie Lao" and "Yu Lao" represent a particular stage in the development of Han Feizi's thought, perhaps an early stage, and hence they explain the differences between those chapters and the rest of the work as simply reflecting a discrepancy between Han Feizi's younger and more mature views. Still others have been inclined to think that the "Jie Lao" and "Yu Lao" are not by Han Feizi at all, but were rather inserted by some later editor into the collection of materials that now bears Han Feizi's name. These various ways of responding to the puzzle are discussed at greater length in Eirik L. Harris' essay in this volume, so we will not pursue them further here, but it is worth noting that if the last of the three possibilities mentioned above is correct, then one important basis for dating the commentaries to at or before 233 BCE is removed.

Even apart from the attribution to Han Feizi, though, there is other evidence from within the "Jie Lao" and "Yu Lao" that supports dating them to around his lifetime. In particular, the era in which Han Feizi lived, now conventionally labeled as the Warring States period, was a time of tremendous social and political chaos, and it ended in 221 BCE when the state of Qin conquered its remaining rivals, thereby bringing to a close a set of conflicts that had been going on for multiple centuries. Despite this momentous achievement, the Qin dynasty lasted only fourteen years before it fell and was replaced by the Han dynasty. As Sarah Queen (2013) has argued, on the one hand, the triumph of Qin and its stunningly rapid downfall were events that could hardly be ignored by anyone concerned with politics and history—and such are prominent concerns in the "Jie Lao" and "Yu Lao"—yet these two commentaries seem to show no awareness of those events and instead display language and concerns that are more typical of late Warring States texts. On the other hand, the "Yu Lao" explicitly references the murder of King Wuling of Zhao (also known as "Zhufu") in 295 BCE, which clearly dates that work (or at least that portion of it) to sometime after that event.[2] In sum, while we cannot determine an exact dating for either the "Jie Lao" or "Yu Lao," and either or both of them may have been composed in whole or in part by someone other than Han Feizi, there is nonetheless a good case to be made that they are both pre-Qin texts, and thus to affirm their status as the earliest surviving commentaries on the *Laozi* (since all other existing commentaries date from the Han dynasty or later).[3]

II. The Laozi as Reflected in the "Jie Lao" and "Yu Lao"

The "standard" version of the *Laozi* known to most readers today is based on the text attributed to the commentator Wang Bi 王弼 (226–249 CE).[4] Now as noted earlier, the "Jie Lao" and "Yu Lao"

[2] See "Yu Lao," section 3, pp. 88–89 in this volume. (Subsequent references to the translations here will use the abbreviated form "JL" for "Jie Lao" and "YL" for "Yu Lao," followed by section sign § and section number, then page number.)

[3] Here we have only sketched two of the most straightforward arguments presented in Queen (2013) for dating the texts to the pre-Qin period. Readers interested in more thorough (and technical) discussion of the evidence are encouraged to consult her essay and that by Sarkissian (2001), which together provide helpful references to and summaries of earlier research on this topic.

[4] We say "attributed" because scholars have noted that Wang Bi's commentary suggests that the *Laozi* he was reading is not identical to the *Laozi* text that has been transmitted with his commentary. See Wagner (1989) for discussion of this issue. For

do not comment on the whole of that text, and indeed, the *Laozi* that is quoted in the "Jie Lao" and "Yu Lao" differs significantly in several respects from the Wang Bi text. If one knew only the Wang Bi version, then it might be tempting to conclude that Han Feizi or whoever wrote the "Jie Lao" and "Yu Lao" either (1) did not possess a complete copy of the *Laozi* or (2) did have a complete copy but chose to comment on it in only a very selective manner, and moreover their copy was badly corrupt, or (3) they misquoted it (perhaps intentionally), or (4) the "Jie Lao" and "Yu Lao" themselves have become so corrupted over time as to deviate significantly from the actual text of the *Laozi*.

Over the past seven decades, archaeological discoveries of copies of the *Laozi* from before the time of Wang Bi have shown, though, that we should not be hasty to draw such conclusions. For example, the "Jie Lao" begins its commentary with what is chapter 38 in the Wang Bi arrangement, which may make it seem as if the "Jie Lao" haphazardly skips to the middle of the *Laozi*, rather than beginning with chapter 1. However, in the silk manuscript copies of the *Laozi* found at Mawangdui (tomb dated to 168 BCE), what is chapter 38 in Wang Bi's version is in fact the first chapter of the text. The "Jie Lao" may thus be following an earlier version of the *Laozi*, rather than simply choosing randomly where to start its commentary.[5] In a similar vein, the copies of the *Laozi* found at Guodian (tomb dated to 300 BCE) contain only some of the chapters found in the Wang Bi version, but the chapters are again in a different order, and some chapters lack lines found in the Wang Bi version, while other chapters in the Wang Bi version are broken into separate chapters

ease of expression, we drop "attributed" in subsequent references and speak simply of "the Wang Bi version" or "Wang Bi's version" of the *Laozi*, but readers should bear in mind that this wording is shorthand for the longer, more qualified phrasing, and is misleading if taken literally.

[5] However, the overall order of chapters in the "Jie Lao" and the "Yu Lao" does not match any of the excavated editions of the *Laozi*, so if the author(s) were following some earlier version of the *Laozi*, it was still organized differently from any version known today.

in the Guodian texts. Moreover, the *Laozi* material at Guodian is spread across three separate bundles of bamboo strips in a way as to suggest that the content of those bundles was not necessarily regarded as belonging to what we now think of as a single work. Given these and other differences between excavated texts and the Wang Bi version of the *Laozi*, many scholars have concluded that the *Laozi* came into being through a process of accretion over a long period of time. Hence, when we see the "Jie Lao" and "Yu Lao" commenting on the *Laozi* in a piecemeal fashion and omitting lines that appear in Wang Bi's version or treating them as if they were in a different order, that may be a genuine reflection of the then-current state of the material that became the *Laozi*,[6] rather than reflecting the lack of a (supposedly) complete copy of the *Laozi* or selective quoting from it or textual corruption. (Of course, it may be that selective quoting from some proto-*Laozi* text or misquoting or other corruption are *also* at work in the "Jie Lao" and "Yu Lao"; the point is simply that since these two commentaries may be working from a different text than Wang Bi's to begin with, one should not view their features as *deviations* from Wang Bi's version.)

Indeed, in light of the idea that the *Laozi* underwent a long process of development before reaching the form it has in Wang Bi's version, the "Jie Lao" and "Yu Lao" can potentially serve as evidence by which to reconstruct one early version of the *Laozi*, rather than being merely documents that elucidate the text. The translation of the commentaries contained in this volume presents one

[6] In addition, it is worth noting that the commentaries do not themselves explicitly mention "Laozi" as a person's name or book title, and the titles of the commentaries, "Jie Lao" and "Yu Lao," which identify the subject of discussion as the *Laozi* (or the thought of the person Laozi) may themselves be labels added by a later editor. So, the fact that the chapters have such titles does not by itself tell us much about the state of the *Laozi* text at the time the commentaries were composed: we cannot be sure, for example, that the author(s) of the commentaries associated the material being discussed with the label "Laozi" at all. The alternative title *Daodejing* was given to the *Laozi* in the Han dynasty by Emperor Jing (r. 156–141 BCE), so unless the "Jie Lao" and "Yu Lao" somehow turn out to have been produced much later in time than most scholars believe, the author(s) definitely could not have conceived the works as being commentaries on a book with the title *Daodejing*.

possible version of such work for readers, by providing at the start of each section a reconstruction of the primary text that is culled from the quotations or paraphrases given in the commentaries and hence translated as the commentaries themselves construe the lines. It is beyond the scope of this volume to engage in detailed comparison between this reconstructed version of the *Laozi* and other versions, because there are too many different versions that would make useful objects for comparison, and so that task is left to readers as an exercise to undertake on their own.[7]

III. The "Jie Lao" and "Yu Lao" as Commentaries

China has a long and rich tradition of commentarial writing. This tradition arose at least partly as a response to the terseness and ambiguity of many ancient texts, and as a result, over time not only the *Laozi* but indeed all the most important works accrued a substantial body of literature explaining the lessons of the texts. Moreover, because of the reverence with which the Classics were regarded in Chinese society, commentaries were not (as they are sometimes regarded in the West) arcane, pedantic productions of interest to only a handful of narrowly specialized scholars. For instance, after it became common for candidates for government service—which was the premier route to success and fame in pre-modern China—to be tested on their understanding of the Classics, familiarity with the commentaries became important for virtually *all* well-educated men, and the commentaries informed the practice of government to at least some degree. The writing of commentaries thus formed an important aspect of philosophical, religious, and even political debates, and while important intellectual work was done through many other genres of writing as well, commentaries

[7] Kim (2010) provides one such study, but the essay presumes that readers know Chinese and thus is not very accessible to non-specialists.

themselves constitute a significant repository for much original and profound thinking that was done in China. Arguably, any attempt to study the history of Chinese thought without taking account of the commentarial literature would wind up with a deeply impoverished picture.

It is not known exactly when commentaries began to be written in China, but the "Jie Lao" and "Yu Lao" are almost surely not the first. Nevertheless, they are clearly among the earliest commentaries on any Chinese text that have survived to us. Thus, even apart from their place in the history of the development and reception of the *Laozi*, the "Jie Lao" and "Yu Lao" are also of interest for their place in the growth of commentarial writing in China more broadly. Or to frame the point in slightly different terms, the chapters are an important data point for the history of Chinese hermeneutics, and hence are worth examining for the interpretive strategies they adopt and how those strategies compare with other Chinese (and non-Chinese) approaches to reading and understanding texts. Y. K. Lo's essay in this volume addresses such matters at length, so for now we will offer only a few brief observations that will perhaps be useful for readers to know before looking at the translations and Lo's analysis.

The first point to note is simply the style in which the "Jie Lao" and "Yu Lao" are written. The vast majority of Chinese commentaries are *interlinear*: a sentence or two of the primary text is presented, and then immediately afterwards, the commentary on that portion is presented, and then another sentence or two of primary text is given, followed by the commentary on that portion, and so on. (In many traditional printed Chinese books, where the text is arranged in vertical columns that are to be read from top to bottom and right to left, the primary text is given in larger characters that occupy the width of a whole column, and the commentary is given in smaller characters that occupy half a column, and so the commentary is visually set apart from the primary text in a conspicuous way.) In contrast with that format, the "Jie Lao" and "Yu Lao" are written as continuous essays, and usually the line that is being expounded is quoted after the explanation is given.[8] One effect of this mode of presentation is to make the commentary seem less subordinate to the primary text, at least in comparison with an interlinear commentary. That is to say, in an interlinear commentary, it is clear—and especially so when the commentary itself is rendered in smaller characters—that the commentary exists mainly to elucidate the primary text. The "Jie Lao" and "Yu Lao," on the other hand, often speak as if they are first and foremost presenting lessons on various subjects, and only subsequently are those lessons claimed to be what the primary text is (also) teaching. Hence, even if the content and flow of the "Jie Lao" and "Yu Lao" are in a sense ultimately dictated by the primary text, that fact is not foregrounded in those commentaries.[9]

A second noteworthy feature of the "Jie Lao" and "Yu Lao" is the approach taken to elucidating the text, which differs significantly between the two works. The "Yu Lao" consistently uses very concrete, historical episodes as examples that function both to specify the meaning of what the primary text is saying and to demonstrate the truth of the claims made in the primary text. The "Jie Lao," while also referencing historical events, more often presents its claims in terms of generalizations about human psychology, politics, and the world. To that extent, the "Jie Lao" might be called more "theoretical" and "abstract" than the "Yu Lao," though it still understands the teachings of the primary text in fairly practical terms. This difference

[8] This feature may be somewhat obscured in Eric Hutton's translations of the "Jie Lao" and "Yu Lao" presented in this volume, since as noted earlier, he breaks the commentaries up into sections roughly according to the chapters of the Wang Bi version and gives a reconstructed version of the *Laozi* at the head of each section, which is not present in the original Chinese version. While the obscuration of this feature of the commentaries is perhaps regrettable, we felt that the tradeoff in terms of providing clarity and intelligibility to first-time readers of the "Jie Lao" and "Yu Lao" was worthwhile.

[9] In addition to the contrast with interlinear commentaries, this feature of the "Jie Lao" and "Yu Lao" also sets them apart from a number of other forms of (non-interlinear) commentarial writing that date from earliest times. For more on this point, see Y. K. Lo's contribution to this book.

between the chapters has led some to suspect that they were written by two different people (and perhaps Han Feizi was neither of them). While we may never be in a position to settle that matter definitively, the difference in approach between the two chapters by itself highlights two significant alternatives for how to engage with the *Laozi* that are well worth pondering further.

Related to this last point, Alan Chan's essay in this volume explores in greater detail how the interpretation of the *Laozi* given in the "Jie Lao" and "Yu Lao" compares with the interpretations of the *Laozi* found in three other important early commentaries by Yan Zun 嚴遵, Heshang Gong 河上公, and Wang Bi,[10] but for now it may be helpful to note the following. Over the course of its history, the *Laozi* has been understood in an incredibly wide variety of ways. Some have read it as a handbook for rulers on how to control people. Some have seen it as a manual for personal psycho-physical cultivation that is potentially applicable to anyone. Some have taken it as a record of a mystical religious experience that others can use as a roadmap to achieve that same experience. Some have regarded it as issuing a call to "return to nature." There are yet other interpretations distinct from these, and some interpretations combine a number of these different elements. Against this background of possibilities, the particular stance taken by the "Jie Lao" and "Yu Lao" is by itself significant. Namely, the commentaries read much of the primary text in a political vein, while also taking parts of the primary text to be about personal cultivation. Far from being a mysterious or inscrutable text, on such a reading the *Laozi* emerges as responding to fairly conventional concerns and offering advice that is sensible and practical (even if sometimes presented in a

[10] Wang Bi has already been introduced earlier (p. 4). Yan Zun flourished around 83 BCE–10 CE. Heshang Gong is a mythical figure ("Heshang Gong" is an epithet, rather than a typical Chinese name, and it means "the Old Man [or Duke] above the River"), and for that reason, there has been substantial debate about the dating of Heshang Gong's commentary. For discussion of Heshang Gong as a figure, see Chan (1991a), and for an argument in favor of dating the Heshang Gong commentary to the second century CE, see Chan (1991b).

less-than-straightforward fashion). Whether that is the most compelling interpretation is a question we leave for readers to consider.

IV. Overview of Key Concepts and Themes

For the benefit of readers who may not have much experience in reading ancient Chinese texts, here we provide an overview of the ideas in the "Jie Lao" and "Yu Lao" to help them navigate what may otherwise seem a dense and disorganized thicket. However, since the essays in the latter half of this volume provide sustained discussion of a number of important terms and themes in the commentaries, our treatment here will be highly selective, in order to minimize redundancy.

Now, the alternative title by which the *Laozi* is commonly known, *Daodejing*, comes from the two main concepts that feature in the two chapters that form the heads of the two sections or books into which the Wang Bi version is divided, namely *dao* 道 in chapter 1, and *de* 德 in chapter 38. (The honorific label *jing* 經, which means "classic" or "scripture," is said to have been bestowed on the *Laozi* by the Emperor Jing of the Han dynasty in the second century CE, centuries after the time when the "Jie Lao" and "Yu Lao" were most likely composed, which helps to explain why neither commentary is named after or explicitly refers to the text it explains as the "*Daodejing*.") Since the "Jie Lao" begins by discussing material that corresponds—though with some significant disparities—to chapter 38 in the Wang Bi text, we shall begin our overview by focusing on the notion of *de* 德.

De 德

This term figures prominently in many early Chinese texts, and from its various appearances one can identify at least three distinct uses of the word.[11] First, it can refer to a kind of *force* or *power* that accrues to a person. This force can be primarily individual in its character, as a kind of power that keeps one alive or that gives one abilities to do certain things. However, such abilities may include the capacity to influence or sway other people, and on such a conception *de* is also a kind of political force or power that one may use to govern. In some texts—most prominently, those typically classed as belonging to the Confucian tradition—this latter understanding of *de* is closely tied to being a good person: *de* is a power that comes from and/or manifests itself in moral excellence. Deployed in this manner, *de* refers to a person's *virtue* (especially its ability to affect others), and this is the second use worth noting. Third, *de* sometimes refers specifically to *kind or favorable treatment* toward others.

Although *de* forms an important element of the terminology shared among early Chinese texts, they importantly differ from each other not only in terms of which of the above three uses of *de* they emphasize but also in how they understand each of them individually and how they take them to be related. In adopting those different positions, the texts are engaging in a debate over a number of significant questions: What is the source of individual vitality and power? What is the source of political power? How are the two sorts of power related to each other? How, if at all, are they related to virtue? If they are somehow derived from or expressed in being virtuous, what are the relevant virtues? Do those virtues consist in traits that are conventionally recognized as virtues, or are they some set of traits not ordinarily considered to be virtues? To what extent does kindness toward others count as virtuous, and to what role should it play in a sovereign's approach to governing?

[11] For two classic studies of *de* that examine its use in some of the very earliest Chinese writings, see David Nivison's essays "'Virtue' in Bone and Bronze" and "The Paradox of 'Virtue'" in Nivison (1996).

The *Laozi* sketches answers to many of these questions through its discussions of *de*, but the vague and elusive wording of the text means that its positions on these topics are often open to being further fleshed out in a variety of ways. The treatments of *de* in the "Jie Lao" and "Yu Lao" thus offer a set of more definite stances on the issues while also serving as a proposal for how to understand the *Laozi*. Here is not the place to offer a detailed reconstruction of those stances, but the following may perhaps serve as a useful preview for what readers will find in the translations presented in this book.

To begin with, all three uses of *de* noted above are at work in the commentaries. Section 1 of the "Jie Lao" clearly explains that *de* is manifested in a set of traits and behaviors that would have conventionally been recognized by many early Chinese (and especially Confucian) readers as morally praiseworthy,[12] and hence the common English rendering of *de* as "virtue" is employed in the translations here. However, the more prominent way in which *de* is used in the commentaries is to refer to a kind of power. The commentaries treat it, on the one hand, as a vital force that keeps one alive and hence should be preserved and nurtured in order to achieve and maintain an excellent bodily state.[13] On the other hand, that same state is envisioned by the commentaries as also bringing with it a kind of skillfulness in deliberation, such that a person of great *de* will be especially successful in their actions, including in the political arena.[14] Thus, *de* is simultaneously an individual and political power. The commentaries recognize, moreover, that successful rule must at some level involve acting so as to benefit the people, and such "kind treatment" is discussed by the texts as *de*.[15] That usage overlaps to an extent with how *de* can refer to "virtue," but insofar as "kind treatment" of the people is also presented as an

[12] See JL §1, p. 40.
[13] See JL §1, p. 37; JL §3, p. 53; JL §12, p. 77.
[14] See JL §3, p. 51.
[15] See JL §1, p. 41; JL §4, pp. 55–56; JL §5, p. 57; YL §4, p. 90; YL §6, pp. 95–96.

important factor in governing well, this conception of *de* carries with it an association of political power as well.

The "Jie Lao" and "Yu Lao" do not offer a well-developed and explicit account of how these various aspects of *de* are related to each other, and so reconstructing such an account is left as a task for interpreters, a task that exceeds the scope of this Introduction. Nonetheless, this much may be observed. One general theme that appears repeatedly in the commentaries is the value of what could in English be called "restraint," understood as an umbrella term used to cover multiple different Chinese formulations.[16] The restraint advocated by the texts is, in the first instance, restraint toward the desire and pursuit of various external goods.[17] As depicted in the commentaries, striving after such goods consumes both physical and mental energy, and the desire for them can warp one's evaluations and deliberations, leading one to bad decisions that bring one no closer to obtaining those goods or, worse yet, put them further out of reach or even bring one to ruin. Especially for rulers, the consequences of such bad decisions are liable to be particularly catastrophic, as they may lead to losses on the battlefield that endanger the state and the ruler's own life as well.[18] Restraint toward external goods, by contrast, allows one to conserve one's mental and physical energy, which is thus one straightforward way to maintain one's vitality (i.e., *de*, per one usage noted above).[19] In addition, such restraint diminishes the distorting effects of desire and so allows one to perceive and to think more clearly and—most important of all, according to the commentaries—to grasp the Way (*dao* 道, more on which below),[20] which in turn allows one to better understand, predict, and respond to circumstances. Such a

[16] For a similar use of "restraint" as a label for a theme manifested in different ways throughout the "Jie Lao," see Hendrischke (2022).

[17] See JL §4, p. 54; JL §5, pp. 58–60; JL §12, p. 77; YL §8, p. 99.

[18] See YL §1, p. 85.

[19] See JL §1, p. 36; JL §3, pp. 49–50.

[20] See JL §3, p. 50; YL §9, pp. 101–102.

person thus becomes far more able to avoid disasters and achieve successes, both individually *and* politically, and therein we can see how the nurturing of *de* as life-force might lend itself to *de* as political power. (It is worth noticing as well that the ability to avoid disasters and achieve successes is itself another, indirect means for preserving and extending one's life.)

The commentaries further suggest that this restraint simultaneously also conduces to ethical behavior, and in more than one manner. For one thing, the texts portray unethical behavior as tending to bring harm to the wrongdoer, and since much unethical behavior is driven precisely by a lack of restraint with regard to external goods,[21] someone motivated to practice restraint from concern for their own well-being will also have reason to behave ethically. Second, at various points the commentaries suggest that the Way itself contains certain ethical norms.[22] Insofar as the development of restraint enables one—as noted above—to grasp and follow the Way, that in turn will then lead a person to live more ethically. Framed in terms of the notion of *de* from which we started, we might roughly say that on the view in the "Jie Lao" and "Yu Lao," the nurturing of one's vital energies, if properly done, must become a process of *moral* cultivation as well, and hence what is nurtured is really just as much a matter of *virtue* as it is a matter of vitality. (Or in other words, even if the notions of life-force and moral excellence seem quite distinct conceptually, the world is such that they go hand-in-hand in practice, according to the commentaries.) Finally, in sketching out the kind of restraint that is involved in developing *de*, the texts point out and sometimes even emphasize how that restraint will take the form of treating others well, as a characteristic of superior individuals generally but also especially of superior rulers, since ill-considered policies and other misguided political decisions can harm great multitudes of common

21 See JL §4, pp. 54–55; JL §5, pp. 58–59.
22 See JL §1, p. 40; JL §2, p. 47; JL §5, p. 57.

people.[23] The welfare of those people is taken by the commentaries to be an important source for the strength of the state, and thus virtue includes—as one might expect—an element of kindness, which also turns out to be yet another source of political power.

To sum up, in terms of the set of questions mentioned earlier, the discussions of *de* in the "Jie Lao" and "Yu Lao" tend to focus on how an individual's energies may be drained and wasted through misguided pursuits, in particular pursuit of unnecessary, external goods. They treat the development of individual vitality and political power as intertwined, with virtue as a concomitant of the former and a contributor to the latter. The virtue recognized by the commentaries is not wholly unconventional in its form, though as we shall see later, the texts do at times also make proposals that tend to subvert conventional ways of thinking. Along with that last point, while the texts present being virtuous and treating others kindly as part of the recipe for political success, they also clearly point out that there are factors beyond these that are crucial for successful rule, some of which will be noted in what follows.

Dao 道

The term *dao* is, like *de*, one that is shared by many different early Chinese texts propounding a variety of competing views, and their disagreements are likewise in part both constituted and represented by how they conceive the notion of *dao*.[24] In general, though, we can identify two broad uses of the term that appear in many texts. One is as a *normative* standard: the *dao* is the "way" that one *ought* to behave or the "way" that the world *ought* to be. The other prominent conception of the *dao* is as a *descriptive* fact: the *dao* is the

[23] See JL §4, p. 54; JL §5, p. 57.

[24] A helpful introduction to and overview of uses of the word *dao* in a number of early Chinese texts can be found in Allan (1997, 66–79), though her discussion there is in service of a larger argument about the importance of water metaphors to early Chinese thought that is potentially controversial in certain respects.

"way" the world in fact operates, at least at some deep level. Again, texts differ in prioritizing one of these conceptions over (or even to the exclusion of) the other, or where both are present, differences arise from how the two are related, and especially in the case of the descriptive notion, exactly what the relevant "facts" about the world are. On the whole, however, when both conceptions are present in a given text, the descriptive notion tends to ground the normative one. That is to say, the text takes the world to operate in some particular "way," but those operations do not necessarily determine exactly how all events in the world unfold, and thus it is possible for human beings and their societies to behave in a manner that runs counter to that "way." Such behavior will, on the view of those texts, tend to result in highly undesirable consequences (e.g., chaos, ruin, sickness, and/or death). Following the "way" the world operates becomes, by contrast, the means to avoid such consequences and flourish—either as an individual and/or as a society—and thus that "way" *also* turns out to be the "way" that one *should* live or that society *should* instantiate.

On a fairly common interpretation, the *Laozi* is either the first text or among the first in early China to adopt this sort of view that grounds the normative conception of the *dao* in the descriptive conception of it. The "Jie Lao" and "Yu Lao" likewise attribute this sort of approach to the *Laozi*, though as before, they likewise fill out that broad framework with a particular set of more detailed commitments that constitute a substantive philosophical picture addressing a number of different questions.

In constructing this picture, the commentaries invoke a term that is completely absent from the Wang Bi and other "standard" versions of the *Laozi*, namely *li* 理, which most literally means a "pattern" or "order." While this term was not new with the "Jie Lao" and "Yu Lao," again they deploy it in a fairly distinctive manner.[25]

[25] Those wishing to know more about how the use of *li* 理 in the "Jie Lao" compares to its usage in other early Chinese texts may find it helpful to consult Hendrischke (2022), though we do not endorse all her claims.

Namely, according to the texts, there is "pattern" or "order" that all the individual types of things tend to follow.[26] This "pattern" or "order" includes not only physical qualities of things, but also stages through which they pass, such as generation, maturation, decline, and dissolution—in other words, *li* covers both synchronic and diachronic structure.[27] The existence of these various discrete structures makes things identifiable, understandable, and to a large degree predictable. Grasping the *li* is thus crucial for interacting with things successfully, and hence the notion of *li* exhibits the dual usage mentioned previously, that is, it serves both to identify a descriptive fact as well as a normative standard for behavior (and hence in the translations here it is rendered as "governing order" or "proper order" depending on context).

However, distinct from the "pattern" and "order" instantiated by any individual type of thing, the commentaries posit some greater pattern or order that applies to how they *all* inter-relate and function—this is the *dao*.[28] The texts take the *dao* to be to some degree knowable, and yet, given the immense variety of the things in the world, the changes to which they are subject, and the potential configurations of them, the *dao* is not capable of being captured in any set, definite formulation: it can be described and discussed, but not delineated in full detail.[29] This infinite complexity is reflected in the use of the term *dao* itself, which is presented by the "Jie Lao" as a respectful label for something that would be mischaracterized by almost any other more substantive appellation.[30] Thus, "the Way" is effectively a nickname acknowledging the significant challenge of trying to grasp the *dao*, and the commentaries present that achievement as one that only someone with the right sort of mindset can hope to attain.

[26] See JL §6, p. 61.
[27] See JL §8, p. 64; JL §10, p. 71.
[28] See JL §6, p. 61.
[29] See JL §8, p. 65.
[30] See JL §8, p. 65.

This last point returns us to some of the issues discussed in the previous section on *de*. As noted there, one significant theme of the commentaries is offering advice about how to develop the ability to deliberate well, which the texts frame in terms of understanding and following the Way. Desire (or more accurately, misplaced and excessive desire) turns out to be one major impediment to such ability, but in view of the preceding points about the complexity and indefinability of the Way, another significant impediment turns out to be having a too narrow and rigid focus or view. It is only when "one's considerations are unconfined," as the "Jie Lao" puts it, that one can adequately grasp and follow the Way.[31] This idea recurs in various guises throughout the commentaries, and interestingly takes the form at one point—in following and filling out a line from the *Laozi*—of a caution against thinking one can obtain wisdom from books,[32] which thus leaves the reader with a challenge about exactly how to digest the lessons of the *Laozi* and the commentaries themselves.

Regardless of how one deals with that challenge, it highlights and exemplifies a larger issue about the Way that confronts any readers of these texts. Namely, even granting that the Way cannot be completely captured in words and is only adequately grasped by someone who is free from the distorting influence of desires and has a kind of flexible open-mindedness, the Way must still have *some* particular character to it, or else the notion of following the Way will have no content to it. On that score, the commentaries do offer assorted indications of what living an individual life or running a society in accordance with the Way would look like, which help us understand the character of the Way.

At the individual level, as noted earlier, the Way has a moral content that takes the form of certain (commonly recognized) virtues, including care for others, commitment to fulfilling the

[31] See JL §1, p. 37.
[32] See YL §8, pp. 99–100.

responsibilities of one's social role, and respect for various social conventions that are supposed to govern people's interactions. Moreover, the commentaries predict that someone who follows the Way will—because of their ability to deliberate well—achieve wealth and power and live comfortably,[33] though they will not be attached to these things, nor will they allow those goods to make them careless or arrogant.[34] What is noteworthy about this picture is what is *omitted* from it, in comparison with other views from early China (especially, but not only, Confucian views). For one thing, even if following the Way leads one to be virtuous, there is no suggestion that such a person strives to be a model for others or seeks to teach them to be morally better, and indeed the "Jie Lao" explicitly warns about some potential dangers that may arise from such endeavors.[35] Second, although the person who follows the Way has care for others, the texts do not particularly advocate that virtuous care for people should by its very nature extend to others as widely as possible, nor do they stress prioritizing care for particular groups of people, such as close family members, over others. While the texts recognize the importance of familial affection and obligations,[36] they do not treat family relations as either especially central to or problematic in following the Way. Third, though the person who follows the Way may adhere to certain conventional norms for behavior, the texts do not valorize traditionalism: in disparaging book-learning, they reject the idea that one should prize the mastery and preservation of practices transmitted from the past. Fourth, in highlighting the power, wealth, and material comforts that are likely to accrue to one who follows the Way, the texts display no aversion toward holding office in the government, including military service, and no predilection for asceticism or austerity. In sum, the commentaries present the person who lives

[33] See JL §2, p. 45; JL §10, pp. 71–72; YL §1, p. 85.
[34] See JL §2, p. 47; JL §5, p. 59; JL §12, p. 77.
[35] See JL §2, p. 48.
[36] See JL §1, p. 38.

the ideal life in accordance with the Way as someone who is highly involved in human affairs and enjoys worldly success but does not flaunt it, who is recognizably moral yet harbors no aspiration to be a savior or preacher to the entire world, and who can respect tradition but is not enamored of it.

At the level of society, we see correlates to basically all these preceding points, often through the commentaries' discussions of the ideal ruler. In their accounts, a society that conforms to the Way will enjoy peace and prosperity. On the one hand, this is in part because the ideal ruler behaves properly toward the lords of other states and so avoids conflict with them, or if conflict cannot be avoided, such a ruler knows how to govern his people such as to make his state a dominating force.[37] On the other hand—and as an extension of this last point—the peace and prosperity of the ideal society also comes in part from that fact that the ruler takes care of his people and ensures that they behave properly toward each other and toward him. However, there is no suggestion that the ruler strives to be "father and mother to the people," caring for them like a loving parent tending to a feeble infant, nor is there any suggestion that the ideal ruler particularly aims to make his people morally excellent through teaching or encouraging them to follow his example. Rather, through ensuring that neither his nor his people's efforts are expended in pursuit of extravagant and licentious goods, he brings it about that their needs are amply met, which thereby reduces or eliminates the conditions giving rise to most or all domestic problems. The texts do not provide much detail on the exact means by which the ideal ruler achieves this goal, but they suggest clearly enough that it will be accomplished in no small part through the exercise of government power in the form of prohibitions, laws, punishments, and rewards, among the various options at the ruler's disposal.[38] At the same time, the commentaries warn against

[37] See JL §3, p. 51; JL §5, p. 57; JL §10, p. 72; YL §10, p. 104.
[38] See JL §5, p. 57; YL §4, pp. 89–90.

abusiveness and counsel judiciousness in the use of such methods, such as pointing out that frequent changes to commands and laws will cause hardships to the people and impede the ruler's ability to get projects done.[39] Parallel to the summary above, then, we may say that a state governed in accordance with the Way will be powerful and wealthy but free of extravagance; its people will be well-behaved, largely because their needs are met and the conditions that would otherwise encourage misdeeds have been alleviated through the ruler's management of affairs, rather than through any concerted attempts at widespread moral reform; and society will follow stable and predictable norms, though not from any particularly great reverence for the past.

While this picture may not appeal to everyone, hopefully it is not too hard to see how it might have struck the author(s) of the "Jie Lao" and "Yu Lao" as attractive, especially given the turbulent context in which they were most likely composed.

Leveraging the World and Non-Action

While the commentaries repeatedly depict the ideal agent as one who can evade pitfalls and overcome obstacles to achieve tremendous success, one important theme in the texts is that such success should *not* be understood as a matter of simply imposing one's wishes on the world. Rather, they portray this achievement as resting primarily on taking advantage of the various forces and resources in the world, which is part of what it means to follow the Way. Significantly, in section eight of the "Yu Lao," this point is put in terms of relying on how things are "so of themselves" (*ziran* 自然).[40] That phrase is a potent one in the context of early China and can refer to the "natural" condition of things, prior to any

[39] See JL §4, pp. 53–54.
[40] See YL §8, p. 101.

human scheming or cleverness. In the Wang Bi version of the *Laozi*, the phrase appears in multiple chapters, and on a common understanding of the text it represents an original and pure state to which humans should return.[41] However, such a conception is not in evidence in the "Jie Lao" and "Yu Lao." Instead, in those commentaries, the value of how things are "so of themselves" consists in the fact that the operation of natural processes is far more efficacious than what human efforts can achieve, and so human agents do better to work with and *build upon* those processes.

The "Yu Lao" presents this view in commenting on a line of the primary text that also alludes to the notion of "non-action" (*wuwei* 無為) that is repeatedly promoted in the *Laozi* and the commentaries,[42] and thus the view just sketched above has implications for understanding "non-action" as well. In many interpretations of the *Laozi*, "non-action" is typically conceived as a means to and manifestation of following what is "so of itself" or "natural." While the "Jie Lao" and "Yu Lao" do not reject that linkage, they do offer a particular variation on that idea: to engage in "non-action" is to refrain from acting ways that are contrary to or heedless of how things are "so of themselves" or how they are "naturally," but such a condition is *also* still compatible with deliberately and actively pursuing a variety of aims (and in the case of a ruler, also compatible with the exercise of coercive governmental powers).

In taking this stance, the "Jie Lao" and "Yu Lao" elaborate the notions of practicing "non-action" and conforming to what is "so of itself" or "natural" in a manner that is substantially less radical and anti-conventional than they have sometimes been conceived by other readers of the *Laozi* who have taken the text to

[41] For further discussion of the notion of *ziran* (as well as a number of other concepts discussed here) in the context of the *Laozi*, readers may find it helpful to consult Liu (2015) and Csikszentmihalyi (2015).

[42] See JL §1, pp. 37–38; YL §10, p. 103.

be espousing an ideal of living spontaneously that rejects human artifice. Certainly, the "Jie Lao" does claim that the growth of *de* can happen only when one is not consciously focused on it, and that commentary does also criticize forced, inauthentic displays of respect, for example.[43] Yet, such concerns are not at the forefront in the broader context of either the "Jie Lao" or "Yu Lao," both of which far more often warn against rash behavior. Against that background, the themes of "non-action" and following along with what is "so of itself" or "natural" serve more to highlight a form of judiciousness that is integral to choosing and planning wisely, rather than constituting the highest ideals themselves.

Foresight and Perceptiveness

One final theme that the commentaries repeatedly discuss in connection with improving one's ability to deliberate is the development of a kind of foresight. The "Jie Lao," however, explicitly disparages attempts to develop "magical" powers such as extrasensory perception or the like.[44] Instead, on the picture sketched in the texts, the relevant skill rests mainly in the ability to be attentive to certain small and subtle matters that, because of how the world operates, are often indicators of potential future problems (or opportunities).[45] The agent who perceives these clues is then able to adjust their behavior accordingly so as to avoid harms or secure benefits.

Insofar as this sort of perceptiveness is key to deliberating well, it is again easy to understand why restraint of desire emerges as an important topic in the texts, for desire tends to focus on some future state of affairs or on goals that have yet to be attained, rather than on the conditions immediately before one, and hence it is liable to

[43] See JL §1, pp. 41–42.
[44] See JL §1, pp. 42–43.
[45] See YL §5–7, pp. 92–97.

misdirect one's attention.[46] That problem is especially dangerous for those with grandiose political ambitions. Not only do they fail to grasp and respond to the conditions around them that portend catastrophe, but they also fail to recognize their own shortcomings and vulnerabilities that may contribute to a disastrous outcome.

Drawing out the implications of this last point a little further, we may say that the perceptiveness advocated by the texts also includes as one of its important elements a sort of perceptiveness about oneself.[47] As before, to appreciate this picture being offered, it will help to notice what is absent from it. In particular, the self-perception in question is not about obtaining deep insights into one's own nature or mind. Nor is it focused on moral self-evaluation, despite the fact that (as noted earlier) the commentaries present the ideal life as one that is quite moral. Rather, what the texts are promoting is a sort of sober assessment of one's own circumstances and abilities to act, one that serves as a crucial complement to perceiving the Way and is indispensable for following it.

Interestingly, while perceptiveness and foresight are personal abilities, many of the discussions about these topics in the commentaries are framed as stories of ministers offering counsel to rulers, and the rulers who disregard that counsel pay for that mistake dearly. Given such framing, the texts may be seen as suggesting, beyond the advice simply to be attentive, that one should heed others who are perceptive, if one does not yet have the requisite ability oneself. At the same time, though, that suggestion is tempered—at least in the political case—by warnings in the commentaries about the ways in which ministers may try to take advantage of the ruler.[48]

This last observation provides a convenient point with which to close: although the "Jie Lao" and "Yu Lao" explain the *Laozi* in such

[46] See YL §9, p. 102.
[47] See YL §11, pp. 105–106.
[48] See YL §4, pp. 90–91.

a way as to make it much less mysterious and paradoxical than it might first appear, their understanding of its advice amounts at the end to a vision that remains quite challenging to live up to in practice. To the extent that the attractive yet challenging features of such a vision underlie the enduring appeal of the *Laozi* to readers across the ages, perhaps we may judge that despite whatever shortcomings they may have as interpretations, the "Jie Lao" and "Yu Lao" do succeed in doing justice to the *Laozi* to at least that degree.

PART I

TRANSLATIONS

Translator's Foreword

Eric L. Hutton

The "Jie Lao" and "Yu Lao" chapters of the *Han Feizi* have attracted the attention of scholars in large part because of what we might learn from them about the *Laozi*, on the one hand, and because of the puzzle these chapters present for how to relate them to the rest of the *Han Feizi*, on the other hand. These features that make the chapters intriguing, however, also present a special challenge when it comes to editing, reading, and translating them. As with many other texts that have been transmitted from ancient times to the present, there are numerous small but sometimes significant variations among the different editions that survived from pre-modern times, and there are places where the wording of the chapters is quite difficult to understand, so difficult that one is led to suspect that the texts are corrupt in those locations due to miscopying and other errors of transmission over the centuries. In addition, the chapters are clearly commenting on material in (what became) the *Laozi*, but in many cases, the version of the *Laozi* discussed in the commentary does not seem to match either the received or excavated versions of that text, which then sometimes complicates the process of figuring out what the commentary itself is saying. When one is thus faced with the problem of selecting among textual variants, trying to make sense of possibly corrupt passages, and assessing what the chapters are saying about the *Laozi* material, there are then competing considerations that may pull one in different directions. Since these chapters have been handed down to us as part of the *Han Feizi*, one may feel inclined

Eric L. Hutton, *Translator's Foreword* In: *Explaining and Illustrating the* Laozi. Edited by: Eirik Lang Harris and Eric L. Hutton, Oxford University Press. © Oxford University Press 2026.
DOI: 10.1093/9780197514948.003.0002

to make choices that cause them to conform more closely to the rest of that text. In contrast, where the chapters do not fit with the received or excavated versions of the *Laozi*, it can be tempting to make choices that would bring the chapters more into line with one of those versions. Indeed, it seems probable that at least some of the textual variations among the surviving editions of the "Jie Lao" and "Yu Lao" from pre-modern times are due to past editors struggling with these same issues and making different choices, without always explicitly marking and elucidating that process in the texts.

My own approach to these challenges—which I will explain but not try to defend fully here—is as follows. Since there is substantial scholarly debate over whether Han Feizi authored the "Jie Lao" and "Yu Lao" and over how, if at all, these chapters are meant to fit with the rest of the *Han Feizi*, I have preferred to translate in such a way that is relatively neutral on this score and does not prejudge the issue by favoring those choices (when choices need to be made) that would more strongly connect the "Jie Lao" and "Yu Lao" with the rest of the *Han Feizi*. Rather, I hope that my translation will permit readers who are familiar with other parts of the *Han Feizi* to appreciate how the chapters present a puzzle that has prompted much discussion among scholars. On the other side of the equation, in relation to the *Laozi*, I have generally tried to resist the temptation to "correct" the quotations in the "Jie Lao" and "Yu Lao" to conform with the received or excavated versions of the *Laozi*. Instead, my primary concern has been to translate the chapters in such a way that readers can clearly understand how the commentary responds to the *Laozi*, even if its version of the *Laozi* happens to differ substantially from any other known version. However, in some cases, the commentary seems to presume knowledge of parts of the *Laozi* that it does not actually quote, and in those cases, the commentary would not be intelligible, especially for non-specialists, without having those other parts filled in for the reader. In those cases, drawing the needed supplementation from the received and excavated versions of the *Laozi* is unavoidable, but I have tried to make clear with brackets and notes when, why, and how I am providing supplementation based on the received and excavated versions of the *Laozi*. My hope is that readers who compare this translation with other translations of the *Laozi* will be able to see how in some cases the "Jie Lao" and "Yu Lao" give very unusual interpretations of the exact same lines that appear in other versions of the *Laozi*, while in other cases the "Jie Lao" and "Yu Lao" seem to be based on a completely different version of the *Laozi* altogether.

The translations of the "Jie Lao" and "Yu Lao" offered here are intended in large part for the benefit of undergraduates and general readers, rather than solely for specialists. For that reason, I have emphasized intelligibility and clarity, though that has sometimes meant adopting renderings that are not entirely literal or that fill in some wording that goes beyond the sparse language of the original text. For the same reason, footnotes here are limited to information that will be most useful to the intended audience, while technical apparatus has been kept to a bare minimum. Furthermore, in order to enable readers who do not know any Chinese to be able to track the occurrence of important terms and concepts throughout the chapters, I have striven to maintain as much consistency as possible in the rendering of various words and to render distinct Chinese words with different English words. This approach has entailed some occasional awkwardness of diction, and complete consistency was not possible, but I hope that readers who wish to study the texts closely will find this feature of the translations useful.

In preparing the translations, I have consulted a wide variety of commentaries and translations. My base text here is that as edited by Chen Qitian 陳啟天 (Chen 1969), so specialists seeking explanation for choices among textual variants should consult that work first. I have not always followed Chen's reading or understanding of particular lines as reflected in his commentary, though. In places where I do not follow Chen or where I offer original readings of my own that depart from most commentaries, an explanation for my approach is provided in the endnotes designated with superscript letters. The endnotes are intended only for those who possess proficiency in classical Chinese and who have access to the relevant commentaries—no attempt has been made to render them accessible to non-specialists. For the benefit of those who can read Chinese, a version of the complete Chinese text on which the translations are based, including modifications from Chen's edition, is available from OUP's website at www.oup.com/us/laozicommentaries. Paragraphing in the translation mostly follows Chen but with occasional departures, either for the convenience of English readers or based on scholarly considerations.

In addition, various portions of both the "Jie Lao" and "Yu Lao" chapters are rhymed or contain textual parallels with early Chinese works other than the *Laozi*. Given the already formidable challenges involved in rendering these chapters into readable English, I have not attempted to highlight the rhymes and parallel passages in any extensive manner, especially since this information is not crucial for non-specialist readers. Those interested in these matters are advised to consult Harbsmeier (2025), Long (1963), Queen (2010), and Queen (2013).[†]

Conventions

The Chinese texts of the "Jie Lao" and "Yu Lao" do not first present the primary text of the *Laozi* on which they comment. However, both for the reader's convenience and to facilitate comparisons

[†] The present translation was basically finalized before Harbsmeier (2025) was published. Any instances of overlapping wording with that translation are therefore a matter of coincidence, in which he and I independently happened to pick very similar or identical English phrases to render the same underlying Chinese text. I have benefited from consulting other previous English translations of the "Jie Lao" and "Yu Lao," including those by Cleary (2009), Liao (1939), Queen (2013), and Sarkissian (2001). I have also consulted various modern Chinese *baihua* translations, such as Chen and Wang (2008), Gao et al. (2015), Lai and Fu (1997), Shao (1990), and Zhang (1996).

between the "Jie Lao" and "Yu Lao" versions of the *Daodejing* and others, here the primary text has been reconstructed and translated at the start of each section, based on how the commentary explains it. In particular, where lines of the "Jie Lao" and "Yu Lao" versions differ substantially from the highly influential version attributed to Wang Bi, an asterisk (*) has been added at the end of the line to note that difference for readers. For those who cannot read Chinese, the absence of such an asterisk should be taken to indicate that in Chinese the line is identical to the Wang Bi version in all significant respects, but the English translation here may still diverge substantially from most translations of the Wang Bi version, given the particular way in which the commentary understands the line. Also, when the Wang Bi version contains one or more lines that are not discussed in the "Jie Lao" and "Yu Lao" (and hence not included in the reconstructions here), the mark ∓ in superscript is added to the reconstructions to indicate the existence of such material in the Wang Bi version that *precedes* a given line discussed in the "Jie Lao" or "Yu Lao," and the mark ± in superscript is used to indicate that the Wang Bi version contains other material that comes *after* what is discussed in the "Jie Lao" or "Yu Lao." As mentioned earlier and as explained in the Introduction to this volume, though, such discrepancies between the Wang Bi version of the *Daodejing* and that reconstructed from the "Jie Lao" and "Yu Lao" should not necessarily be understood as cases where the version of the *Daodejing* read and discussed by the author(s) of the "Jie Lao" and "Yu Lao" was *missing* material that was *supposed* to be there and *is* there in the Wang Bi version. Hence, the ∓ and ± symbols here should not automatically be interpreted as signaling an *omission*, but rather merely flag for the reader that some other versions of the *Daodejing* have further lines above or below the one that is so marked. I leave it to the reader to assess whether the absence of those lines from the versions here is an omission of something originally present, or whether those other lines constitute an *addition* of something new to the *Daodejing*, creating an expanded version that had not been seen by the author(s) of the "Jie Lao" and "Yu Lao." Conversely, where the "Jie Lao" and "Yu Lao" versions of the *Daodejing* contain a line that is absent in some or all editions of the Wang Bi version, that difference is marked with a superscript ◊ symbol. Finally, where a line in the "Jie Lao" and "Yu Lao" versions matches that of the Wang Bi version but appears in a different position from the ordering of the Wang Bi version, those instances are flagged with a superscript ∿ symbol.

Readers should also bear in mind that the English translations of individual Chinese terms given here are intended as only approximations, rather than as exact equivalents for the original Chinese terms. No single English word can capture the full range of meanings of any of the most important Chinese philosophical notions. The glossary at the end of this book lists alternative translations of several significant terms that the "Jie Lao" and "Yu Lao" deploy. The list is intended to help orient readers who may be familiar with other translations of these terms, but it can also help provide readers with a sense for the broader range of connotations the translated terms may have.

1

Jie Lao 解老

Explaining the *Laozi*

Translated by Eric L. Hutton

Section One[1]

[Primary Text]

One with highest virtue does not possess virtue, and thereby has virtue.⫫
*One with highest virtue takes no action, but leaves nothing undone.**⫪⫫
One with highest humaneness acts on it, but has nothing for which he acts.⫪
One with highest appropriateness acts on it, but has something for which he acts.
One with highest ritual propriety acts on it, but no one matches him;
*He then rolls up his sleeves and redoubles his efforts.**
*When one loses the Way, then one loses virtue.**
*When one loses virtue, then one loses humaneness.**
*When one loses humaneness, then one loses appropriateness.**
*When one loses appropriateness, then one loses ritual propriety.**

[1] Section divisions and headings are provided here for the convenience of the reader; they do not appear in the original Chinese text. This section corresponds to chapter 38 of the *Daodejing* in the Wang Bi arrangement.

Eric L. Hutton, *Jie Lao* 解老: *Explaining the* Laozi In: *Explaining and Illustrating the* Laozi. Edited by: Eirik Lang Harris and Eric L. Hutton, Oxford University Press.
DOI: 10.1093/9780197514948.003.0003

Insisting on ritual is the impoverishment of loyalty and good faith, and the start of chaos.
Practicing foreknowledge is a flowery exhibition of the Way, and the start of foolishness.
The great man dwells in what is rich and does not dwell in what is impoverished,
Dwells in what is genuine fruit and does not dwell in what is flowery exhibition,
Discards the latter and chooses the former.

[Commentary]

Virtue involves what is internal.[2] Possession involves what is external. "One with highest virtue does not possess virtue"[3] means that one's spirit is not drawn out by external things.[4] When one's spirit is not drawn out by external things, then one's self is kept

[2] The term translated here as "virtue" is *de* 德, which has a range of senses that cannot be captured with a single English term. In addition to the moral connotation of "virtue," *de* can mean more specifically "kindness," but *de* can also refer to a kind of "potency" or "power," where such "potency" or "power" can be something like one's basic "life-force" or (especially in Confucian texts) a "moral charisma" that influences those around one. The commentary plays on different senses of *de* in different places and sometimes relies on a fusion of various senses. To allow readers to track the occurrences of the term throughout the text, the term is consistently rendered as "virtue" or variants thereof. In this first section, the commentary seems to treat *de* as *both* life-force and moral excellence.

[3] In a word play that is hard to capture in English, the commentary begins by distinguishing between "virtue" (*de* 德) and "taking possession" (*de* 得) of a thing, but then employs the latter idea to explain an apparently pejorative use of the character *de* 德 in the primary text. To reflect the application of this explanation to the pejorative *de* 德 and the merging of *de* 得 with *de* 德 in that usage, along with the seemingly paradoxical character of the primary text, I have rendered the pejorative *de* 德 as "possess virtue" or "take virtue as a possession" according to the context.

[4] Here, the text again seems to play on two senses of the word *yin* 淫 in a manner not easily captured in English. The term can refer to water overflowing or—by extension—to what is immoderate, decadent, and thereby tempting. In the former sense, the text is warning against letting one's spirit "flow to the outside" (and so depleting one's life-force), while in the latter sense, it is warning against a pre-occupation with "external things" leading one to misunderstand virtue and how to cultivate it. The use of the English phrase "drawn out" here is intended to reflect both the liquid metaphor and the sense of temptation. Later in this translation, *yin* is rendered as "enticing" or "licentious" or related word forms.

whole.[5] For one's self to be kept whole is called virtue. Thus, virtue is tantamount to possessing one's own self. In every case of virtue, one collects it by means of non-action, completes it by means of non-desiring, secures it by means of non-thinking, and solidifies it by means of non-use. If one acts on it and desires it, then virtue will have no place to lodge. If virtue has no place to lodge, then it will not be whole. If one uses it and thinks about it, then it will not be solid. If it is not solid, then it will lack achievements. This lack of achievements arises from taking virtue as a possession. Thus, if one takes virtue as a possession, then one lacks virtue. And if one does not take virtue as a possession, then one has virtue. And so the text says,[6] "One with highest virtue does not possess virtue, and thereby has virtue."

The reason to value non-action and no-thought for achieving emptiness[7] is that in such conditions one's considerations are unconfined. A person who lacks the right technique will intentionally try to use non-action and no-thought in order to become empty. If one intentionally tries to use non-action and no-thought in order to become empty, then in one's considerations one never forgets emptiness, and so one winds up confined by trying to be empty. Emptiness means that one's considerations are unconfined. So now if one is confined by trying to be empty, then this is not true emptiness. In the non-action involved in becoming empty, one does not

[5] The term rendered here as "self" is *shen* 身, which more literally means "body" and is rendered that way in certain occurrences later on here. I have also occasionally translated it as "person" when that fits the context better than either of those other English words.

[6] In the Chinese, the grammatical subject of the verb "say" is not explicit. In such cases, I have rendered it as "the text" for the sake of clarity, based on the instances later in the chapter that expressly reference what the "book" (*shu* 書, more literally "document") discusses. Readers should nonetheless be aware that in these cases where the grammatical subject is implicit, it could instead be a person such as "he" (or even "she" or "they").

[7] Although the Chinese word here, *xu* 虛, means "emptiness," in this and several other instances in the "Jie Lao," it clearly does not mean literally to be absolutely devoid of all thoughts, but rather means not being confined in one's thinking and approach to things. For that reason, "receptiveness" or "openness" comes closer to the sense of *xu* in such cases, but I have retained the translation "emptiness" for the sake of consistency with instances elsewhere in the texts where *xu* is used in a more literal sense.

take non-action as a constant tenet. If one does not take non-action as a constant tenet, then one becomes empty, and if one is empty, then one's virtue flourishes. When one's virtue flourishes, this is called the highest virtue. And so the text says, "One with highest virtue takes no action,[8] but leaves nothing undone."

Humaneness[9] means that in one's innermost heart one joyfully cares for people. One delights in their having good fortune and abhors their having misfortunes. This is born from something that the heart cannot help but feel, and not from seeking for some recompense. And so the text says, "One with highest humaneness acts on it, but has nothing for which he acts."

What is appropriate[10] concerns the services between lord and minister, superior and subordinate; the distinctions between father and son, noble and lowly; the links between acquaintances and associates, friends and comrades; and the divisions between close and distant relatives, insiders and outsiders. For the minister to serve the lord is proper. For the subordinate to cherish the superior is proper. For the son to serve the father is proper. For the lowly to honor the noble is proper. For acquaintances and associates and friends and comrades to help each other is proper. For close relatives to be insiders and distant relatives to be outsiders is proper. Appropriateness means being proper in each of these things.[11]

[8] Up to this point, the characters *wuwei* 無為 have been used as a noun phrase, and hence have been translated as "non-action." Here in the primary text, however, they are used as a sentence predicate, and so I translate as "takes no action" to reflect that difference, but readers should be aware that the same two characters appear here and are what the commentary's discussion of "non-action" is referencing.

[9] The Chinese term here is *ren* 仁 (often translated as "benevolence"), which was a major virtue in Confucian and Mohist thought. The commentary's explanation of the term is highly similar to explanations of it in Confucian texts.

[10] The term translated here is *yi* 義, which, like *ren* (see previous footnote), was also a major concept in Confucian and Mohist thought, and again the commentary's explanation here greatly resembles what one sees in Confucian texts. *Yi* can refer to a particular standard for conduct or the virtue of abiding by that standard. In other texts, the former usage is often translated as "duty" and the latter usage is often translated as "righteousness."

[11] Here the text plays on the fact that the words for "appropriateness" (*yi* 義) and "proper" (*yi* 宜) sounded alike in ancient Chinese.

Because something is proper, one acts on it. And so the text says, "One with highest appropriateness acts on it, but has something for which he acts."

Ritual[12] is that by which one provides an exterior display for one's inner essence.[13] It is the ornamentation and adornment of the various things that are appropriate. It is the fitting interaction between lord and minister, father and son. It is that by which noble and lowly, worthy and unworthy are all differentiated. In one's innermost heart one may cherish others without it being understood by them, and so one hurries before them and humbly bows in order to make it clear. In one's true heart one may care for others without it being known to them, and so one refines one's words and embellishes one's phrases in order to attest to it. Ritual is that by which external adornment makes understood what is internal. And so I have said that ritual is for providing an exterior display for one's inner essence. Whenever people act for the sake of external things, it is because they do not understand that these rituals are for themselves. The masses perform ritual merely to put on a show of respect toward others, and so at times they do it vigorously and at times they are slack. The gentleman,[14] however, performs ritual

[12] "Ritual" is the standard translation for *li* 禮, which covers a wide range of standards for behavior, including what we would nowadays think of as etiquette. The term *li* is also used to describe a person's devotion to these standards, and that usage is translated here as "ritual propriety." As with *ren* and *yi*, ritual and ritual propriety were very important concepts for Confucian thinkers, but not so for Mohists. The commentary's discussion of the value of *li* in this paragraph again tallies well with a number of early Confucian treatments of it, and especially that found in the *Xunzi*.

[13] "Essence" is used here to translate *qing* 情, which more literally refers to the true or genuine "condition" of a thing. As applied to people, it often refers to the emotions in particular, and that is probably included in its intended sense here, though subsequent appearances of the word in this chapter clearly do not have that sense, so "essence" has been chosen to allow for a more consistent way of rendering the term throughout the translation.

[14] "Gentleman" translates the term *junzi* 君子. The term is especially prominent in Confucian texts, where the *junzi* represents a highly cultivated person whose judgment and conduct are exemplary. Those texts often treat the *junzi* as equivalent to the ideal or highest type of person, namely the "sage" (*sheng ren* 聖人), and such thinking is reflected here as well, since this paragraph slides from talking about the gentleman to talking about the sage in its explanation of the primary text. The word *junzi* originally meant "the son of a lord," i.e., a prince, but over time—and especially due to the influence of

for his own self. He does it for his own self, and so he venerates it to the point of achieving the highest ritual propriety. A person of highest ritual propriety venerates it, but the masses waver in it, and so they cannot match him.[a] They cannot match him, and so the text says, "One with highest ritual propriety acts on it, but no one matches him." Although the masses waver in it, at this the sage doubles his courtesy and respect, tending to every detail of ritual with his hands and feet, without slackening. And so the text says, "He then rolls up his sleeves and redoubles his efforts."[b]

In following the Way[15] there is a process of accumulation, and this accumulation results in an achievement. Virtue is the achievement that comes from following the Way. This achievement has its fruition, and this fruition has a radiant expression. Humaneness is the radiant expression of virtue. This radiant expression has shining instances, and these shining instances take the form of concrete activity. Doing what is appropriate is the concrete activity of humaneness. For this concrete activity there are rituals, and in these rituals there is ornamentation. Ritual is the ornamentation for what is appropriate. And so the text says, "When one loses the Way, then one loses virtue. When one loses virtue, then one loses humaneness. When one loses humaneness, then one loses appropriateness. When one loses appropriateness, then one loses ritual propriety."[16]

Confucians—that aristocratic sense was largely abandoned in favor of using it as a term of moral appraisal. That transition was mostly complete by the late Warring States period when the "Jie Lao" and "Yu Lao" were likely written, but occasionally the word was still used in ways that rely on its older sense, e.g., "Yu Lao" §3, p. 88.

[15] For more explanation of how the Way (*dao* 道) is understood in this text, see §6–8 below and the introduction to this volume.

[16] The *Laozi* text as quoted by the "Jie Lao" is ambiguous and could be understood as a claim about the world or society generally that might alternatively be translated thus: "With the loss of the Way comes the loss of virtue. With the loss of virtue comes the loss of humaneness. With the loss of humaneness comes the loss of appropriateness. With the loss of appropriateness comes the loss of ritual propriety." However, based on what precedes the quotation, the "Jie Lao" apparently interprets the lines as applying first and foremost to the individual, and so that is how they are rendered above.

Ritual then becomes a merely exterior display simulating inner essence, and ornamentation then becomes a mere adornment covering over underlying substance.[c] The gentleman chooses that which is essential and discards what is merely exterior display, delights in that which is substantial and hates what is mere adornment. When something relies upon its exterior display for judging its essence, its essence is ugly. When something depends upon its adornment for judging its substance, such substance is defective. How do I conclude this? The jade disk of Mr. He was not adorned with the five colors, and the pearl of the Marquis of Sui was not adorned with gold and silver.[17] Their substances themselves were extremely beautiful, and so other things were unworthy of adorning them. As for things that must await adornment and only afterwards are acceptable, their substances are not beautiful. Thus, between father and son, ritual is to be simple and not explicitly demanded.[d] And so the text says, "Insisting on ritual is . . . impoverishment . . . ."[18,e] In every case, opposed things cannot simultaneously flourish; *yin* and *yang* are an example of this.[19] Opposed governing orders[20] take from and yield to each other; threats and virtue[21] are an example of

[17] The jade disk of Mr. He and the pearl of the Marquis of Sui were famous treasures.

[18] Here ellipsis points are added to indicate that the commentary quotes an abbreviated version of a line from the primary text; they do not represent a lacuna in the original Chinese text of the commentary.

[19] *Yin* and *yang* were conceived as two basic forces or polarities in the world. Although they could (and often did) co-exist within an individual entity, they were thought of as going through alternations in which one would be in ascendance and the other in decline—in no case could both of them reach their maximal state simultaneously.

[20] The words "governing order" here translate the Chinese term *li* 理, which most literally refers to the "pattern" a thing does or should follow in its behavior, and is an important concept in this text. This usage can sometimes be translated with the English word "principle," but since this same character *li* can be used as a verb meaning "to order" or "be ordered" and is so used later in the chapter, I translate the noun with "order" here and elsewhere to bring out the connection between the various occurrences of the term. "Governing" is added to reflect the idea (highlighted in §6 below) that the *li* of a thing determines its behavior to some degree. That addition also happens to fit the particular political connotation with which the term is being used in this sentence. In most other places in this chapter, *li* as a noun is rendered as "proper order."

[21] The primary sense of *de* 德 here (see note 2 above) appears to be "kindness," and the commentary seems to have in mind specifically the contrast between two ostensibly opposed principles of governing: coercing people through fear and winning them over through kindness.

this. When the actuality of something is rich, to make a display of it is impoverishing; rituals between father and son are an example of this. Looking at the matter from this perspective, when ritual is burgeoning, then people's true hearts are in decline. Nevertheless, the performance of ritual is for working at opening up people's simple hearts. When the masses perform ritual, if people give a matching response then they are light-hearted and happy, and if they do not give a matching response then they criticize and are resentful. Now performing ritual is for working at opening up the simple hearts of people, but if one uses it as an item for criticizing others, can there be no conflict? If there is conflict then there will be chaos, and so it says, "Insisting on ritual is the impoverishment of loyalty and good faith, and the start of chaos."

To anticipate the state of affairs in one's conduct and to anticipate the order of things in one's movements is called practicing foreknowledge. To practice foreknowledge is to baselessly and recklessly consider and measure things. How do I conclude this? Zhan He[22] was sitting, and a disciple was waiting upon him. There was a cow that mooed outside the door. The disciple said, "It is a black cow, and it has a white forehead." Zhan He said, "Right. It is a black cow, but the white is on its horns." They sent someone out to look at it, and it indeed turned out to be a black cow with a white cloth wrapped around its horns. However, if you take the technique of Zhan He to stir up the heart of the masses, that is a flowery exhibition and dangerous. And so the text says that it is "a flowery exhibition of the Way."[23] If one tries to do without the

[22] Zhan He appears in a few other stories in early Chinese texts, so he was at least a somewhat known figure among Chinese writers, but those other stories unfortunately do not really provide any substantial information about him that would be helpful for understanding the discussion of him here.

[23] Below (see §3), the commentary suggests that there is a sense in which a sage is sensitive to early signs of danger and so takes steps to avoid disaster, and in that respect following the Way *does* provide a kind of foresight. So, I take it that the commentary's point here is to criticize those who mistakenly focus on the achievement of such foresight as the primary achievement in following the Way (and then turn it into a spectacle), much in the same way that the preceding paragraphs criticize other instances of focusing on the wrong thing.

acute perception of Zhan He and just sends a foolish young child[24] to look at the cow, one will also discover that it was a black cow with a white cloth wrapped around it horns. And so in seeking the acute perception of Zhan He one may give one's heart bitter toils and harm one's spirit but in the end wind up having the same result as what a foolish young child can achieve, and thus the text says that it is "the start of foolishness." And so the text says, "Practicing foreknowledge is a flowery exhibition of the Way, and the start of foolishness."

When the text speaks of "the great man," it is speaking of the greatness of his intelligence. What is meant by saying that he "dwells in what is rich and does not dwell in what is impoverished" is that he carries out the actuality of what is essential[25] and discards merely exterior displays of ritual. What is meant by saying that he "dwells in what is genuine fruit[26] and does not dwell in what is flowery exhibition" is that he is sure to follow the proper order and does not take short cuts.[27] What is meant by saying that he "discards the latter and chooses the former" is that he discards merely exterior displays of ritual and taking short cuts and chooses following the proper order and the actuality of what is essential. And so the text says that he "discards the latter and chooses the former."

[24] Here and in the next sentence, the text references an ancient system of measurement and literally says "a child five *chi* tall." Five *chi* would have been somewhere in the range of about 100–116 cm or 3.28–3.8 feet.

[25] E.g., he develops the genuine relation of affection that is supposed to obtain between father and son and that is supposed to underlie the rituals concerning their interactions.

[26] The word *shi* 實 can mean what is "actual," "real," "true," or "genuine," but it can also mean "fruit." Here the text seems to play on both senses simultaneously: in contrasting it with *hua* 華 (lit. "flower"), *shi* refers to the "fruit," but insofar as *hua* in this case refers more specifically to displaying special powers like those of Zhan He that are at best epiphenomena of the Way, *shi* by contrast also refers to the genuine substance of the Way. Hence, I have translated it as "genuine fruit" to try to reflect both senses at once.

[27] Here "short cuts" refers to the kind of foreknowledge practiced by Zhan He as mentioned earlier, which seeks to proceed by some method for gaining knowledge that bypasses more typical methods such as using one's eyes.

Section Two[28]

[Primary Text]

Misfortune, indeed, is what good fortune rests upon.∓
Good fortune, indeed, is where misfortune lies in wait.
Who knows where their limits lie?±
The days that people have spent being lost indeed stretch over a long time already!∓
[And so the sage] has rectitude but is not cutting,
Is principled but is not hurtful,
Is upright but is not aggressive,
Is radiant but is not dazzling.

[Commentary]

If a person has misfortunes then his heart will be fearful and cautious. If his heart is fearful and cautious, then his conduct will be correct and upright. If his conduct is correct and upright, then his thoughts and deliberations will be thorough. If his thoughts and deliberations are thorough, then he will grasp the proper order for affairs. If his conduct is correct and upright, then he will avoid misfortune and harm. If he avoids misfortune and harm, then he will complete his Heaven-allotted years. If he grasps the proper order for affairs, then he is sure to be successful. If he can complete his Heaven-allotted years, then he will remain whole and be long-lived. If he is sure to be successful, then he will become rich and achieve noble status. Being whole, long-lived, rich, and noble is called good fortune, but good fortune has its root in having misfortunes. And so the text says, "Misfortune, indeed, is what good fortune rests upon," in order to aid one in achieving success.

If a person has good fortune, then riches and nobility will come. If riches and nobility come, then one's clothing and food will be fine.

[28] This section corresponds to chapter 58 of the *Daodejing* in the Wang Bi arrangement.

If one's clothing and food are fine, then one's heart will become arrogant. If one's heart becomes arrogant, then one's conduct will become deviant and perverse, and one will abandon proper order in one's actions. If one's conduct is deviant and perverse, then one will die an untimely death, and if one abandons proper order in one's actions, then one will lack successes. Having the calamity of untimely death press in upon one's person, while also lacking any successes to one's name in the wider world, is a great misfortune, and this misfortune is at its root born from having good fortune. And so the text says, "Good fortune, indeed, is where misfortune lies in wait."

For one who follows the proper order of the Way in pursuing his affairs, there is nothing that he cannot achieve. When there is nothing he cannot achieve, then at the greatest he can achieve the power and prestige of the Son of Heaven,[29] and at the least he can still easily come to possess the rewards and stipend of a grand minister, prime minister, or general. As for one who deviates from the proper order of the Way and behaves recklessly, even if such a one at the greatest had the power and prestige of the Son of Heaven or the feudal lords,[30] or at the least had the riches of Yi Dun, Tao Zhu, or Bu Zhu,[31] he would still lose his populace and forfeit his wealth. The reason why the masses lightly abandon the proper order of the

[29] "Son of Heaven" (*tianzi* 天子) was the official title of the king of the Zhou dynasty, who was considered to be the rightful ruler of "all under Heaven" (*tianxia* 天下). The word translated as "power" in this paragraph is *shi* 勢, which figures as a very important concept in other chapters of the *Han Feizi*. In a broad sense, the term refers to "circumstances," but chapter 40 of the *Han Feizi* argues that one's ability to rule depends in large part on the institutional "circumstances" in which one occupies a position of authority. On such usage, *shi* has the sense of "power." Elsewhere in the translation, when the text is especially emphasizing the connection between such power and one's particular institutional position, I render it as "authoritative power."

[30] The "feudal lords" (*zhuhou* 諸侯) were given hereditary rule over specific territories by the Zhou king, to whom they were in principle subordinate. The rank of feudal lord was thus one of the highest positions possible. By the time this passage was written, likely during the Warring States period, the actual power of many feudal lords exceeded that of the Zhou king.

[31] According to other sources, Yi Dun was originally a poor farmer who went from rags to riches after asking Tao Zhu for advice on becoming wealthy. Tao Zhu is said to be the same as Fan Li 范蠡, who once played a prominent role in the government of the state of Yue in first half of the fifth century BCE, but then left government service, moved

Way and easily behave recklessly is because they do not know that the depths and magnitudes of misfortune and good fortune and the breadth and vastness of the Way are like this. And so the text tries to make people understand by saying, "Who knows where their limits lie?"[32]

Among people, there are none who do not desire to be rich, noble, whole, and long-lived, yet none can avoid the misfortunes of poverty, low status, and untimely death. When one's heart desires riches, nobility, wholeness, and long life, but one now faces poverty, low status, and untimely death, this is a case of being unable to go where one desires to go. Whenever a person misses the road to where he desires to go and recklessly wanders off, this is called being lost. If one is lost, then one will simply never be able to go where one desires to go. Now the masses are thus unable to go where they desire to go, and so the text says that they are "lost." The inability of the masses to go where they desire to go has continued from the time Heaven and Earth first split apart from each other down to the present day, and so the text says, "The days that people have spent being lost indeed stretch over a long time already!"

away, changed his name, and became a successful businessman. The placement of the two characters *bu zhu* 卜祝 in parallel with Yi Dun and Tao Zhu suggests that it is a person's name (which is how it is rendered here), but if so, the person is unknown. Some commentators suggest taking *bu zhu* as instead meaning "prognosticators and priests" who preyed on people's superstitions to become rich. Other commentators suggest that the two characters *bu zhu* are a corruption, and the sentence either had some other well-known rich person's name or the whole phrase originally read "ten times the riches of Yi Dun and Tao Zhu."

[32] Even with the commentary, this sentence from the primary text remains ambiguous. As I understand it, the point is that the Way sets certain limits on how wealth and power can be possessed. To understand these limits is simultaneously to understand the "breadth and vastness of the Way" and the "depths and magnitudes of misfortune and good fortune," e.g., how far one can go before good fortune leads to misfortune. Note that the commentary does not take the question "Who knows?" as suggesting—as it often does in contemporary English—that no one does or can know the answer, but rather as suggesting that there *is* a genuine understanding of this issue to be had, and one that the sage *does* have, as the commentary goes on to explain.

What the text calls having "rectitude" is for one's inner states and outer performances to match each other and for one's words and actions to correspond to each other. What the text calls being "principled" is to respect the necessity of what has been mandated[33] in living and dying and to regard wealth lightly. What the text calls having "uprightness" is to ensure that one is unprejudiced and fair in enacting what is appropriate, and to be neither biased nor partisan in one's heart. What the text calls being "radiant" is for one's official position and salary to be prestigious and noble and one's clothes to be majestic and beautiful. Now as for a well-bred man[34] who holds to the Way, even though inside and outside he is trustworthy and accommodating, he does not use this to disparage those who behave poorly or demean those who fall short. Even though he is willing to die in upholding proper regulation and regards wealth lightly, he does not use these to insult those who are enervated or shame those who are greedy. Even though he does what is appropriate and correct and is not partisan, he does not use these to purge those who go astray or condemn those who are selfish. Even though his power is prestigious and his clothing is beautiful, he does not use these to brag before those who are lowly or bully those who are poor. What is

[33] The Chinese text here is difficult to translate and is ambiguous because of its use of the word *ming* 命, which literally means "mandate." In many early Chinese texts, it refers to what the cosmos or Heaven has mandated for human beings, i.e., fate or destiny, in which case the point would be that the principled person lives and dies in accordance with his proper destiny, which is a kind of moral integrity. However, the word *ming* can also refer to what a human ruler has mandated or "commanded" for his subordinates, in which case the point would be that the principled person lives and dies in accordance with the orders he has been given, which is a form of political devotion. The commentary may be intentionally playing upon both these senses simultaneously.

[34] The term translated here as "well-bred man" is *shi* 士, which originally referred to minor aristocrats who served various lower-level functions in government. The term later came to be used—as it is here—to designate a person of virtue and intelligence, much like the term *junzi* 君子 ("gentleman"; see note 14 above). As with that latter term, the "well-bred man" is also sometimes treated as more or less tantamount to the "sage," which can again be seen in the manner in which this paragraph of the commentary slides between the two concepts as if they are nearly equivalent. In a few other instances in the "Jie Lao" and "Yu Lao," the term *shi* is used in a military context, where it is not meant to convey moral or intellectual excellence, but instead just designates a certain set of members of the army, and in those cases I have rendered it simply as "officer."

the reason for this? If there is one who has missed the right road but is willing to listen to those who are practiced and ask those who are knowledgeable, then he will not become lost. Now the masses desire to be successful but in the end wind up being defeated because they do not understand the proper order of the Way and are unwilling to ask those who are knowledgeable and listen to those who are capable. Since the masses are not willing to ask those who are knowledgeable and listen to those who are capable, if the sage forcefully uses their misfortunes and failures to reprove them, then they will be resentful. The masses are many but the sages are few. That the few do not prevail over the many is simply a matter of numbers. Now if one adopts actions yet becomes an enemy to all under Heaven, this is not the way to keep one's self whole and make one's life long, and so in following the right track the sage moderates his actions and then adopts them. And so the text says that he "has rectitude but is not cutting, is principled but is not hurtful, is upright but is not aggressive,[f] is radiant but is not dazzling."

Section Three[35]

[Primary Text]

For ordering human affairs and serving Heavenly affairs, nothing is as good as frugality.
*When one is called frugal, this is due to submitting early.**
As for submitting early, this means repeatedly amassing virtue.
If one repeatedly amasses virtue, then there is nothing that one does not overcome.
If there is nothing that one does not overcome, then no one will know where one's limits lie.

[35] This section corresponds to chapter 59 of the *Daodejing* in the Wang Bi arrangement.

If no one knows where one's limits lie, then one can hold the state.
By means of the mother of holding a state, one can last long and endure.
Make deep the root, make solid the base—this is the way to long life and enduring sight.

[Commentary]

Acuteness, clarity, and sharp intelligence—these are Heavenly affairs.[36] Activity and calm, thinking and deliberation—these are human affairs. Humans rely upon Heavenly clarity[37] in order to see, rest on Heavenly acuteness in order to hear, and lean on Heavenly intelligence in order to think and deliberate. And so if one's vision is forcibly strained, then one's eyes will not be clear. If one's hearing is taxed too much, then one's ears will not be acute. If one's thinking and deliberation are excessive, then one's intelligence and discernment will be confused. If one's eyes are not clear, then one cannot judge the difference between black and white. If one's ears are not acute, then one cannot distinguish high and low sounds. If one's intelligence and discernment are confused, then one cannot assess the conditions for gain and loss. If one's eyes cannot judge black and white colors, then we call that person blind. If one's ears cannot distinguish high and low sounds, then we call that person deaf. If one's heart cannot assess the conditions for gain and loss, then we call that person witless. If one is blind, then one cannot evade the dangers of daytime. If one is deaf, then

[36] The sense in which these are "Heavenly" is ambiguous in Chinese. On the one hand, it can mean that these are qualities of Heaven itself. On the other hand, it can mean that these are qualities given to people by Heaven. The text goes on to speak in ways that lean more toward the latter sense, but the former may be intended as well (i.e., these are qualities that Heaven itself has, but which it also endows in people, and thus these qualities in people resemble those of Heaven). In order to reflect these various senses, I have rendered the Chinese here simply as "Heavenly."

[37] Here the text appears to be playing on two senses of *tian ming* 天明. The term can mean "Heavenly (i.e., Heaven-given or Heaven-like) clear vision," but it can also mean "the brightness of Heaven," i.e., sunlight.

one cannot know the menace of thunderstrokes. If one is witless, then one cannot avoid the misfortunes imposed by laws and decrees among humans. What the book calls "ordering human affairs" is to conform to proper measure for activity and calm, and to decrease one's effort expended in thinking and deliberating. What it means by "serving Heavenly affairs" is to refrain from pushing the powers of acute hearing and clear vision to the extreme and to refrain from exhausting one's intelligence and discernment. If one pushes them to the extreme and exhausts them, then one's expenditure of spirit will be great. If one's expenditure of spirit is great, then the misfortunes of blindness, deafness, and unruly witlessness will arrive. Therefore, one is to be frugal with these things. Being frugal with these things is to use one's energy and spirit sparingly and to use one's intelligence and discernment frugally. And so the text says, "For ordering human affairs and serving Heavenly affairs, nothing is as good as frugality."

The way the masses use their spirit is frenetic. Since it is frenetic, it involves great expenditure of effort. Having great expenditure is called being extravagant. The way the sage uses his spirit is calm. Since it is calm, it involves little expenditure of effort. Having little expenditure is called being frugal. The kind of frugality that constitutes the right technique is born from the proper order of the Way. So when someone is able to be frugal, this is someone who follows the Way and submits to its proper order. The masses meet with troubles and fall into misfortune, and still they do not know to withdraw, nor do they submit to and follow the proper order of the Way. Even though the sage has not yet seen the full form of misfortunes and troubles, he is empty and unfilled, and he submits to and follows the proper order of the Way, and with this he is called "submitting early." And so the text says, "When one is called frugal, this is due to submitting early."

As for one who knows how to order human affairs, his thoughts and deliberations are calm. As for one who knows how to serve Heavenly affairs, the orifices and cavities of his body are empty.

If one's thoughts and reflections are calm, then one's original virtue[38] will not depart, and if the orifices and cavities of one's body are empty, then harmonious *qi*[39] will daily enter. And so the text speaks of "repeatedly amassing virtue." One who can ensure that his original virtue does not depart and that new harmonious *qi* arrives daily is one who submits early. And so the text says, "As for submitting early, this means repeatedly amassing virtue." When one amasses virtue, then one's spirit is calm. When one's spirit is calm, then one's harmoniousness increases.[40] When one's harmoniousness increases, then one's plans are successful. When one's plans are successful, then one can harness the power of the ten thousand things. If one can harness the power of the ten thousand things, then it is easy to prevail over one's opponents in battle. When it is easy to prevail over one's opponents in battle, one's proclamations are sure to dominate one's era. One's proclamations are sure to dominate one's era, and so the text says, "There is nothing that one does not overcome." Having nothing that one does not overcome has its root in repeatedly amassing virtue, and so the text says, "If one repeatedly amasses virtue, then there is nothing that one does not overcome." If one easily prevails over one's opponents in battle, then one will annex and own every place under Heaven. If one's proclamations are sure to dominate one's era, then the populace will follow. If upon marching out, one annexes every place under Heaven, and upon marching back, one has the populace following,

[38] As mentioned earlier (note 2 above), here the term *de* 德 is used more in the sense of "life-force," though I have continued to render it as "virtue" in English in order to allow readers to track the term throughout the translation.

[39] *Qi* 氣 designates a quasi-substance, quasi-energy that was thought by many early Chinese to circulate throughout the environment and living bodies, and the presence or absence of various kinds of good or bad *qi* was taken to explain health or illness. Hence, one sees passages such as this one advocating methods for drawing in good types of *qi* for the sake of physical and mental vigor. In this particular case, the sense of *qi* approaches that of *de* 德 as "life-force," and so the commentary treats the accumulation of *qi* as part of the process of "repeatedly amassing virtue."

[40] The "harmoniousness" in question could be a harmony solely within one's person, or it could be instead (or in addition) an ability to work harmoniously with one's surrounding environment.

then this person's technique is far-reaching, and the masses will not see his beginning and end. No one sees his beginning and end, and therefore no one knows where his limits lie. And so the text says, "If there is nothing that one does not overcome, then no one will know where one's limits lie."

In every case where one has a state and then loses it or has a body and then injures it,[g] this cannot be called being able to hold one's state or being able to protect one's body. As for being able to hold one's state, one must certainly be able to safeguard one's altars of soil and grain,[41] and as for being able to protect one's body, one must certainly be able to live out one's Heaven-allotted years. Only afterwards can one be called able to hold one's state and protect one's body. If one is going to be able to hold one's state and be able to protect one's body, one must, moreover, embody the Way. If one embodies the Way, then one's intelligence will be profound. If one's intelligence is profound, then one's comprehension will be far-reaching. If one's comprehension is far-reaching, then none among the masses will be able to see where one's limits lie. Only when one is able to embody the Way can one cause people to be unable to see where the limits of one's affairs lie. When others cannot see where the limits of one's affairs lie, then one can protect one's body and hold one's state. And so the text says, "If no one knows where one's limits lie, then one can hold the state."

When the text speaks of "the mother of holding a state," the "mother" is the Way. As for the Way itself, it gives birth to the technique by which one holds a state.[h] It is this technique by which one holds a state, and so the text calls it the "mother of holding a state." In following the Way so as to revolve and turn along with the era, one establishes one's life in a manner that makes it long-lasting, and one maintains one's salary in a manner that makes it enduring. And so the text says, "By means of the mother of holding a state, one can last long and endure."

[41] The "altars of soil and grain" (*she ji* 社稷) were important sites symbolizing the authority of a state's ruling family.

Trees have spreading roots and tap roots. The tap root is what the book calls the "base." The base is that by which the tree establishes its life. The spreading root is that by which the tree maintains its life. Virtue is that by which a person establishes his life, and a salary is that by which a person maintains his life. Now as for one who establishes himself on the proper order, he will maintain his salary enduringly, and so the text says, "Make deep the root." As for one who embodies the proper Way, the days of his life will long, and so the text says, "Make solid the base." If the base is solid then one's life will be long. If the root is deep then one's sight will be enduring,[42] and so the text says, "Make deep the root, make solid the base—this is the way to long life and enduring sight."

Section Four[43]

[Primary Text]

Ordering a large state is like cooking a small fish.
If you use the Way to oversee all under Heaven, then ghosts will lack spirit force.
It is not that ghosts really lack spirit force. Rather, their spirit force does not injure people.
The sage also does not injure the people.
If the two do not injure each other, then in their interaction virtue will reside with them.

[Commentary]

If a laborer frequently changes occupation, then one is deprived of some of his output. If a worker is frequently disturbed and

[42] Here, "enduring sight" is metonymy for life more broadly, similar to how in English the remark "She has seen many things come and go" serves as another way of saying that the person in question has lived a long time.
[43] This section corresponds to chapter 60 of the *Daodejing* in the Wang Bi arrangement.

reassigned, then one loses some of his output. If half of a person's work is lost each day, then in ten days one will lose five people's output. If half of the work of ten thousand people is lost every day, then in ten days one will have lost fifty thousand people's output. Thus, where occupations are frequently changing, the greater the number of people involved, the greater the losses. Whenever laws and decrees are changed, then what is beneficial and what is harmful also change. If what is beneficial and what is harmful change, then the people will devote effort to changing, too. When the people devote effort to changing, this means that they are changing occupations. And so looking at this from the perspective of proper order, if you are giving tasks to large masses of people and frequently disturb them, then you will achieve few accomplishments.[i] If you are keeping a large vessel and frequently move it, then it will suffer much damage.[44] When you cook a small fish and frequently turn it, then you ruin its texture. When you rule a large state and frequently change the laws, the people will suffer from it. Therefore, the ruler who holds to the Way values emptiness and calmness and views changing the laws as a weighty matter. And so the text says, "Ordering a large state is like cooking a small fish."

When people experience sickness then they value doctors. When they have misfortunes then they fear ghosts. When a sage is in power, the people reduce their desires. If the people reduce their desires, then their blood and *qi* will be well regulated, and their actions and behavior will be well ordered. If their blood and *qi* are well regulated and their actions and behavior are well ordered, then this will reduce their misfortunes and harms. If from within there is no harm from boils, tumors, ulcers, and swellings,

[44] This sentence may contain a double entendre. I have translated it as most commentaries understand it, but the word *qi* 器 ("vessel") was also sometimes used metaphorically to refer to talented people suited for government positions. Understood that way, the sentence would be saying, "If you are keeping (i.e., employing) greatly talented people and frequently move (i.e., re-assign) them, then you will suffer much failure and injury." Such a reading also fits with the context. I thank Eirik L. Harris for highlighting to me this feature of the text.

and from without there are no misfortunes from punishments, penalties, laws, and executions, then they will have very little concern over ghosts. And so the text says, "If you use the Way to oversee all under Heaven, then ghosts will lack spirit force."[45] The people of an ordered age do not engage with ghosts and spirits in such a way as to do harm to each other. And so the text says, "It is not that ghosts really lack spirit force. Rather, their spirit force does not injure people." When ghosts haunt and sicken people, this is called ghosts injuring people. When people banish and exterminate them, this is called people injuring ghosts. For the people to violate laws and decrees is called the people injuring their superiors, and for the superiors to punish and execute the people is called the superiors injuring the people. Now if the people do not violate the laws, then their superiors will correspondingly not carry out punishments. When the superiors do not carry out punishments, this is called the superiors not injuring the people. And so the text says, "The sage also does not injure the people." The superiors and the people do not harm each other, and people and ghosts do not injure each other, and so the text says, "The two do not injure each other." If the people do not dare to violate the laws, then their superiors will neither target their bodies with the application of punishments and penalties nor target their belongings with efforts to confiscate profits from their products and occupations.[j] If the superiors neither target their bodies with the application of punishments and penalties nor target their belongings with efforts to confiscate profits from their products and occupations, then the people will thrive. The people thrive and then their harvests flourish. For the people to thrive and their harvests to flourish is called having

[45] The term *shen* 神, which elsewhere in this translation is rendered simply as "spirit," can be used in Chinese to refer to a kind of power or efficaciousness that is immense and operates in mysterious ways, i.e., the sort of power that superhuman entities are typically thought to possess. I have rendered *shen* in such instances as "spirit force," in order to retain a clear link in English between this use of the term and its use to refer to spirits, and hence to allow readers who do not know Chinese to track various occurrences of the term *shen* across the translation.

virtue.[46] In every case of what are called hauntings, one's *hun* and *po*[47] are dispersed and one's energy and spirit are disordered. If one's energy and spirit are disordered, then one lacks virtue. If ghosts do not haunt people, then their *hun* and *po* will not be dispersed. If their *hun* and *po* are not dispersed, then their energy and spirit will not be disordered. For their energy and spirit not to be disordered is called having virtue. When their superiors make the harvest flourish and ghosts do not disorder their energy and spirit, then virtue will fully rest in the people. And so the text says, "If the two do not injure each other, then in their interaction virtue will reside in them." This says that virtue in the interaction of superior and inferior will flourish and will fully reside in the people.

Section Five[48]

[Primary Text]

When all under Heaven hold to the Way, then swift horses are relegated to carrying dung.
When all under Heaven lack the Way, then war horses are born from the suburbs.
Of crimes, none is greater than approving desires.◊

[46] The meaning of "having virtue" here is ambiguous, and perhaps deliberately so. On the one hand, the text may be using it in the sense of a life-giving force, and the point would be that the common people are amply supplied with the means to live. On the other hand, "virtue" may instead (or also) be meant in the sense of "kindness," and the point would be that the common people enjoy the kindness of their superior's rule (and in this latter case, "virtue" would be something that both the superior and the common people "have," though in different senses).

[47] The *hun* 魂 and *po* 魄 were two different "vital energies" or "souls" that were believed to dwell within people. (Based on etymology, the two are sometimes rendered, respectively, as "cloud-soul" and "white-soul" by other translators.) It was believed that at death, the two left the body, and the *hun* 魂 ascended to Heaven while the *po* 魄 descended into the Earth. In this particular case, the "dispersal" of *hun* and *po* seems to refer to something like psycho-physical dysfunction, rather than death.

[48] This section corresponds to chapter 46 of the *Daodejing* in the Wang Bi arrangement. This material is also discussed in §1 of the "Yu Lao" chapter, and readers are invited to compare the two treatments.

Of misfortunes, none is greater than being insatiable.
*Of faults, none is more agonizing than desiring benefit.**±

[*Commentary*]

As for a ruler who holds to the Way, outside the state he harbors no resentment or enmity against his neighbors and rivals, and inside the state he shows virtue[49] and generosity toward his subjects. Since outside the state he harbors no resentment or enmity against his neighbors and rivals, when he meets with the feudal lords, he follows the rituals and standards for what is appropriate.[50] Since inside the state he shows virtue and generosity toward his subjects, in his ordering of human affairs he works at what is fundamental. If when meeting with the feudal lords he follows the rituals and standards for what is appropriate, then the occasions for military conscriptions will be few. If in ordering the affairs of the people he works at what is fundamental, then licentiousness and extravagance will cease. When horses are used extensively, it is for providing armor and weapons outside the state and supplying licentiousness and extravagance inside the state. Now the ruler who holds to the Way rarely uses armor and weapons outside the state, and he forbids licentiousness and extravagance inside the state. When the superiors do not employ horses in fighting wars and pursuing retreating forces, and the people do not use horses to transport licentious goods over great distances, then their accumulated strength is devoted to the fields. When their accumulated strength is put into the fields, then they must, moreover, fertilize them with dung and irrigate them. And so the text says, "When all under Heaven hold to the Way, then swift horses are relegated to carrying dung."

[49] Here, the term *de* 德 ("virtue") seems to be used primarily in its sense as "kindness."
[50] The phrase "standards for what is appropriate" here translates the term *yi* 義. For more explanation, see note 10 above.

If the ruler of people lacks the Way, then inside the state he will tyrannize and abuse his people, and outside the state he will invade and bully his neighboring states. If inside the state he engages in tyranny and abuse, then the people's productivity will be disrupted. If outside the state he invades and bullies, then troops must often be raised. If the people's productivity is disrupted, then the birth of livestock will decrease. If troops must often be raised, then one will run out of officers and soldiers. If the birth of livestock decreases, then war horses will be in short supply. If one runs out of officers and soldiers, then the army will be in grave danger. If war horses are in short supply, then pregnant mares will be sent out. If the army is in grave danger, then close ministers will be conscripted. Horses are something used extensively by the army. "The suburbs" refers to what is close. Now in this case what the army is provided with are pregnant mares and close ministers. And so the text says, "When all under Heaven lack the Way, then war horses are born from the suburbs."

If people have desires, then their plans and calculations will become chaotic. If their plans and calculations become chaotic, then their having of desires will become even greater.[51] When their having of desires become even greater, then a deviant heart will prevail in them. If a deviant heart prevails in them, then in their affairs they will take short cuts. If in their affairs they take short cuts, then misfortunes and difficulties will arise. Looking at the matter from this perspective, misfortunes and difficulties are born from a deviant heart, and a deviant heart is led astray in approving desires. As for the kinds of things that happen in approving desires, when it progresses it teaches upstanding subjects to be scoundrels, but

[51] The thought here is somewhat ambiguous. On the one hand, the text could mean that because people are unable to plan effectively for how to obtain what they desire, their existing desires will go unsatisfied and hence grow even more intense. On the other hand, the text could mean instead (or in addition) that people's inability to plan well will lead them to desire things that they would not otherwise pursue (because they would normally realize that such things are beyond their ability to acquire, or that such things are not worth desiring in the first place), and so the scope or range of things they desire expands inappropriately.

even when it is curtailed it causes good people to have misfortunes. If scoundrels arise then above they will infringe upon and weaken their ruler. If misfortunes arrive then the populace will suffer many injuries. And so, the kinds of things that happen in approving desires will infringe upon and weaken rulers above and do injury to their subjects below. As for infringing upon and weakening one's ruler above and doing injury to his subjects below, this is a great crime. And so the text says, "Of crimes, none is greater than approving desires." Therefore, a sage is neither led on by the five colors nor enticed by lovely sounds and music,[52] and an intelligent ruler despises frivolous enjoyments and gets rid of enticing beauties.

Humans have neither feathers nor fur, and so if they do not clothe themselves then they will be unable to withstand the cold. They are not part of Heaven above, nor are they attached to Earth below. Their intestines and stomachs serve as their roots, and so if they do not eat then they cannot live. Thus, they cannot avoid having a heart desirous of benefit. If this heart desirous of benefit is not eliminated, then it will become a distress for their persons. And so as for the sage, if his clothing is enough to withstand the cold and his food is enough to fill his empty stomach, then he has no distress. As for the masses, it is not so. Even if at greatest they were to become feudal lords, or if at least they were to have wealth in excess of a thousand pieces of gold, the distress that comes from their desire to possess things would still not be eliminated. Convicts sometimes receive a pardon, and those who have committed capital crimes sometimes get to live. Now the distress of those who are insatiable[53] will not be alleviated to the end of their lives. And so the text says, "Of misfortunes, none is greater than being insatiable."

[52] The thought expressed in this sentence is somewhat reminiscent of chapter 12 of the *Daodejing* in the Wang Bi arrangement, though depending on exactly how one interprets that chapter, the point made here may not be the same. Neither the "Jie Lao" nor "Yu Lao" comment directly on chapter 12, so it is unclear whether the author(s) of these commentaries had seen that material.

[53] More literally, "those who do not know when to be satisfied."

And so, if one greatly desires benefit, then one will be distressed. If one is distressed, then anxiety[54] will arise. When anxiety arises, then one's intelligence and wisdom decline. If one's intelligence and wisdom decline, then one will lose the ability to measure and weigh. If one loses the ability to measure and weigh, then one will select actions recklessly. If one selects actions recklessly, then misfortunes and harms will arrive. When misfortunes and harms arrive, then one's anxiety will disturb one's innards. If one's anxiety disturbs one's innards, then one will feel pain, and if misfortunes press from outside, then one will feel suffering. When suffering and pain are strewn among one's intestines and stomach, then the injury to the person will be agonizing. If it is agonizing, then one will retire and fault oneself. Retiring and faulting oneself is thus born from desiring benefit. And so the text says, "Of faults, none is more agonizing than desiring benefit."[k]

Section Six[55]

[Primary Text]

The Way is that which orders them.◊
They draw on it and thereby die,◊
They draw on it and thereby live.◊
They draw on it and are thereby defeated,◊
They draw on it and are thereby completed.◊

[54] The word *ji* 疾, rendered here as "anxiety," can also mean "illness," which is a sense that it clearly has elsewhere in this text. As I understand it, this passage appears to be playing on both senses, showing how what starts as "anxiety" leads to genuine "illness" afflicting one's organs.

[55] The primary text as reconstructed from the commentary does not appear in any extant versions of the *Daodejing*, but it does bear some resemblance to chapter 39 of the *Daodejing* in the Wang Bi arrangement. Some commentators have also suggested that the explanations in this section of commentary may be intended to expand on ideas found in chapters 14 and 23 of the *Daodejing* in the Wang Bi arrangement, though the wording of those chapters is even more unlike the text quoted here. This discrepancy between all known versions of the *Daodejing* and the text as discussed here has led some scholars to regard this entire section of the commentary as an interpolation.

[Commentary]

The Way is that to which the ten thousand things conform, and that wherein their ten thousand governing orders unite. These governing orders are the patterns of completed things. The Way is that by which the ten thousand things are brought to completion. And so the text says, "The Way is that which orders them." Things have their governing orders and they cannot encroach upon each other.[56] Things have their governing orders and they cannot encroach upon each other, and so the manner in which the governing orders regulate things is that things each have a different governing order. The ten thousand things each have different governing orders, but the Way comprehensively unites the governing orders of the ten thousand things, and so it cannot but undergo transformations. It cannot but undergo transformations, and so it has no constant deportment. It has no constant deportment, and thus the *qi* associated with life and death are received from it, the ten thousand intelligences pour in lesser or greater measure from it,[l] and the ten thousand affairs arise from and cease in it.

Heaven draws on it and thereby is high.[57] Earth draws on it and thereby has stores.[58] The Pole Star draws on it and thereby completes its awe-inspiring majesty. The sun and moon draw on it and thereby make lasting their light. The Five Constants draw on it and thereby make constant their stations.[59] The arrayed stars

[56] Even in the original Chinese text, the wording here is vague and the point is not entirely clear, but I take its meaning to be roughly that there are distinct, natural patterns for things (their "governing orders"), and these "governing orders" do not and cannot extend to things to which they do not originally apply. So, for example, the pattern governing the life-cycle of a butterfly cannot come to govern horses, and vice versa, so that butterflies and horses remain distinct (kinds of) things.

[57] Beginning with this sentence and continuing to the end of this section of commentary, the original Chinese text is extensively rhymed, but I have not attempted to reflect this in the translation.

[58] The sense of "stores" here is somewhat ambiguous, but it could refer to the "capaciousness" of Earth to contain the myriad things generally, or it could (also) refer more specifically to the precious stones and metals that humans have found "stored" within the Earth.

[59] The exact referent of the "Five Constants" is unclear, but given the position of this remark between the remarks about the sun and moon and the arrayed stars, perhaps the most plausible suggestion is that of Chen (1969), who takes the term as referring to the Five Planets, namely Saturn, Jupiter, Mars, Venus, and Mercury.

draw on it and thereby make straight their paths. The four seasons draw on it and thereby steer their changing *qi*. Xuan Yuan drew on it and thereby reigned over all four corners of the world.[60] Chi Song drew on it and joined together with Heaven and Earth.[61] Sages draw on it and thereby complete their patterning and adornments. The Way gave Yao and Shun complete intelligence, it gave Jieyu complete madness, it gave Jie and Zhòu complete destruction, and it gave Tang and Wu complete glory.[62,m] Do you believe it is close by? In fact, it goes out to the four poles. Do you believe it is far away? In fact, it is constantly at one's side. Do you believe it is obscure? In fact, its light shines brilliantly. Do you believe it is clear? In fact, its substance is most mysterious. Yet, its achievements complete Heaven and Earth, and its

[60] Xuan Yuan, also known as the Yellow Emperor, was a (mythical) early, pre-dynastic sage king often lauded in Daoist texts, though he is not actually mentioned by name in any extant version of the *Daodejing*. Some chronologies put his reign at the beginning of the twenty-seventh century BCE.

[61] Chi Song (lit. "Red Pine") is described by early texts as an ancient seeker of immortality, and he serves as an inspirational figure in many Daoist texts, though again no extant version of the *Daodejing* explicitly refers to him. Commentators explain that the sense in which he "joined together with Heaven and Earth" is that he achieved a longevity matching theirs.

[62] The figures listed here are often mentioned in early texts across a wide range of philosophical orientations, but are especially important in Confucian discourse. Yao, Shun, Tang, and Wu were all ancient sage kings. Yao and Shun were pre-dynastic rulers, whereas Tang was believed to have founded the Shang dynasty (traditionally dated to ca. 1766 BCE), and Wu was credited with founding the Zhou dynasty (traditionally dated to ca. 1122 BCE). Jie and Zhòu were infamous arch-tyrants who were overthrown, respectively, by Tang and Wu to start the new dynasties. (This translation uses "Zhòu" for the name of the arch-tyrant and "Zhou" for the name of the dynasty founded by King Wu, in order to help English readers distinguish the two.) Jieyu was a famous "madman" from Chu who is depicted as crossing paths with Confucius in *Analects* 18.5. It is somewhat unclear exactly why and how Jieyu is being invoked as an example here. Several early stories about him depict him as deliberately avoiding political involvement, and some portray his madness as an intentionally feigned ruse to avoid being drawn into government, which could be dangerous business. Since the other figures mentioned in this sentence of the commentary are clear examples of political success or failure, Jieyu's lack of political involvement is perhaps why he is contrasted with Yao and Shun. On the other hand, since the cases of intelligence, destruction, and glory listed here are likely being presented as *genuine* instances of those things, then it may be that Jieyu's "madness" is likewise here conceived as being genuine, and hence that he serves as a negative example, namely as someone who wrongly and stupidly avoided government service.

harmoniousness transforms thunderstorms.[63] All things in the universe rely upon it and thereby are completed. In every case, the essence of the Way has no limit, has no form, is supple and yielding, flows with the times, and matches the governing orders of things. The ten thousand things draw on it and thereby die, draw on it and thereby live; the ten thousand affairs draw on it and are thereby defeated, draw on it and are thereby completed. You can compare the Way to water: a drowning person drinks too much of it and dies, while a thirsty person drinks just the right amount of it and lives. You can compare it to swords and halberds: if a stupid person uses them to carry out his anger, then misfortunes arise, while if a sage uses them to execute the violent, then good fortune is completed. And so the text says, "They draw on it and thereby die, they draw on it and thereby live. They draw on it and are thereby defeated, they draw on it and are thereby completed."

Section Seven[64]

[Primary Text]

. . . the shape of that without shape, the image of
that without substance.[*∓±]

[Commentary]

People rarely see live elephants, but they have obtained the bones of dead elephants and followed their outlines in order to imagine

[63] The latter half of this sentence is rather ambiguous. I suggest that the sense in which the harmoniousness of the Way "transforms" thunderstorms is that it calms them, such that the point of the remark is to ascribe to the Way both the power to generate tremendous forces of nature and the power to pacify the more destructive ones among them.

[64] This section corresponds to chapter 14 of the *Daodejing* in the Wang Bi arrangement. Some editors, who take §6 of the commentary as also explaining that same chapter of the *Daodejing*, combine this section with the previous one. Since I do not find their grounds for doing so to be persuasive, here I present it as a separate section.

what elephants look like when alive. And so, that by which everyone considers and imagines things are all called "images."[65] Now even though the Way cannot be heard or seen, the sage grasps its visible achievements in order to dwell amidst its visible forms. And so the text says, ". . . the shape of that without shape, the image of that without substance."[66]

Section Eight[67]

[Primary Text]

A way that can be delineated is not the constant Way.[±]

[Commentary]

In every case, the governing orders [of things] are what divide square from round, short from long, coarse from fine, and hard from brittle. And so, when there is a fixed governing order [for something], only then can it be delineated. Thus, the fixed governing orders [for things] contain preservation and loss, contain death and birth, and contain flourishing and decay. As for the way that things at one time are preserved and at another time are lost, suddenly die and suddenly are born, flourish in the beginning and later decay, this cannot be called constancy. Only that which was born together with the splitting asunder of Heaven and Earth and which until the

[65] Here, the text plays on the fact that the character *xiang* 象 can mean both "elephant" and "image" to provide an etymology of the latter as derived from the former.

[66] In most extant editions of the *Daodejing*, the words from the primary text that are quoted here are preceded by either *shi wei* 是謂 ("This is called . . .") or just *shi* 是 ("This is . . ."), but neither of those variants appears here. In their absence, the quotation is ambiguous. On the one hand, it could be a grammatically incomplete fragment of what was originally a longer line, which is how I have translated it here. On the other hand, it could also be read as a grammatically complete sentence (by taking the *zhi* 之 in the original Chinese—which is usually read as a possessive particle—as instead being a loangraph for *zhi* 至, "arrive"), in which case it would mean, "That without shape comes to have a shape. That without substance comes to have an image."

[67] This section corresponds to chapter 1 of the *Daodejing* in the Wang Bi arrangement.

dissolution and dispersal of Heaven and Earth does not die or decay can be called constant. And that which is constant has nothing that replaces it and lacks a fixed governing order.[n] In lacking a fixed governing order, it is not situated with any constant bearings,[o] and hence it cannot be delineated. The sage, observing its mysterious emptiness and making use of its all-encompassing movement, gives it a forced style-name, "the Way," and thus it can be discussed.[68] And so the text says, "A way that can be delineated is not the constant Way."

Section Nine[69]

[Primary Text]

Coming out at birth and going in at death,
The followers of life are thirteen in number,
The followers of death are thirteen in number.
*As for the life of the people, they are born and become active.**
In being active they all arrive at places of death, and these are also thirteen in number.±
[As for] one who is good at nurturing his life,[70] ∓

[68] In pre-modern China, it was impolite to address or speak of people with whom one was not thoroughly familiar by using their personal name, and so instead people were commonly referenced using a "style" or "courtesy" name (*zi* 字) that they chose for themselves. In depicting the sage as assigning "the Way" as a forced style-name, the commentary highlights both that the Way does not choose any name for itself and that even the sage in some sense lacks complete familiarity with it. Some scholars suggest that "the sage" here refers specifically to Laozi, and thus this comment serves to explain the basis on which the primary text is composed. Additionally, the wording of this sentence is highly reminiscent of what is now chapter 25 of the *Daodejing* in the Wang Bi arrangement, and the commentary might be alluding to that material, but since that chapter is not discussed elsewhere in the "Jie Lao" or "Yu Lao" chapter, we cannot be certain that the author of the commentary had seen that material and is deliberately referencing it here.

[69] This section corresponds to chapter 50 of the *Daodejing* in the Wang Bi arrangement.

[70] If we go strictly by the order of discussion in the commentary, this line should be moved after all the others, to serve as the final line of the chapter. However, in both the received and excavated versions of the *Daodejing*, this line appears right before the line referencing "rhinos and tigers." Moreover, in its mention of "one who treats his life as a weighty matter," the "Jie Lao" commentary itself seems to presume the existence of something like this line in its explanation of the remark referencing "rhinos and tigers"

When traveling on land, he does not meet with rhinos and tigers.
When walking into an army, he does not prepare armor and weapons.
The rhino has nowhere to thrust its horn.
The tiger has nowhere to sink its claws.
The soldier has nowhere to lodge his blade.[±]
There is no place of death in him.[∓]

[Commentary]

A person begins at birth and ends at death. The beginning is called "coming out," and the end is called "going in." And so the text says, "Coming out at birth and going in at death." A person's body has three hundred and sixty joints, four limbs, and nine orifices, and these are his main equipments. The four limbs and the nine orifices together make thirteen. The activity and calm of these thirteen are all subordinated to providing life for him. As subordinates, they are called "followers." And so the text says, "The followers of life are thirteen in number." When he dies, these thirteen equipments all reverse course and are subordinated to dying, and thus the followers of death are also thirteen in number. And so the text says, "The followers of life are thirteen in number, the followers of death are thirteen in number."

In every case, the life of the people is such that those who are born and live are sure to be active. When such activity reaches its limit then it is damaging, but their activity does not stop, and thus the damage does not stop. If the damage does not stop, then life reaches its limit. For life to reach its limit is called death, and then the thirteen all become places for dying and death. And so the text says, "As for the life of the people, they are born and become active. In being active they all arrive at places of death, and these are also

and the lines after that. So, in this case, I have placed this line in its traditional location in my reconstruction of the primary text.

thirteen in number." Therefore, the sage uses his energy and spirit sparingly and values dwelling in calmness.[p]

The following are much more pervasive than the harms from rhinos and tigers,[q] for rhinos and tigers have set territories and their periods of activity and calm have set times, and so if you avoid their territories and watch their times, then you can completely avoid harm from rhinos and tigers. The people understand only that rhinos and tigers have claws and horns, but none of them understand that the ten thousand things also all have claws and horns, and so they fail to evade harm from the ten thousand things. How do I conclude this? When the seasonal rains fall and collect, and the open plains are peaceful and calm, if people intrude upon the mountains and rivers between dusk and dawn, then the claws and horns of winds and dew harm them. If in serving a superior they are not loyal and think little of disobeying prohibitions and decrees, then the claws and horns of punishments and laws harm them. If their manner of dwelling in their villages is not properly regulated and their hatreds and loves have no proper measure, then the claws and horns of conflict and fighting harm them. If their appetites and desires have no proper limits, and their periods of activity and calm are not properly regulated, then the claws and horns of boils and tumors harm them. If they are fond of employing their intelligence for self-centered aims while disregarding the proper order of the Way, then the claws and horns of nets and snares harm them.[71] Rhinos and tigers have their set territories, and the ten thousand harms have their particular wellsprings. If you avoid their territories and block up their wellsprings, then you can evade the various harms.

[71] It is unclear what sort of "nets and snares" (*wangluo* 網羅) are being referenced here. The term *wangluo* often has a legal connotation, i.e., it means the "nets and snares" of the law, but it might also refer simply to various deceptions or "traps" used by others, where those in turn might be devious means employed by a ruler to test the honesty of his subordinates (a technique advocated in other chapters of the *Han Feizi*), or perhaps frauds perpetrated by other unscrupulous people in pursuit of selfish gain.

In every case, weapons and armor are that by which one prepares against harms. As for one who treats his life as a weighty matter, even if he walks into an army, he has no heart for angry conflict. Since he has no heart for angry conflict, then he has no need for preparation to save himself from harm.[72] This applies not just to an army encamped in the wilds. The sage, in roaming about the world, has no heart for harming other people. Since he has no heart for harming other people, then surely there will be no others who harm him. If there are no others who harm him, then he does not prepare against others, and so the text says, "When traveling on land, he does not meet with rhinos and tigers."[73] When walking into an army[r] he does not rely on preparations to save himself from harm, and so the text says, "When walking into an army, he does not prepare armor and weapons." He keeps the various harms at a distance, and so the text says, "The rhino has nowhere to thrust its horn. The tiger has nowhere to sink its claws. The soldier has nowhere to lodge his blade." To omit making preparations yet surely remain unharmed is the proper order of the Way that is followed by Heaven and Earth. He embodies this Way that is followed by Heaven and Earth, and so the text says, "There is no place of death in him." Since in his activities there is no place of death, it calls him "one who is good at nurturing his life."

[72] The text here is ambiguous, and the line of thought it traces is difficult to make out. Following Zhang Jue (1996 and 2010), I take the sense in which this ideal individual "walks into" (*ru* 入, lit. "enters") an army to be a literal case of a person going into the encampment of an army of which he is not a member. The point of the commentary, as I understand it, is that this ideal individual makes it understood that he is *neither an enemy nor a threat*, and hence not a *target* for the army. For that reason, he can escape being harmed by the army, and so has no need for weapons and armor that would normally be used to defend himself from that army.

[73] Here, too, the line of thought articulated in the text is difficult to follow, but based on the reading sketched in the previous footnote, the commentary would seem to be explaining the primary text in a non-literal way: the sage avoids being an enemy to others, and so they are not enemies to him, and that is the sense in which he does not meet with "rhinos and tigers."

Section Ten[74]

[Primary Text]

*One who is caring is thereby able to be dauntless.*ᵀ
One who is restrained is thereby able to be expansive.
*One who does not dare to be ahead of anything under Heaven is thereby able to be a leader in completing affairs.**±
*One who is caring in battle will prevail.*ᵀ
One who uses this in defense will be solid.±
*[Heaven's sustainment will be fully realized therein, as if protecting him with caring.]** [75]
*I have these three treasures that I hold onto and treasure.**~

[Commentary]

One who loves a child takes care of that child.[76] One who treats his life as a weighty matter takes care of his person. One who esteems achievements takes care of affairs. The manner in which a caring mother behaves toward her child when it is still feeble is that she endeavors to bring about good fortune for it. In endeavoring to

[74] This section corresponds to chapter 67 of the *Daodejing* in the Wang Bi arrangement.

[75] This bracketed line is inserted here, because in both the received and excavated versions of the *Daodejing* there is a line that follows the sentence "One who uses this in defense will be solid," and the "Jie Lao" seems to be explaining something like that line. However, the primary text on which the "Jie Lao" is commenting is not completely clear, and it appears to differ substantially from both the received and excavated versions of the *Daodejing*, so this reconstruction of the primary text is speculative. See footnote 81 below, and endnote s.

[76] In this section, the text uses the word *ci* 慈 repeatedly and in multiple ways that are difficult to capture with a single English term consistently. I have chosen to employ "care" and its variants to translate *ci*, but the problem is that *ci* as used here implies some kind of *action* that may or may not also involve some kind of affectionate sentiment, whereas the available English expressions ("be caring," "care about," "care for," "take care of," etc.) may tend to systematically suggest either the absence or presence of that sentiment or the absence or presence of action. Readers should therefore bear in mind that the "care" discussed in this section is conceived predominantly in terms of action, but spans a range from a relatively unsentimental "care" toward things like "implements and gear" (as mentioned below in the main text) to a highly sentimental "care" toward one's own children.

bring about good fortune for it, she works at averting misfortunes for it. If she works at averting misfortunes for it, then her thoughts and deliberations will be thorough. If her thoughts and deliberations are thorough, then she will grasp the proper order for affairs. If she grasps the proper order for affairs, then she will surely bring about many achievements. If she is sure to bring about many achievements, then in carrying them out she will be unhesitating. To be unhesitating is called being dauntless. The sage's approach to the ten thousand affairs is just like the manner in which a caring mother deliberates for the sake of her child when it is still feeble, and so he sees the Way that is sure to go through.[77] When he sees the Way that is sure to go through, then in undertaking affairs he will also be unhesitating, and to be unhesitating is called being dauntless. Being unhesitating is thus born from being caring, and so the text says, "One who is caring is thereby able to be dauntless."

The Duke of Zhou said, "If the winter days do not firmly seal up the ice, then the growth of grasses and trees in the spring and summer will not be luxuriant."[78] Heaven and Earth cannot constantly be extravagant, constantly be expending. How much more so in the case of human beings! And so, there are sure to be both flourishing and decay among the ten thousand things, there are sure to be both relaxation and exertion among the ten thousand

[77] The phrase translated here as "the Way that is sure to go through" (*bi xing zhi dao* 必行之道) is syntactically and semantically ambiguous in the original, and could also mean "the Way that must be followed" or "the Way that operates inevitably." Any of the three could fit this context, and each will yield slightly different understandings of the argument, though it seems to me that the parallel with the mother who is "unhesitating" because she "is sure to bring about many achievements" (*bi cheng gong* 必成功) slightly favors the first of these, and so I have translated accordingly.

[78] The Duke of Zhou was the younger brother of King Wu, who founded the Zhou dynasty—see §6 of the commentary above and note 62 there. The Duke of Zhou was often regarded as a sage in early China, especially by Confucians. The relevance of the quote to what follows seems to be that a "mild" or "warm" winter often portends poor growth in the summer and spring (because, e.g., as modern science now explains, ice and snowpack serve as natural water reservoirs, which rapidly become depleted when conditions are too warm or warm too quickly). So, if Heaven and Earth do not substantially "withhold" their warmth and other life-giving powers during the winter, their effects will be diminished later on, and hence the text warns against constant "expenditure" and "extravagance."

affairs, there are sure to be both cultured and martial activities for the state and its clans, there are sure to be both rewards and penalties among the regulations for officials. Therefore, if an intelligent, well-bred man uses his wealth in a restrained fashion, then his clan will be rich. If the sage treasures his spirit in a sparing manner, then his energy will flourish. If the lord of the people takes sending his soldiers to do battle as a weighty matter, then his people will be numerous. If his people are numerous, then the state will be expansive, and therefore the text praises this, saying, "One who is restrained is thereby able to be expansive."

In every case, those things that have a definite form are easy to dissect and easy to cut to pieces. How do I conclude this? When there is a definite form, there is short and long. When there is short and long, there is small and big. When there is small and big, there is square and round. When there is square and round, there is hard and brittle. When there is hard and brittle, there is light and heavy. When there is light and heavy, there is illumination and shadow. Short and long, small and big, square and round, hard and brittle, light and heavy, illumination and shadow are called governing orders. With a fixed governing order, things are easy to cut to pieces. And so, if you are presenting arguments in the grand court and speak last, then you establish your view.[79] A well-bred man who engages in weighing and arguing will understand this. And so in desiring to complete a circle or square, if you follow after the carpenter's compass and square, then the achievement [of circles and squares] in ten thousand affairs will take form. For each of the ten thousand things there is a compass and square, and a well-bred man who argues and makes speeches will plan and calculate on the basis of these compasses and squares. On every occasion, the sage follows after the compasses and squares of the ten thousand things, and so

[79] As Chen Qitian (1969) nicely explains, the connection between this point and the remarks that precede it is that those who speak first in the debate have given their view a definite form and fixed its governing order by putting it into words, and later speakers then have a clear target to attack and "cut to pieces," and hence the one who speaks last is most likely to prevail in the debate.

he is called "one who does not dare to be ahead of anything under Heaven." If one does not dare to be ahead of anything under Heaven, then one's affairs will all be effective, one's achievements will all be meritorious, and one's arguments will surely dominate one's era, so even if one desired in no way to occupy the position of a great official, would that be obtainable? To occupy the position of a great official is called being a leader in completing affairs, and therefore the text says, "One who does not dare to be ahead of anything under Heaven is thereby able to be a leader in completing affairs."[80]

One who cares for a child does not dare to cut off its supply of clothing and food. One who cares for his own person does not dare to deviate from the law and its measures. One who cares for the squareness and roundness of things does not dare to discard his compass and square. And so if in overseeing soldiers you care for your officers and aides, then in battle you will prevail over your enemies. If you care for your implements and gear, then your fortifications will be firm and solid. And so the text says, "One who is caring in battle will prevail. One who uses this in defense will be solid." One who can keep himself whole, and who on every occasion follows after the governing order of the ten thousand things, is sure, moreover, to receive Heaven's sustainment. Such Heavenly sustainment consists in sustainment of [the ambitions of] his heart.[81,s] Accordingly, the ways of everything under Heaven will be

[80] The primary text originally has a paradoxical flavor that is difficult to reflect in English here, given how the commentary unfolds. In particular, the word *xian* 先 can mean "to be ahead of" something in either time or place, but the latter sense also gives rise to an extended, metaphorical meaning as "to take the lead." Based on this last meaning, the primary text appears at first glance to present the paradox that "one who does not dare to take the lead . . . is thereby able to be a leader," but the commentary relies more on the temporal sense of *xian* in explaining the line, namely as meaning that "one who does not dare to act rashly, before the circumstances are understood and the timing is opportune . . . is thereby able to be a leader," which resolves the puzzle. Simultaneously, as another aspect of the text that is likewise hard to reflect in English, the term rendered here as "completing" (*cheng* 成) can also mean "successful," and that sense of the word is probably intended as well in this context.

[81] The Chinese text from here to the end of this paragraph is very difficult to understand and may well be corrupt. The translation represents my best effort to make sense of it without any substantial emendations, but remains tentative. For an explanation of

such as to fully realize this sustainment, as if protecting him with caring. When one's affairs are sure to be whole in all ten thousand cases, and in one's actions there is nothing that is not fitting, then this is called a "treasure." And so the text says, "I have these three treasures that I hold onto and treasure."[82]

Section Eleven[83]

[Primary Text]

[When traveling along]the great Way,[84] ⸆
Displays that are aberrant [are to be feared.]
[The great Way is very smooth,]
*[Yet the people] take short cuts right through what is great.**

my approach, see the endnote. As I understand it, the commentary is interpreting the remark in the primary text about "Heaven's sustainment" (which could—but need not—be understood in a theological vein) in a non-literal way. Namely, in being caring and "following after the governing order of the ten thousand things," the caring person wins the cooperation of the myriad things and so enjoys tremendous success in his pursuits, as if the tremendous power of Heaven were protecting him, and that phenomenon is what "Heaven's sustainment" amounts to.

[82] In both the received and excavated versions of the *Daodejing*, this line appears before all the other lines from the chapter that are quoted here, and serves to introduce the "three treasures," which are subsequently identified as being caring, being restrained, and not daring to be first among any under Heaven. Since the "Jie Lao" comments on this line last and does so in a way that apparently makes it a comment on what has been mentioned earlier, that suggests that the version of the *Daodejing* from which the author was working had this line last, and so I have placed it last in my reconstruction of the primary text. However, in that case, the referent of the "three treasures" is no longer so clear. It could be—as many scholars have thought—that it still refers to being caring, being restrained, and not daring to be first among any under Heaven, as in the received and excavated versions of the *Daodejing*. However, given its current position, the "three treasures" could have other referents instead: it could refer to "keeping oneself whole," "following after the governing order of the ten thousand things," and "Heaven's sustainment," which would correspond roughly to the commentary's explanation of lines 3–6 of the primary text as given in the reconstruction here.

[83] This section corresponds to chapter 53 of the *Daodejing* in the Wang Bi arrangement.

[84] The commentary in some cases explains only grammatically incomplete fragments of what must have originally been longer, complete lines. In order to provide a comprehensible reconstruction of the primary text, I have filled in some of the apparently missing words based on the received and excavated versions of the *Laozi*. These

The court is kept very clean,
But the fields go fallow,
*And the storehouses and granaries are empty.**
Some don ornaments and decorations,
But they carry sharp swords.
They claim to be satisfied with their food and drink,
But they have resources and goods in excess.
This is called the piping of thievery.≐*

[Commentary]

What the book calls "the great Way" is the correct Way. What it calls "displays that are aberrant" are deviant ways.[t] What it calls "taking short cuts right through what is great" are grandeur and splendor.[85,u] Such grandeur and splendor are part of deviant ways. That "the court is kept very clean" is due to accusations and litigations proliferating.[86] When accusations and litigations proliferate, then the fields will go fallow.[87] If the fields go fallow, then the storehouses and granaries will be empty. If the storehouses and granaries are empty, then the state will become poor. The state becomes poor but the people's customs are licentious and extravagant. If the people's customs are licentious and extravagant, then

supplementations are marked in square brackets. In addition, the commentary at points discusses certain phrases that appear as lines in the received and excavated versions of the *Laozi*, but without quoting them as such. I have added these into the reconstruction of the primary text, but without marking the difference between them and the lines that are quoted in the commentary.

[85] The point of this remark, as I understand it, is that although following "the great Way" can lead—as other parts of the "Jie Lao" claim—to wealth and power, many people mistakenly focus simply on the trappings of wealth and power, and hence take "short cuts" for acquiring them that bypass what is truly "great" in the Way. As a result, the "deviant ways" that they follow instead wind up achieving only mere "displays" that mask deep problems and hence are "aberrant."

[86] As the Japanese scholar Ōta Hō explains this line, the point is that since many people are coming to court, it is frequently swept and kept well maintained.

[87] I.e., because the common people are frequently engaged in criminal and civil proceedings at the court, they do not do their farm work.

the production of clothing and food will be cut off. If the production of clothing and food is cut off, then the people cannot help but adorn themselves with chicanery and deceit.[88] If they adorn themselves with chicanery and deceit, then they will know decoration and ornamentation. To know decoration and ornamentation is called "donning ornaments and decorations." When accusations and litigations have proliferated, but the granaries and storehouses are empty, and there are those who adopt licentiousness and extravagance as their customs, then the injury to the state is like using a sharp sword to stab it, and so the text says that "they carry sharp swords." When various men adorn themselves with crafty intelligence and designs to the point of harming the state, their own private clans are sure to grow rich. Since their own private clans are sure to grow rich, thus the text says that "they have resources and goods in excess." If the state has people like this, then the foolish common people cannot help but take their course from and imitate them. If they imitate them, then petty thieves are born. Looking at the matter from this perspective, if great scoundrels arise then petty thieves will follow. If great scoundrels sing the lead then petty thieves will chime in. The pitch-pipe is the leader of the five tones. And so the pitch-pipe plays first and the bells and zithers all follow; the pitch-pipe sings the lead and the various musical instruments all chime in. Now when great scoundrels arise, then the vulgar among the people will sing the lead. When the vulgar among the people sing the lead, then petty thieves are sure to chime in. And so in the case where "Some don ornaments and decorations, but they carry sharp swords. They claim to be satisfied with their food and drink,[v] but they have resources and goods in excess," then "This is called the piping of thievery."

[88] In other words, since the people cannot satisfy their licentious and extravagant customs through "honest" manual labor, they instead turn to "dishonest" schemes to procure money and goods.

Section Twelve[89]

[Primary Text]

One who is established [well] will not be uprooted.
[One who has taken a good grip] will not be thrown off.
As son and grandson, [one uses this so that one's] familial sacrifices will not be cut off.
Cultivate it in one's person, and one's virtue will be genuine.
Cultivate it in the clan, and its virtue will be abundant.
Cultivate it in the village, and its virtue will be extensive.
Cultivate it in the state, and its virtue will be bountiful.
Cultivate it in the empire, and its virtue will be ubiquitous.
Use what pertains to the person to look at the person.
Use what pertains to the clan to look at the clan.
Use what pertains to the village to look at the village.
Use what pertains to the state to look at the state.
Use what pertains to the empire to look at the empire.
How do I know what is so for all under Heaven?
By this.

[Commentary]

Whether intelligent or foolish, nobody fails to have predilections and aversions. When reposed and calm, none fail to know the origins of misfortune and good fortune. But when they are in the grip of likes and dislikes or aroused by licentious things, then they become confused. The reason this is so is that they are led on by external things and confused by frivolous likes. In repose, they grasp what is appropriate among predilections and aversions, and when calm, they recognize plans leading to misfortune and good fortune. But now they are changed by frivolous likes and led on by

[89] This section corresponds to chapter 54 of the *Daodejing* in the Wang Bi arrangement. This material is also discussed in §2 of the "Yu Lao" chapter, and readers are invited to compare the two treatments.

external things. Being led on, they go off, and so the text speaks of being "uprooted."[90] A consummate sage is not like this. Once he establishes his predilections and aversions, even if he sees something that he likes, he cannot be led on. To be incapable of being led on is called "not being uprooted." He is unified in his essence, and so even if desirable sorts of things are present, his spirit will not be moved by them. For his spirit not to be moved by them is called "not being thrown off." In being a person's son or grandson, he embodies this Way in order to preserve his ancestral temple. When one's ancestral temple is not destroyed, this is called "familial sacrifices not being cut off." In the case of a person, virtue[91] consists in accumulated energy. In the case of a clan, virtue consists in wealth and resources. In the case of the village, the state, and the empire,[92] virtue for each consists in [the wellbeing of] the people. Now in bringing order to one's person, external things cannot confuse one's energy and spirit, and so the text says, "Cultivate it in one's person, and one's virtue will be genuine." This genuineness is for one's virtue to be solid. In bringing order to a clan, if useless objects cannot move them from their plans, then they will have an abundance of wealth, and so the text says, "Cultivate it in the clan, and its virtue will be abundant." If one bringing order to the village practices this regimen, then the clans that have abundance

[90] The word *yin* 引, translated here as "led on," most literally refers to "pulling" something, so in Chinese it is fairly natural to re-describe being "led on" as being "uprooted" (*ba* 拔, lit. "pull up/out").

[91] Here and in the next few lines, the term *de* 德 ("virtue") is best understood in its sense as "power" or a source of power. So, the point being made is that an individual person draws his power from having accumulated energy, and a clan draws its power from possessing substantial wealth and resources, and the village, state, and empire each draw their power from a flourishing population.

[92] The term *tianxia* 天下 most literally means "(all/everything) under Heaven," which is how I have rendered it in the vast majority of instances. However, in some cases—such as here—it seems to refer more specifically to a political unit, and in particular the most expansive level that encompassed multiple states and populations. I have rendered those usages of *tianxia* 天下 as "empire" to convey that political sense of the term. Readers should bear in mind, though, that particular conceptions of what constitutes an "empire" may not fit the Chinese concept, and so "empire" as used here is merely a convenient stand-in for the Chinese term, and not an exact equivalent.

will become more numerous, and so the text says, "Cultivate it in the village, and its virtue will be extensive." If one bringing order to the state practices this regimen, then the villages that have virtue will become more numerous, and so the text says, "Cultivate it in the state, and its virtue will be bountiful." If one overseeing the empire practices this regimen, then in the lives of the people none will fail to reap from his generosity, and so the text says, "Cultivate it in the empire, and its virtue will be ubiquitous." If in cultivating one's person, one uses this to differentiate being a gentleman from being a petty person, and if in bringing order to the village, bringing order to the state, or overseeing the empire, one examines and looks at gain and loss in each case according to these items,[93] then in ten thousand times one will not err even once. And so the text says, "Use what pertains to the person to look at the person. Use what pertains to the clan to look at the clan. Use what pertains to the village to look at the village. Use what pertains to the state to look at the state. Use what pertains to the empire to look at the empire. How do I know what is so for all under Heaven? By this."

[93] The "items" in question are the abundance of virtue in the village, the bountifulness of virtue in the state, and the ubiquity of virtue in the empire—those are the standards against which gain and loss are to be measured at these various levels, according to the text.

Textual Notes for Jie Lao

a. Although it is more common to render 應 here as "respond," in this translation I render it with "match" or "matching response" to try to maintain a link in English between these occurrences and the line later in this chapter 內外相應, where 應 more clearly has the sense of "match" or "correspond." Also, as I understand this particular case, the point in context is that because the masses are inconsistent in their practice of ritual (sometimes vigorous, sometimes slack), the masses both are *not as good* at ritual practice as the gentleman/sage and also regularly *fail to give the called-for response* to his ritual gestures toward them, and these two points can both be described as a failure to "match" him.

b. Most commentators on the "Jie Lao" seem to understand 仍 as meaning 因 or 就, and so take 仍之 as meaning something like "keeps at it" or "completes it." However, among the meanings of 仍 attested by dictionaries (e.g., 康熙字典, 中文大辭典) is 重 or 再. Since the "Jie Lao" chapter starts its explanation of the line 攘臂而仍之 with the words 復恭敬, understanding 仍 as 重 or 再 seems to better capture how the commentary is explaining the line than merely "keeps at it" or "completes it," so in the translation I render 仍 as "redouble."

c. There is a long-standing puzzle here because of the way that the commentary's discussion of ritual suddenly switches from endorsing it to criticizing it. Lu Wenchao, for example, suggests that the text is discussing a different sense of "ritual," since in this paragraph it uses the phrase 情貌 whereas previously it had used the phrase 貌情. Similarly, Ōta Hō (2014 [1783]) suggests that here "ritual" refers to "vulgar ritual" as opposed to the "highest ritual" discussed earlier. Although both these readings go some way toward solving the puzzle, neither really explains *why* the text suddenly—and apparently without any explicit marking—introduces a new sense of "ritual." I propose that the answer is to be found in seeing the text as picking up from the immediately preceding line discussing 失禮. I take it that what 失禮 refers to is not a condition in which knowledge of what ritual demands is lost, but rather a condition in which one no longer practices ritual in the correct manner and with the correct motivations, if one practices it at all (and hence I render 禮 there as "ritual propriety"). In *that* case, ritual practice can be only a formal display. I translate the 為 in this line as "then becomes" to reflect this construal of the underlying thought here. As support for this approach, note first that in commenting on the line which appears in the Wang Bi version of the *Daodejing* as 上禮為之而莫之應則攘臂而扔之, the version quoted in the "Jie Lao" lacks the 則 indicating that 攘臂而仍之 is the consequent of 上禮為之而莫之應, though in other cases—such as the opening line 上德不德是以有德—it clearly includes the 是以 indicating an antecedent-consequent relation. This suggests that the version of the *Daodejing* used by the "Jie Lao" author(s) itself lacked the 則 that appears in the Wang Bi version. Even so, the "Jie Lao" clearly *does* treat the 攘臂而仍之 as the consequent of 上禮為之而莫之應. In that case, since the "Jie Lao" infers an antecedent-consequent relation without any explicit marker such as 則, then it is at least plausible that the line 禮為情貌者也 . . . stands in an antecedent-consequent relation to the previous line, despite the lack of any explicit linguistic markers.

d. Many commentators on the "Jie Lao" seem to understand 明 as 顯明, where in context that means something to the effect that the ritual observances between fathers and sons are not highly formal, or not especially showy or ostentatious. However, on my understanding of what the passage is trying to identify as potentially problematic in ritual practice (see note e below), that reading of 明 is not really the right point for the context. Instead, I understand 明 in the way it is used in phrases such as 明

禮義 in the *Xunzi*, or 明法 in the *Han Feizi*, where to 明 some standard is to make it known that there is some behavior that is demanded of people.

e. I understand the use of 禮 here by reference to the way the "Jie Lao" treats it further below. Namely, what the commentary treats as the start of chaos is not ritual *per se*, but rather the condition when people *demand* that others show them proper respect according to ritual, while failing to care about the ways in which the ritual performances are or are not genuine reflections of virtue, humaneness, etc. Hence, I translate 禮 as "insisting on ritual" to reflect the particular pejorative sense it has in the primary text, as elaborated in the commentary.

f. Here I follow the suggestion of Zhang Jue (1996) to understand 肆 as 突.

g. Here I follow those editions that have 後 instead of 復.

h. Here I follow Shao (1990) in reading 於 as 為.

i. Both Chen Qitian (1969) and Lai and Fu (1997) have 事大眾而數搖之則多敗傷 here, but as far as I know, all other editions have 事大眾而數搖之則少成功, 藏大器而數徙之則多敗傷. I have not as yet been able to identify the source of the discrepancy, since neither Chen nor Lai and Fu indicate what edition they are following here, and no other commentators seem to discuss this variant. However, I strongly suspect that the difference is due to a printing error in Chen's text that was followed by Lai and Fu. I therefore follow the other editions with the longer version of the sentence and translate accordingly.

j. Here I follow the interpretation of Zhang Jue (1996 and 2010) as regards 內, 外, and 利, but in order to avoid making the English translation of the sentence long and cumbersome, I have adopted a relatively non-literal rendering. Compare Zhang's own *baihua* translation in Zhang Jue (1996).

k. Here I follow those editions that have 咎莫憯於欲利, instead of emending the text to 咎莫憯於欲得 to match the received version of the *Laozi*.

l. Here I follow the explanation given by Zhang Jue (2010) of 斟酌, but not the exact interpretation he gives of the line as a whole.

m. Most scholars seem inclined to read 與 as the preposition "with" and to read 俱 in the sense of "together." However, that reading is problematic when we get to the part of the sentence that says 與桀紂俱滅, since it would imply that the Way was destroyed together with Jie and Zhòu, but the text goes on to say in §8 of the commentary that the Way is indestructible. For that reason, I opt instead to read 與 as the verb "give" and take 俱 in the sense of 具 ("complete"), since the two characters were often used interchangeably in early Chinese texts.

n. Here I follow the explanation given by Zhang Jue (2010) of 攸易.

o. Many commentators seem inclined to read the 所 here in a fairly literal sense as "place." However, they appear to overlook the problem this creates, in that such a reading sets up a contradiction between this claim understood as saying that the Way "does not rest in any constant place" (非在於常所) and the claim made earlier in this chapter (§6) that the Way is "constantly at one's side" (常在吾側). For that reason, it seems preferable to understand the 所 here in a less literal sense, such as one sees in the following passage from the 儒行 chapter of the 禮記: 儒有忠信以為甲冑, 禮義以為干櫓; 戴仁而行, 抱義而處, 雖有暴政, 不更其所. 其自立有如此者. In this case, the 所 is not meant literally as the "place" where the 儒 is located, but rather means something more like the "position" or "stance" he takes, i.e., the way he goes about doing things (Legge, for instance, translates 不更其所 as "does not change his course," which conveys the right sense, but is not very literal). My translation of 所 as "bearings" is meant to be analogous to the notion of a "stance" and capture the sense of a figurative location but also a *direction*, since the passage seems to be emphasizing that the Way has no set direction of development. So understood, the phrase 非在於常所 can be seen as an echo of the claim earlier in the text (§6) that the Way "has no constant deportment" (無常操).

p. Here I follow those editions that have 處, instead of emending the text to 虛.

q. There is a problem here, caused mainly by the demonstrative 此 ("this"). On a very natural reading, it would refer to the description of the sage in the previous sentence, but that would result in a nonsensical claim. That difficulty (together with the fact that the commentary seems to omit discussion of some lines in the received and excavated versions of the *Daodejing*) has led some scholars to suspect that the text is corrupt here, and that either there is a lacuna prior to this sentence or that this sentence has fallen out of place from somewhere else. Zhang Jue (1996 and 2010) suggests taking the referent of 此 to be the injurious behavior of the people that brings them to death. While that proposal allows him to avoid positing a lacuna or emending the text, it is likewise not fully satisfactory, because the discussion that follows this sentence does not focus solely or even primarily on the type of injurious behavior mentioned previously, and so Zhang's approach makes the sentence into a very awkward and inadequate bridge between the preceding and subsequent lines. As an alternative, I suggest that we take the referent of 此 to be the sources of harm that are mentioned in what follows. In other words, the text should be read as if the prior discussion had concluded and the author was turning to a new subject by saying, "Now, *these* things do much greater harm than rhinos and tigers: [followed by a list]." In order to convey this idea clearly, however, I have rendered the 此 as simply "the following" in the translation.

r. Here I follow Chen Qiyou (2000) and emend 山 to 軍.

s. Here is not the place to offer a complete defense of my approach to these difficult sentences at the end of §10, so what follows is simply an explanation to try at least to clarify to specialists how I arrived at the translation I offer.

Let me start with the parsing of the lines, since scholars differ on this matter. In particular, following Chen Qitian (1969) and Chen Qiyou (2000) and unlike a number of other scholars, I group the characters 若以慈衛之也 with what precedes them, rather than with what follows them, for a couple of reasons. The first is that in the received versions of the *Daodejing*, 以慈衛之 is meant to be a continuation from 天將救之, and likewise in the Mawangdui versions, 女/如以茲垣之 is meant to be a continuation from 天將建之. The "Jie Lao" chapter seems to be working from a different text than either 天將救之 or 天將建之, but the reference to 天生 in this section of the "Jie Lao" chapter makes it appear that the author is referencing a line that was something like 天將救之 or 天將建之, so it seems more reasonable to construe 若以慈衛之也 as more closely connected with the discussion of 天生 that precedes these words. Second, if one reads 若以慈衛之也 with what follows, as 若以慈衛之也, 事必萬全而舉無不當, 則謂之寶矣, that seems to create an awkward double conditional construction with 若 and 則 that simply strikes me as rather unlikely. Moreover, it treats 若以慈衛之也 as somehow introducing the line in the primary text 吾有三寶, 持而寶之, but not only is that not how either the received or Mawangdui versions treat 以慈衛之/以茲垣之, but such a connection also seems very difficult to understand on its own (in other words, 若以慈衛之, 吾有三寶, 持而寶之 does not make a lot of sense as a sequence, *especially* if 慈 is taken as one of the 三寶). However, although I do not read 若以慈衛之也 together with 事必萬全而舉無不當, 則謂之寶矣, nevertheless I do think a good interpretation of the lines should try to make sense of the transition from the preceding sentence to 事必萬全而舉無不當, 則謂之寶矣, and that is one motivating consideration in my approach (more on which below).

Next, on the sense of 生 in 天生, I understand it in roughly the sense of "keep alive," which I gather is also how Wang Xianqian understands it, given his paraphrasing of 天生 as 有善心故天救而生之. As should be apparent from that paraphrasing, adopting this view has a benefit in that, while the primary text on which the "Jie Lao" is commenting ostensibly differs from the known versions that have 天將救之 or 天將建之, this reading keeps the sense of 天生 in the same general ballpark as 天將救之 or 天將建之, rather than being simply a major and rather mysterious divergence. (I thank Y. K. Lo for impressing upon me the value of this reading.) My translation in the remainder of the paragraph is based on trying to keep the sense of 生 consistent throughout the passage, but since it is used as both a noun and verb, and since its usage is explained in the passage in a manner that makes a literal notion of "keeping alive" not fully applicable, I have settled on "sustain" and its variants for rendering it into English.

As for the 心 in 生心, I take it as having roughly the same sort of sense as it does in a couple of other places in early texts where it refers more specifically to something like ambitions or plans, rather than the "heart" or "mind" generally. See, e.g., *Zuozhuan*, Duke Zhuang, year 28, 宗邑無主, 則民不威. 疆場無主, 則啟戎心. 戎之生心, 民慢其政, 國之患也, which Durrant et al. (2016, 213) translate thus: "If the site of the Ancestral Temple is without a master, then the people will not stand in awe of your authority. If the border regions are without masters, then you will give the Rong ideas. If the Rong get ideas and the people disrespect their government, it will be trouble for the domain." My reason for preferring this sort of construal is that such an understanding of 心 seems to me to fit better with how the passage moves from speaking of 生心 to 事必萬全而舉無不當. The claim that is being made, as I see it, is that being caring will help bring one's plans to fruition (as long as they are formulated in accordance with the Way to begin with), and that is why the text also describes the situation as one in which it is as if Heaven were protecting the person. In the translation, though, I have adopted the formulation "[the ambitions of] his heart" to allow readers who do not know Chinese to be able to track the occurrence of 心 in the text here.

In addition, there is some disagreement among scholars about how to understand the second 之 in 故天下之道盡之生也, 若以慈衛之也. I read it with the sense—as one sees in other cases in early Chinese texts—of the demonstrative 是, and take 之生 as a noun phrase that is the direct object of the verb 盡. Compare Chen Qitian (1969), who glosses the 之 as 其 and so treats 之生 as equivalent to 其生.

Finally, in light of comparison with the Mawangdui and the received versions of the *Laozi*, then given the way the commentary unfolds, namely its reference to 天生, followed by the remark about 盡之生 (however we construe that), and then the remark 若以慈衛之, it seems to me that the version of the *Laozi* on which the text is commenting would likely have had something like either 天生盡之, 若以慈衛之 or 天生盡焉, 若以慈衛之. That is the basis for my reconstructed translation of the line from the primary text that precedes the commentary.

t. Here I follow the majority of commentators on the "Jie Lao" in reading 施 as 迆. Although Chen Qitian (1969) suggests excising 貌, here I retain it, because I am not persuaded by the arguments for deleting it, and the text seems quite intelligible to me with it included.

u. Here I retain 大 after 徑, instead of excising the 大 as most scholars seem inclined to do, since I think the phrase 徑大 can be made sense of as it stands. In particular, since 徑 as a transitive verb with a grammatical object can mean "to pass through" or "to take a shortcut through" some location, we can understand 徑大 as meaning "taking a shortcut through what is great," i.e., rather than arriving at or resting in what is truly great (namely, the Way), one merely passes through it in attempting to reach something else, such as conditions that seem to be good but are not really so.

v. Since the commentary does not explain 厭飲食, and 厭 can have several different senses, it is hard to be certain how to translate these words. It seems to me that the basic point of the commentary's explanation of the previous lines is to stress cases where things look as if all is well, but in fact mask underlying problems. On that basis, then, I take 厭 in the sense of 足, but where 足 has the connotation of being a display only: these people "treat as sufficient" their food and drink, but in reality they are hoarding excessive wealth.

2

Yu Lao 喻老

Illustrating the *Laozi*

Translated by Eric L. Hutton

Section One[1]

[Primary Text]

When all under Heaven hold to the Way, then swift horses are relegated to carrying dung.
When all under Heaven lack the Way, then war horses are born in the outlands.
Of crimes, none is greater than being desirable.◊
Of misfortunes, none is greater than being insatiable.
Of faults, none is more agonizing than desiring gain.
*Knowing when to be satisfied is truly satisfying.**

[Commentary]

In the case where all under Heaven hold to the Way, there are no urgent troubles, and hence there is no use for rapid communications. And so the text says that "swift horses are relegated to carrying dung." In the case where all under Heaven lack the Way, attacks and ambushes do not pause, and defense against others goes on for numerous years incessantly. Armor and helmets breed lice and their

[1] This section corresponds to chapter 46 of the *Daodejing* in the Wang Bi arrangement. This material is also discussed in §5 of the "Jie Lao" chapter, and readers are invited to compare the two treatments.

Eric L. Hutton, *Yu Lao* 喻老: *Illustrating the* Laozi In: *Explaining and Illustrating the* Laozi.
Edited by: Eirik Lang Harris and Eric L. Hutton, Oxford University Press.
 DOI: 10.1093/9780197514948.003.0004

young, swallows and sparrows inhabit the screening and tents, and still the soldiers do not return home. And so the text says that "war horses are born in the outlands."[2]

A man of Di offered to Duke Wen of Jin a gift of pelts from giant foxes and dark leopards.[a] Duke Wen accepted the visitor's pelts and said with a sigh, "These creatures make criminals of themselves by the beauty of their pelts."[3] Among those who manage a state, some become criminals by means of their good name and title—King Yan of Xu is such a case.[4] Some become criminals by means of their cities and territories—the states of Yu and Guo are such cases.[5] And so the text says, "Of crimes, none is greater than being desirable."[6]

[2] The commentary's quotation of the primary text here is the same in Chinese as that in §5 of the "Jie Lao," but the translation differs because of an ambiguity in the term *jiao* 郊, which most literally refers to the area outside a city. However, the term could refer to land just outside the city, or much further outside the city. Section 5 of the "Jie Lao" clearly reads it in the former sense, and so there *jiao* is translated as "suburbs." While the "Yu Lao" commentary does not explicitly discuss the term *jiao*, its remarks about soldiers living away from home for years in tents suggest that their location is somewhere more remote, and hence here it is rendered as "outlands." The point would seem to be that military campaigns last so long that the army winds up breeding horses where it is carrying out operations.

[3] This remark may be a double entendre. Duke Wen of Jin (r. 636–628 BCE), also known as Prince Chong'er before he became duke, was a famous Chinese ruler. Prior to ascending the throne, however, he had been forced out of his state during a power struggle. On his mother's side, he was descended from the Di people (who were considered "barbarians" by the ancient Chinese), and at one point during his exile, he took refuge with them. It is unclear when the story recounted here is supposed to have happened—ancient texts sometimes refer to him as "Duke Wen" even before he officially became ruler—but one possibility is that the story is set when he was in exile and was renewing his ties with the Di people. In that case, the Duke's remark could also be about the Di people or even himself: it could be translated as "These people make criminals of themselves with the beauty of these pelts" (i.e., in allying themselves with him, the Di people have made themselves criminals in view of his enemies in Jin), or as "This is to make a criminal of myself with the beauty of these pelts" (i.e., in building ties with an "unfriendly" power, he is solidifying his status as a "criminal" enemy of the ruling powers in Jin). For more on Duke Wen, see §6 of this chapter.

[4] According to various early stories, the ruler of the state of Xu was renowned and admired for his practice of virtue, so much so that other states subordinated themselves to him, and he proclaimed himself "King" (*wang* 王), which was a title normally reserved for only the Zhou dynasty sovereign, who in principle was chief over all the states. As a result, King Yan of Xu was regarded as a threat by some, and the state of Chu attacked and eliminated Xu.

[5] Yu and Guo are discussed later in this chapter, but the stories there have a somewhat different focus. Here the point is that, like the pelts of foxes and leopards, the desirability of their cities and territories brings destruction upon them.

[6] Again, the commentary's quotation of the primary text here is the same in Chinese as that in §5 of the "Jie Lao," but the translation differs because of a difference in how the phrase *ke yu* 可欲 seems to be understood in the two commentaries.

Earl Zhi annexed the holdings of the Fan and Zhonghang clans and attacked Zhao incessantly.[7] Han and Wei turned against him, and his army was defeated at Jinyang. He himself died east of Gaoliang, and then he[8] was ultimately dismembered, and they lacquered his skull and made it into a cup for wine.[9] And so the text says, "Of misfortunes, none is greater than being insatiable."

The lord of Yu desired the horse team of Quchan and the jade disk of Chuiji, and did not listen to Gong Zhiqi, and so his state perished and he himself died.[10] And so the text says, "Of faults, none is more agonizing than desiring gain."

When a state settles for survival as its constant aim, then becoming a hegemon or true king[11] is feasible, and when a person settles for staying alive as his constant aim, then achieving wealth and nobility is feasible. If one does not harm oneself through desiring, then one's state will not be led to perish, and one's person

[7] Earl Zhi headed one of six ministerial families that in effect controlled the state of Jin, each with their own territory. The others were the Fan, Zhonghang, Han, Wei, and Zhao clans. After defeating the Fan and Zhonghang clans, Earl Zhi initially induced the Han and Wei clans to join him in eliminating Zhao, but they later betrayed him at the critical battle of Jinyang in 453 BCE, which is why the text says they "turned against him." Earl Zhi was already wealthy and powerful before annexing the Fan and Zhonghang holdings, but he pursued expansionist aims, and so serves as an example of someone who "does not know when to be satisfied" or "is insatiable." Another chapter of the *Han Feizi* offers a lengthy account of Earl Zhi and makes a similar point. For a translation, see Watson (2003, 56–62).

[8] Based on other versions of the story, some scholars suggest emending the text here so that rather than "then he," the sentence would say "his land" instead.

[9] The last two characters of this sentence are ambiguous. They might mean "a piss pot" instead of "a cup for wine."

[10] Section 6 of this chapter recounts these events in greater detail, so readers should look there for the explanation.

[11] As mentioned above (note 4), the title *wang* 王 ("King") was supposed to be reserved for the Zhou dynasty ruler, as chief over all states, but during the Warring States period, rulers of individual states adopted the title for themselves while lacking the *de facto* power over other states that the title would normally connote. In response to that situation, early texts sometimes—as in the present case—use the word *wang* more narrowly to designate specifically a ruler who *does* have supreme *de facto* power, and I use the translation "true king" to convey this sense. The title "Hegemon" (*ba* 霸) was originally bestowed by a Zhou king on the ruler of an especially powerful state, and later on came to be a label for any ruler capable of dominating most other states. So, talk of "becoming a hegemon or true king" stands for ruling the world.

will not be led to die. And so the text says, "Knowing when to be satisfied is truly satisfying."[12]

Section Two[13]

[Primary Text]

One who is established well will not be uprooted.
One who has taken a good grip will not be thrown off.
*His sons and grandsons will take up the familial sacrifices and go on for generation upon generation unendingly.**±

[Commentary]

After King Zhuang of Chu had prevailed over the state of Jin [in battle] at Heyong, he went home and rewarded Sunshu Ao.[14] Sunshu Ao asked for some territory in the vicinity of the Han River, a place of sand and rocks. According to the laws of the Chu state, ministers with directly heritable emoluments were to have their territory taken back after the second generation, but only Sunshu Ao stands apart from this. The reason why his enfeoffment was not taken back is that it was unproductive, and so even after nine generations, the familial sacrifices conducted there have not broken off. And so when the text says, "One who is established well will not be uprooted. One who has taken a good grip will not be thrown off. His sons and grandsons will take up the familial sacrifices and go

[12] Even with the commentary, the line from the primary text remains somewhat ambiguous. It could also be translated as the imperative "Know that being satisfied is truly satisfying!"

[13] This section corresponds to chapter 54 of the *Daodejing* in the Wang Bi arrangement. This material is also discussed in §12 of the "Jie Lao" chapter, and readers are invited to compare the two treatments.

[14] Sunshu Ao was a minister in Chu who was credited for Chu's rise to power, and that is why the king rewards him.

on for generation upon generation unendingly," it is referring to a Sunshu Ao.[15]

Section Three[16]

[Primary Text]

To be heavy is to be the root for what is light.
To be still is to be lord over what is restless.
*To the end of his days, a prince, when on the march, does not abandon his heavy-transport wagon.**
[Only when he has a walled-in lodge in which to rest at ease, then is he unconcerned.][17]
[Why ever would a ruler who can field ten thousand war chariots make himself a lightweight in the world?][18]
If one becomes light, then one loses the role of root.
If one becomes restless, then one loses the role of lord.

[15] Most literally, the commentary says that the *Laozi* "is referring to Sunshu Ao," but the claim is probably not meant literally as an actual historical claim about the basis on which the *Laozi* was composed. As in English, where a personal name can be used to designate a type (e.g., "He will be the next Elvis!"), Chinese texts likewise sometimes use names to designate types (see, e.g., the use of the name "Bian Que" in §6 of this chapter), and such is more probably the intended usage here, so I have translated it as "a Sunshu Ao."

[16] This section corresponds to chapter 26 of the *Daodejing* in the Wang Bi arrangement.

[17] This bracketed line is inserted here, because in both the received and excavated versions of the *Daodejing* there is a line at this point in the primary text that the "Yu Lao" seems to be referencing. However, the primary text on which the "Yu Lao" is commenting is not completely clear, so this reconstruction of the primary text is speculative. See endnote c for further discussion.

[18] Again, this bracketed line is inserted here, because in both the received and excavated versions of the *Daodejing* there is a line at this point to which the "Yu Lao" seems to be responding but does not quote. However, unlike the line above it, we can be much more confident about what the line was, based on comparison between the various texts.

[Commentary]

When control rests with oneself, that is called being "heavy." When one does not abandon one's position, that is called being "still."[19] When one is heavy, then one can put to use those who are light. When one is still, then one can put to use those who are restless. And so the text says, "To be heavy is to be the root for what is light. To be still is to be lord over what is restless." And so when the text says, "To the end of his days, a prince, when on the march, does not abandon his heavy-transport wagon,"[20,b] the state is the "heavy-transport wagon" for a lord of men. Zhufu, while still alive, handed off his state, and this is a case of abandoning one's "heavy-transport wagon."[21] And so even though he had the delights of Dai and Yunzhong, he had already lost the state of Zhao, yet was unconcerned.[22,c] Zhufu had

[19] The words translated as "still" and "restless" in this section are *jing* 靜 and *zao* 躁, which are rendered elsewhere in this translation as "calm" and "frenetic," respectively.

[20] The Chinese text here contains a word play that is hard to capture in English. Namely, the word *xing* 行, which is here translated as "march" (based on the military connotations of some of the language used in the primary text and the commentary), can also mean "to take action." Also, the characters *zizhong* 輜重 (rendered here as "heavy-transport wagon") could alternatively be read as a noun phrase meaning "what carries heaviness." So, the sentence could also be understood as "To the end of his days, a prince, in taking actions, does not abandon the carrier of his heaviness." The commentary seems to be playing on these two senses in the way it switches from the military metaphor to talking about the conduct of a ruler generally. In addition, the word translated here as "prince" is *junzi* 君子, which in all other cases in the "Jie Lao" and "Yu Lao" is translated as "gentleman" (see note 14 in the "Jie Lao"). It is due to the highly political interpretation of this passage offered by the "Yu Lao" that the older, more aristocratic and literal sense of the term seems more appropriate for rendering it in this instance.

[21] "Zhufu" is a title, literally meaning "Father of the Ruler," that was adopted by King Wuling of Zhao (r. 325–299 BCE, d. 295 BCE) after abdicating the throne to his younger son, apparently so that he could devote himself to military adventures without needing to worry about the other tasks involved in administering a state. Zhufu later regretted his decision and wanted his older son to become a king, and when the older son instigated a coup and failed, the rebels took refuge with Zhufu. The ministers involved in putting down the coup confined Zhufu in his palace until he starved to death, a rather gruesome end. Hence, Zhufu serves as a negative example of a ruler who failed to maintain control, and it is these events that the "Yu Lao" commentary is referencing.

[22] Dai and Yunzhong were territories forcibly taken by Zhufu from the rival state of Zhongshan. Given this history, the phrase "the delights of Dai and Yunzhong" might refer to the entertainments Zhufu enjoyed at those locations after capturing them, or it might refer to the excitement and pleasure Zhufu felt in the very attempt to capture them. Either way, I take the basic point of this sentence to be criticizing Zhufu for enjoying himself while having blithely surrendered the one thing that was most important for being secure, namely his control of the state of Zhao.

been a ruler who could field ten thousand war chariots, but made himself a lightweight in the world. To lack authoritative power is called being "light,"[23] and to abandon one's position is called being "restless." For such reasons, one's life becomes dim and one dies.[24] And so when the text says, "If one becomes light, then one loses the role of root. If one becomes restless, then one loses the role of lord," it is referring to a Zhufu.

Section Four[25]

[Primary Text]

A fish must not be separated from its watery abode.~
The valuable implements of the state must not be presented to others.~
That which you desire to gather up, you must certainly first spread out.
That which you desire to make weak, you must certainly first strongly exercise.±
*That which you desire to take in, you must certainly first give to.**∓
[This is referred to as] the subtle becomes apparent.
*The diminished and weak prevail over the strong.**

[Commentary]

Weighty authoritative power is the "watery abode" for a lord of men.[26] To be lord over men is for one's authoritative power to

[23] For more on the notion of "authoritative power" (*shi* 勢), see footnote 29 in the "Jie Lao" chapter.

[24] The Chinese text here is ambiguous, and perhaps deliberately so. In addition to making the sort of general claim as translated above, it could be rendered as "For such reasons, [Zhufu] was imprisoned alive and thus died."

[25] This section corresponds to chapter 36 of the *Daodejing* in the Wang Bi arrangement.

[26] The word translated as "weighty" is the same word *zhong* 重 that was rendered as "heavy" in the previous section, so there is a continuity of theme between the two

outweigh that found among one's ministers. Once lost, it cannot be recovered. Duke Jian lost it to Tian Cheng, and the dukes of Jin lost it to the six high ministers, and so their states perished and they themselves died.[27] And so the text says, "A fish must not be separated from its watery abode."

Rewards and penalties are "the valuable implements of the state." When they rest with the lord, then he controls his minister. When they rest with the minister, then he prevails over his lord. When the lord sets out rewards to be made, the minister makes a deduction from them and uses what was deducted for [augmenting his own] virtue.[28] When the lord sets out penalties to be inflicted, the

sections, but it is not easy to capture with a single English term. In addition, here the text is playing on the sense in which the term *shi* 勢 ("authoritative power") can also mean "circumstances"—see footnote 29 in the "Jie Lao" chapter—which makes the metaphorical equating of "power" and "abode" in this sentence a little more natural in the original Chinese than it is in English.

[27] Tian Cheng was a powerful minister in the state of Qi. In 481 BCE, he murdered his ruler, Duke Jian, and replaced him with the duke's younger brother, known as Duke Ping. From then on, the Tian clan had *de facto* control of Qi, until in 386 BCE they were officially recognized as the rulers of Qi by the Zhou king, while the original Lü clan to which Duke Jian and the subsequent dukes had belonged was completely ousted. It is this latter event to which the commentary refers as the "perishing" of Duke Jian's state—the complete destruction of Qi as a distinct political entity did not happen until 221 BCE, when it was eliminated by the state of Qin. The system of "six high ministers" was initially established in Jin by Duke Jing in 588 BCE, and the ministers expanded their power over time. In 514 BCE, the six ministerial clans mentioned in footnote 7 above used legal pretexts to execute many members of the ruling clan of Jin, and eventually, after attacking each other, divided Jin among the remaining three clans of Han, Wei, and Zhao, whose heads were recognized as the official rulers of their respective states in 403 BCE. The last remnants of the Jin ruling clan and its territory were wiped out by these three states in 376 BCE. So, it is in a rather extended temporal sense that the commentary's remark about the perishing of the state and death of the ruler(s) applies to the case of Jin.

[28] Based on the kinds of cases discussed elsewhere in the *Han Feizi*, the phenomenon mentioned here in the commentary is one where a corrupt minister surreptitiously diverts resources that are supposed to be used for rewards ordered by the lord and instead uses them to do private favors for people, thereby garnering goodwill for him personally, rather than for the lord. In this instance, then, the term *de* 德 ("virtue") here refers both to acts of kindness and to the goodwill they generate. The solution to this problem that is proposed elsewhere in the *Han Feizi* is that rather than simply relying on ministers to carry out the lord's directives about what is to be rewarded or penalized, the lord should have the rewards and penalties for various behaviors set forth in publicly promulgated laws. Hence, everyone will know how the ministers are supposed to act, and so their corrupt actions can be easily recognized and reported.

minister increases them and uses the increase for [augmenting his own] awe-inspiring majesty. Thus, when the lord of men sets out rewards to be made, the minister exploits his authoritative power, and when the lord of men sets out penalties to be inflicted, the minister harnesses his awe-inspiring majesty. And so the text says, "The valuable implements of the state must not be presented to others."[29]

The king of Yue had been a captive servant in Wu and later encouraged it to attack Qi in order to wear out Wu.[d] After prevailing over the men of Qi at Ailing, the soldiers of Wu were spread out between the Jiang and Ji Rivers, and they were strongly exercised in going to Huangchi, and so they could be overcome [by Yue] at Wuhu.[30] And so the text says, "That which you desire to gather up, you must certainly first spread out. That which you desire to make weak, you must certainly first strongly exercise." When Duke Xian of Jin desired to ambush the state of Yu, he sent them a jade disk and horses, and when Earl Zhi desired to ambush the Chouyou people, he sent them a wide wagon.[31] And so the text says, "That which you desire to take in, you must certainly first give to." When one starts an affair from a formless state and then attains a great accomplishment

[29] The word translated here as "be presented to" is *shi* 示, which more literally means "be shown to," but the dual senses of the English verb "to present" as "to show" and "to give" nicely capture how the commentary reads the line from the *Laozi* in terms of how political power may be (inadvertently) transferred.

[30] The commentary's understanding of the history mentioned here is not entirely clear, but according to an account in the ancient text *Guoyu* 國語 ("Discourses of the States"), the king of Wu attended a meeting of feudal lords at Huangchi in 482 BCE, and in an attempt to intimidate the rival state of Jin, engaged in a nighttime march with full battle gear, in formation, and with thunderous noise, to within a few hundred yards from the Jin army's encampment, and challenged them to a fight. The sense in which the soldiers of Wu were "strongly exercised" may refer to this particular event, or it may refer more broadly to the whole journey from Wu to Huangchi, which was far from the capital of Wu. The account in the *Guoyu* also mentions that the soldiers of Wu dug canals as part of the expedition, and that may likewise be part of the sense in which they were "strongly exercised" and hence worn out.

[31] For the story about the state of Yu, see §6 below. According to early sources, the Chouyou people, who were regarded as "barbarians," lived in a remote area that was accessible only by narrow roads. As a ruse, Earl Zhi offered the Chouyou ruler a gift of a large bronze bell, so large that it could only be transported in a very wide wagon. In order to accept the bell, the ruler had the roads widened, which then made them passable for Earl Zhi's army.

before all under Heaven—this is referred to as "The subtle becomes apparent." When one occupies the role of the small and the weak and then those who are heavyweights humble themselves, it is referred to as "The diminished and weak prevail over the strong."[e]

Section Five[32]

[Primary Text]

The most difficult affairs under Heaven surely originate from
what is simple.~∓
The most significant affairs under Heaven surely originate from
what is paltry.~
Plan against difficulties while they are still simple.~
Counteract what is significant while it is still paltry.~±

[Commentary]

In the class of things that have form, those that are big are sure to have started from being small. Among creatures that go on for a long time, those that are prolific are sure to have started from being few. And so the text says, "The most difficult affairs under Heaven surely originate from what is simple. The most significant affairs under Heaven surely originate from what is paltry." For this reason, one who desires to control things focuses on them while they are still paltry. And so the text says, "Plan against difficulties while they are still simple. Counteract what is significant while it is still paltry." A dike that is a thousand *zhang*[33] in length may collapse due to holes from mole crickets and ants. A building that is one hundred

[32] This section corresponds to chapter 63 of the *Daodejing* in the Wang Bi arrangement.
[33] The *zhang* is a Chinese unit of measurement. Due to a lack of rigid standardization in ancient China, the exact modern equivalent is difficult to determine, but it would have been in the range of about 2–2.3 meters or 6.6–7.5 feet.

chi[34] in height may burn down because of a spark from a crack in a chimney. And so, when Bo Gui[35] would walk along the dikes, he would plug up the holes, and when elders are being vigilant against fires, they plaster over the cracks. For these reasons, Bo Gui did not face any difficulties due to flooding, and those elders do not face any troubles due to fires. These are all cases of being vigilant about what is simple in order to avoid difficulties, and carefully attending to what is paltry in order to keep at bay something significant.

Section Six[36]

[Primary Text]

[The sage is early to undertake affairs with regard to these.][37]
That which is secure is easy to maintain.
That which has not yet become manifest is easy to strategize against.±

[Commentary]

Bian Que had an audience with Duke Huan of Cai.[38] After standing there for a while, Bian Que said, "My lord, you have an illness in the

[34] As with the *zhang*, it is hard to be certain about the exact modern equivalent of a *chi* as referenced here, but it would have been in the range of about 20–23 cm or 0.66–0.75 feet (i.e., roughly 8–9 inches).

[35] Bo Gui appears or is mentioned in several early texts. He is said to have been a minister in the state of Wei, and in *Mencius* 6B11 he claims to be even better at controlling floodwaters than the ancient sage Yu. So, there may have been a tradition of associating Bo Gui with the building and maintaining of dikes, etc., that is being referenced here.

[36] This section corresponds to chapter 64 of the *Daodejing* in the Wang Bi arrangement.

[37] Scholars disagree about whether this line should be attributed to the primary text. As a result, it is also unclear whether it should be treated as belonging to the previous section or this section. For more on this issue, see note 40 below, and endnote g.

[38] Bian Que was a famous doctor about whom there are many stories. However, the chronology reflected in those stories would make his lifetime far removed from that of Duke Huan of Cai, which has led scholars to speculate that the text here is corrupt, and that some other ruler's name was originally written here. Since I do not feel confident about any of their proposed alternatives, and since the exact identity of the ruler seems immaterial to the point of the story, I have simply left the name as "Duke Huan of Cai."

pores of your skin. If left untreated, I fear it will go deeper." Duke Huan said, "We have no illness." Bian Que left, and Duke Huan said, "The fondness of doctors for treating those who are not sick is because it is a means for them to accrue merit."

After ten days, Bian Que had another audience with Duke Huan, and said, "My lord, your illness is now in your muscles and flesh. If left untreated, it will go even deeper." Duke Huan did not respond to him, so Bian Que left, and Duke Huan was again displeased.

After ten more days, Bian Que had another audience with Duke Huan, and said, "My lord, your illness is now in your intestines and stomach. If left untreated, it will go even deeper." Duke Huan did not respond to him, so Bian Que left, and Duke Huan was again displeased.

After ten more days, Bian Que took one look at Duke Huan, then turned around and hurried off. Duke Huan made a point of sending someone to question him. Bian Que said, "When an illness is in the pores of the skin, it is something that soaking and hot compresses will get at.[f] When it is in the muscles and flesh, it is something that needles of metal and stone will get at. When it is in the intestines and stomach, it is something that potions prepared with fire will get at. When it is in the bones and marrow, then that falls within the purview of the Supervisor of Fates,[39] and there is nothing for me to do. At present, the illness is in our lord's bones and marrow, and for this reason I as his servant had no requests to make."

After five days, Duke Huan's body was in pain and he sent someone to ask for Bian Que [to come], but Bian Que had already fled to the state of Qin, and Duke Huan subsequently died. And so, the way that good doctors treat sicknesses is to attack them while they are still in the pores of the skin—these are all cases of struggling against them while they are still small. As for misfortune and good fortune in affairs, they also have a "pores of the skin"

[39] The "Supervisor of Fates" (*siming* 司命) was the name of a spirit or deity with control over matters of life and death.

stage. And so the text says, "The sage is early to undertake affairs with regard to these."[40,g]

In the past, when Prince Chong'er of Jin fled [his state],[41] he passed through the state of Zheng. The lord of Zheng did not treat him in accordance with ritual.[42] Shu Zhan remonstrated with the ruler, saying, "This man is a worthy prince. If you, my lord, treat him generously, you can accumulate virtue."[43] The lord of Zheng did not heed him, so Shu Zhan remonstrated again, saying, "If you are not going to treat him generously, then it would be better to kill him, so that you do not cause there to be troubles later." Again, the lord of Zheng did not heed him. When the prince had returned to the state of Jin [and become ruler], he raised troops and attacked Zheng and greatly shattered it, taking eight cities from there. [On a different occasion,] Duke Xian of Jin was trying to use the jade disk of Chuiji to borrow passage through the state of Yu to attack the state of Guo. Grand minister Gong Zhiqi remonstrated with the ruler [of Yu], saying, "This is not to be allowed. If the lips

[40] Because no such sentence appears in either the received or excavated versions of the *Laozi*, and because a parallel passage in the early text *Xinxu* 新序 lacks the word *yue* 曰 ("[the text] says") in its version of this last sentence, some scholars suggest emending the line so that it is not a direct quotation, in which case it would say simply, "And so the sage is early to undertake affairs with regard to them." If that is correct, then there is no basis for attributing this remark to the *Laozi* primary text that the "Yu Lao" is explaining. I have tentatively kept it as a quotation and included it in my reconstruction of the primary text, in order to highlight the issue for readers. See endnote g for further discussion.

[41] For more on this history, see footnote 3 above.

[42] It is unclear exactly how the lord of Zheng violated ritual protocol. Generally, royalty visiting another state would have been formally received and lavishly entertained by the ruler, and so the violation may have consisted simply in failing to host Chong'er with the same generosity and respect normally given to princes. Shu Zhan's remarks tend to suggest this explanation. On the other hand, early accounts say that Chong'er had unusual "fused ribs" and that in the state of Cao, the ruler was curious about this and so spied on him while Chong'er was undressed, an egregious violation of ritual. The *Han Feizi* contains a version of that story, but the text runs together elements of the stories about what happened in Zheng and Cao (e.g., Shu Zhan appears as a minister to both the rulers of Zheng *and* Cao and offers similar advice to both). Since the text somewhat conflates the two stories, then when speaking of the lord of Zheng, the "Yu Lao" author might have in mind the violation of ritual that is otherwise typically attributed to the ruler of Cao.

[43] On the sense of *de* 德 ("virtue") here, see note 28 above.

perish, the teeth will grow cold. For Yu and Guo to save each other is not a matter of treating one another virtuously.[44] If Jin destroys Guo today, then tomorrow Yu will surely follow it in perishing." The lord of Yu did not heed him, but rather accepted the jade disk and lent them passage. After Jin had already taken Guo, then on the way back it destroyed Yu. These two ministers were struggling against what was still "in the pores of the skin," but the two lords disregarded them. That being the case, then Shu Zhan and Gong Zhiqi were the Bian Ques for Zheng and Yu, but the two lords did not heed them, and so Zheng thereby was shattered, and Yu thereby perished. And so the text says, "That which is secure is easy to maintain. That which has not yet become manifest is easy to strategize against."

Section Seven[45]

[Primary Text]

To take notice of what is small is called "sharp-sightedness." ∿∓
To persevere in a position of weakness is called "strength." ∿±
The way sages become unafflicted is by not being afflicted at things. *∿∓
Therefore they come to have no afflictions. ∿

[Commentary]

In the past, Zhòu created chopsticks of ivory, and Jizi became scared,[46] thinking, "Ivory chopsticks surely are not to be used with earthenware dishes, so he is sure to adopt vessels of rhinoceros horn

[44] I.e., the issue is not one of whether they ought to be kind to each other.
[45] This section comments on material from chapters 52 and 71 of the *Daodejing* in the Wang Bi arrangement. For further discussion of this arrangement, see note 52 below.
[46] For the ruler Zhòu, see the "Jie Lao," note 62. Jizi (also known as the Viscount of Ji) was Zhòu's uncle and advisor and is famous in Chinese history for having tried (unsuccessfully) to persuade Zhòu to give up the evil ways that eventually led to his overthrow.

and jade. With ivory chopsticks and jade vessels, one is surely not to consume stew of beans and leaves, so he is sure to have yak, elephant, and leopard placenta.[47] With yak, elephant, and leopard placenta, one is surely not to wear coarse garments and eat under a thatched roof, so he is sure to have embroidered clothes with multiple layers, spacious chambers, and towering pavilions. I fear how this ends, so I am scared at this beginning." Within five years, Zhòu created a meat garden, set up a roasting pillar, ascended a hill of grain mash, and oversaw a lake of wine.[48] Zhòu subsequently perished because of these things.[49] Thus, Jizi took notice of the ivory chopsticks and thereby knew the impending misfortune for the empire.[50] And so the text says, "To take notice of what is small is called 'sharp-sightedness.'"

When [the king of Yue] Goujian entered into captive servitude in the state of Wu, he personally walked before the king of Wu's horse team, holding a shield and dagger-axe, and so he was able to kill [the king of Wu] Fuchai at Gusu.[51] When King Wu was insulted [by

[47] The Chinese here has an ambiguity that I have deliberately left in the English translation as well. Namely, it is unclear whether the three items listed are two types of animal meat in general (yak and elephant) and a specific part of one animal (leopard placenta—though the term might also refer to a leopard fetus), or whether what is listed is the same part in three different animals, i.e., the placenta (or fetus) of a yak, that of an elephant, and that of a leopard.

[48] One early text records an explanation of the "meat garden" as follows: "Zhòu hung up meats to make a forest, and then ordered men and women to go naked and chase each other among them" (*Lunheng* 論衡, "Yu zeng" 語增 chapter). The "roasting pillar" was a metal pillar set over a fire pit and heated to a high temperature. Infamously, Zhòu would punish people by forcing them to walk across the pillar barefoot, until their feet got burned and they fell into the fire and died. Some scholars contend that here the roasting pillar is not being referenced for its use in punishment, but rather as a tool for cooking meat (taken from the "meat garden"), and hence it symbolizes excess, but I find that view less compelling. The grain mash is what is left over after the distillation process, and so a literal hill of it represents production of a significant amount of alcohol.

[49] I.e., they are what led King Wu to overthrow him.

[50] The phrase "misfortune for the empire" is ambiguous: it could refer to the disastrous effects of Zhòu's rule on the people, or it could refer to Zhòu's disastrous loss of his empire.

[51] The job of walking before the king's horse team with a shield and dagger-axe was usually done by fairly low-ranking men, so the position would have been a humiliating one for the king of Yue. Despite the mention of weapons, the sense in which he killed the king of Wu is not that he directly attacked him. Rather, while being a servant, the king of Yue studied the vulnerabilities of Wu, and as noted above in §4, after later returning to Yue he tricked Wu into over-extending itself and then took advantage of that to defeat its

Zhòu] at Yumen,[h] the expression on his face did not change, and later King Wu captured Zhòu at Muye. And so the text says, "To persevere in a position of weakness is called 'strength.'" The king of Yue became a hegemon by not being afflicted by servitude, and King Wu became a true king by not being afflicted by insults. And so the text says, "The way sages become unafflicted is by not being afflicted at things. Therefore they come to have no afflictions."[52]

Section Eight[53]

[Primary Text]

*Desire not to be desirous, and do not value goods that are difficult to obtain.**†

forces in battle. According to various early accounts, the king of Wu committed suicide in order to avoid being taken captive.

[52] This last quotation is from what is now chapter 71 in the received edition of the *Laozi*, whereas the previous two quotations are from chapter 52 in the received edition. My basis for grouping the discussion of the chapter 52 material with that from chapter 71 as a single section here is that the commentary itself closely connects its explanation of the remarks about "affliction" from chapter 71 with its explanation of the remark on "strength" from chapter 52. However, this feature of the commentary raises a question about the primary text from which the "Yu Lao" author was working: did it combine the lines from chapters 52 and 71 in a single chapter (as in the reconstructed translation offered here), or was the author consciously drawing from different chapters? At present, no excavated versions of the *Laozi* combine lines from chapters 52 and 71 as a single section, which somewhat favors the latter scenario. On the other hand, the "Yu Lao" explains the chapter 71 material in a manner that ignores and is even deeply at odds with its meaning in the context of (what has long been) the rest of that chapter, and that feature would be understandable if the author's version of the *Laozi* combined the lines from chapters 52 and 71. Alternatively, it seems that we would have to suppose that the "Yu Lao" author's text either did not contain the rest of chapter 71 or, if it did, that the author is taking the lines completely out of context. There is currently no way to decide among these possibilities, and hence readers should be aware that both my reconstructed translation and my grouping of paragraphs to constitute this section may be misleading and may not accurately reflect whatever principle of organization the "Yu Lao" author was following.

[53] This section corresponds to chapter 64 of the *Daodejing* in the Wang Bi arrangement. It is worth noting that the way the "Yu Lao" divides its commentary on that material into two different sections (namely here and earlier, in §6) corresponds well to how the lines constituting chapter 64 in the Wang Bi arrangement are split into two different chapters in both the Guodian *Laozi* and the Beida *Laozi*.

*Learn not to be learned, and return back to what the masses pass over.**
*Rely upon how the ten thousand things are so of themselves, and do not dare to take action.**

[Commentary]

A yokel from the state of Song obtained an uncarved piece of jade and offered it as a gift to Zihan.[54] Zihan did not accept it. The yokel said, "This treasure should become a vessel belonging to a gentleman [such as yourself]. It should not become the utensil of a paltry man." Zihan replied, "You deem the jade to be a treasure. I deem not accepting your jade to be a treasure." Thus, the yokel was desirous toward jade, but Zihan was not desirous toward jade. And so the text says, "Desire not to be desirous, and do not value goods that are difficult to obtain."

Wang Shou was carrying books on his back[55] and walking along, and met Xu Feng in Zhou. Xu Feng said, "Affairs are composed of actions, and actions arise from the times, so those who are timely have no constant affairs. Books are composed of sayings, and sayings arise from knowledge, so those who are knowledgeable do not collect books. So now why do you so singularly carry them on your back and walk along?"[56] Accordingly, Wang Shou thereupon burned his books and danced over the ashes. And so, those who are knowledgeable do not teach through sayings and discourses, and those who are

[54] There were multiple officials with the style-name "Zihan" in ancient China, so this reference is somewhat ambiguous. Zhang Jue (1996 and 2010) suggests that this Zihan is the man named Yue Xi, a minister in the state of Song who is presented in the historical records as being a worthy person.

[55] In ancient China, "books" were commonly written on bamboo slips that were rolled into bundles, and hence a collection of multiple books would quickly become a weighty burden, which is reflected in the fact that Wang Shou is described as carrying them on his back (*fu* 負).

[56] As with §3 above (see note 20), here the text is probably playing on two senses of *xing* 行, as meaning both "to walk" and "to act," so that Xu Feng's question also amounts to asking "Why are you so singularly encumbered by [the teachings of] books in your actions?"

wise do not learn through collections of books. This [point] is something that the world passes over,[57] but Wang Shou went back to it, and thus he learned not to be learned. And so the text says, "Learn not to be learned, and return back to what the masses pass over."

Things each have their constant features. Accord with and harness these to guide them. By according and following with the features of things, then when at calm one will be established in virtue, and when on the move one will conform to the Way. Among the people of Song, there was one who used ivory to make for the lord the leaf of a paper mulberry tree. It took three years to complete, and its size, veining, texture, and color were such that if one mixed it in with the leaves of a paper mulberry tree, it could not be distinguished. On the basis of such skill, this person subsequently enjoyed a salary from the state of Song. Liezi[58] heard of this and said, "If it took Heaven and Earth three years to complete a single leaf, then the things having leaves would be few indeed!" And so, failing to harness the resources of Heaven and Earth and instead depending on a single person's bodily efforts, or failing to follow the arrangements of the Way and its proper order and instead learning

[57] The commentary here is ambiguous in a way that yields at least two distinct possible meanings, and hence at least two possible readings of the primary text that cannot be simultaneously captured in the English translation. The word *guo* 過 most literally means "to pass beyond," but it can also mean "to go too far," "to overshoot," or "to miss," and by extension from that sort of sense, it can mean more generally "to be mistaken" or "to regard as mistaken." The exact sense of *guo* that is operative here then depends on what the referent of the word *ci* 此 ("this") is taken to be. If the "this" refers to the piece of wisdom conveyed in the immediately preceding sentence, then the sense in which the masses *guo* it would seem to be that they "miss" this realization. On the other hand, if the "this" refers just to skipping book learning, then the sense in which the masses *guo* it would seem to be that they regard it as a mistake (i.e., as laziness). In the next sentence, the text invokes a metaphor of spatial movement with its use of the word *gui* 歸 ("return"), and so I have opted for the former construal in the translation, rendering *guo* as "pass over" to capture the connection to motion. On the latter construal, the commentary would be saying: "This [failure to pursue book-learning] is something that the world considers a mistake, but Wang Shou went back to it, and thus he learned not to be learned. And so the text says, 'Learn not to be learned, and return back to what the masses consider mistaken.'"

[58] Liezi is a famous figure in the Chinese tradition and is often regarded as an early Daoist master like Laozi.

from a single person's intelligence—these are all "single leaf" behaviors.[59] And so, the grain crop from a winter planting is not something that even Hou Ji could make plentiful,[60] and the copious grain of a bountiful year is not something that even lowly menials could bungle. If one makes use of just a single person's strength, then even a Hou Ji will not be enough, but if one follows what is so of itself, then even lowly menials will produce an abundance. And so the text says, "Rely upon how the ten thousand things are so of themselves, and do not dare to take action."

Section Nine[61]

[Primary Text]

By not going out the door, one can know all under Heaven.
By not peering out the window, one can know the Way of Heaven.
The farther out one goes, the less one knows.
[For this reason, the sage] does not venture about and yet is knowledgeable,
*Does not look about and yet sees sharply,**
Does not take action and yet is accomplished.

[Commentary]

One's void-like orifices are the "doors" and "windows" for one's spirit and intellect. But when the ears and eyes are drained by sounds and sights, and one's energy and spirit are drained by external phenomena, then at one's center there will be no ruler. If

[59] I.e., they are not only artificial but also inefficient.
[60] Hou Ji (also known as "Lord Millet") was an ancient sage credited with first teaching people how to grow grain. Here he represents expertise in farming, and the point is that not even an expert could get a good crop from planting in the winter, since the timing is wrong.
[61] This section corresponds to chapter 47 of the *Daodejing* in the Wang Bi arrangement.

at one's center there is no ruler, then even if [the different things leading to] misfortune and good fortune were piled up before one like hills and mountains, one would have no way to recognize them. And so the text says, "By not going out the door, one can know all under Heaven. By not peering out the window, one can know the Way of Heaven." This is speaking of when one's spirit and intellect do not depart from their fullest state.

Master Xiang of Zhao was learning charioteering from Wang Yuqi, and suddenly started racing with Yuqi, but fell behind him three times, even after changing horses three times.[62] Master Xiang said, "In your teaching me charioteering, the technique has not been completely conveyed." Wang Yuqi replied, "The technique has already been completely conveyed, but the way you use it is mistaken. Whenever one drives a chariot, the things to value are that the horses' bodies feel at ease with the chariot and that the person's heart is attuned to the horses. Only then can one make swift pursuits over long distances. In the present case, when you, my lord, fall behind, then you desire to catch up with me, your servant, and when you are ahead, then you fear being overtaken by this servant of yours. In proceeding along some route and contesting over a long distance, if one is not ahead then one is behind, but whether ahead or behind, your heart is in all cases focused on this servant of yours, so just how could it be attuned to the horses? This is why my lord fell behind." [Another illustration of the same point is that] when Duke Sheng of Bo was plotting an uprising,[63] one time upon leaving the court he took hold of his whip upside down, and the sharp metal tip pierced his cheek, and blood flowed to the ground without him even

[62] The text is a little vague here, but the implication seems to be that Wang Yuqi was driving the same horse team the whole time, so Master Xiang's failure to beat him even with a fresh team after three times (which would have normally been a significantly unfair advantage by that point) is what explains Master Xiang's surprise and suspicion.

[63] Duke Sheng of Bo was a member of the royal family in the state of Chu. His father had been killed by the state of Zheng, and so he harbored great hatred for Zheng. When Chu later wound up saving Zheng from being destroyed by another state, he viewed that as a betrayal and instigated a rebellion in Chu.

knowing it. The people of Zheng heard about this and said, "If even his cheek can thus be forgotten, what will he not forget!"[64] And so the text says, "The farther out one goes, the less one knows." This is saying that if one's intelligence revolves around what is far away, then there will be that which one overlooks nearby. For this reason, the sage dispenses with constantly venturing about, and is able to comprehensively know [both the near and the far]. And so the text says that he "does not venture about and yet is knowledgeable." He is able to comprehensively see [both the near and the far], and so the text says that he "does not look about and yet sees sharply." He follows the times in selecting his affairs and accords with the available resources to establish achievements. He employs the capabilities of the ten thousand things and reaps the benefits from atop them. And so the text says that he "does not take action and yet is accomplished."

Section Ten[65]

[Primary Text]

A great vessel is slow to be completed.[下]
A great note makes a faint sound.[上]

[Commentary]

King Zhuang of Chu had been in charge of the government for three years, but no new orders had been issued, and no new government regulations had been enacted.[66] The Supervisor of the Military on the Right was in waiting at the throne, and spoke with

[64] The point of the question is to highlight the worry that Duke Sheng will not forget his hatred for Zheng and will come for them next.

[65] This section corresponds to chapter 41 of the *Daodejing* in the Wang Bi arrangement.

[66] The original Chinese text for the last part of this sentence (*wu zheng wei* 無政為) is very close in its phrasing to the term for "non-action" (*wuwei* 無為), such that the passage may be offering an interpretation of that notion in addition to illustrating the particular piece of primary text under discussion here.

the king in a veiled manner, saying, "There is a bird that has alit upon a knoll in the south. For three years it has not flapped its wings. It neither flies nor calls out, but is silent and without sound. What is its name?"[67] The king replied, "That for three years it has not flapped its wings is for the sake of growing out its feathers and wings. That it neither flies nor calls out is for the sake of observing the norms of the people. Though it has not flown, when it flies it is sure to soar to Heaven. Though it has not called out, when it calls out it is sure to astound people. Pay no heed to this matter. We understand it."[68] After another half a year, the king then personally presided over government business. There were ten people whom he dismissed, and nine whom he promoted. He executed five major ministers and brought into service six well-bred men who had been dwelling in seclusion. Thereupon, the state was greatly ordered. He then raised troops to punish the state of Qi and defeated it at Xuzhou, prevailed over the state of Jin at Heyong, convened a meeting of the feudal lords in the state of Song, and subsequently dominated all under Heaven as a hegemon. King Zhuang did not engage in actions of minor goodness, and so he had great fame. He did not prematurely set out or present [his intentions], and so he had great achievements. And so the text says, "A great vessel is slow to be completed. A great note makes a faint sound."[69]

[67] The Chinese word *ming* 名, here translated as "name," can also mean "title," so the question is simultaneously asking what title the "bird" deserves (i.e., is it a "king" or not?).

[68] These remarks may be subtly responding to Confucian views. Confucians supported a traditional practice of mourning one's deceased parent for three years, during which the mourner was supposed to refrain from almost all other activities, out of sadness and respect for the departed. In *Analects* 4.20 (see also 1.11), Confucius is recorded as saying, "One who makes no change to the ways of his father for three years after his father has passed away may be called a filial son" (trans. Slingerland 2003a). King Zhuang of Chu ascended to the throne after his father (King Mu) died. The fact that King Zhuang issued no new orders and made no changes to the government for three years thus conforms to Confucian ideals (which were not endorsed by some, such as the Supervisor of the Military on the Right in this story), but King Zhuang's words here reveal an entirely different motivation for his actions than what the Confucians would hope to see.

[69] The wording of the commentary and the constraints one faces when trying to translate it into English make it difficult to bring out fully the connection between the commentary and the line in the primary text. The word translated as "fame" is again *ming* 名,

Section Eleven[70]

[Primary Text]

To see oneself is called "sharp-sightedness."[*∓]
To prevail over oneself is called "strength."[*±]

[Commentary]

King Zhuang of Chu[71] desired to attack the state of Yue. Duzi[72] remonstrated, saying, "What is the basis for my king's [planned] attack on Yue?" The king replied, "Its government is in disarray and its military is weak." Duzi said, "As your servant, I worry about cases where a person's intelligence is just like their eyes, which can see what lies more than a hundred paces away, but cannot

which under its sense as "name" typically carries a connotation of creating a noise when the name is spoken. So, the "great note" corresponds to King Zhuang's "great fame" and its "faint sound" corresponds to his "silent" period of observing the conditions in his state. Furthermore, the word translated as "slow" here is *wan* 晚, which more typically means "late" and is regularly contrasted with *zao* 蚤, which means "early" or (as here) "premature." So, the "great vessel" corresponds to King Zhuang's "great achievements," and its "slow" completion corresponds to his waiting three years to unveil his approach to ruling.

[70] This section corresponds to chapter 33 of the *Daodejing* in the Wang Bi arrangement.

[71] A number of the features of the story that follows do not fit with what other early accounts tell us about King Zhuang of Chu, and therefore scholars have suspected that the text is corrupt here, and should instead read "King Wei of Chu," who lived long after King Zhuang of Chu. Since it is not clear whether the text is corrupt, or whether the "Yu Lao" author might simply have believed (perhaps mistakenly) in a different version of history, I have left the original reference to King Zhuang as it stands, but readers who may be struck by the apparent contrast between the depiction of King Zhuang in this section and that in the previous section should be aware that the reference to King Zhuang in this section might be just an error.

[72] There are quotations of this section preserved in other texts, and in some of those, the person mentioned here as Duzi 杜子 (who is otherwise unknown) instead appears as Zhuangzi 莊子. While more than one person in early China was referred to as "Zhuangzi," a quotation of this section in the *Wenxuan* 文選 lists the name specifically as Zhuang Zhouzi 莊周子 ("Master Zhuang Zhou"), which would then definitely be referring to the famous figure of the Warring States period who, along with Laozi and Liezi (see note 58 above), was regarded as one of the main Daoist thinkers of the time.

themselves see their own eyelashes. My king's military was itself defeated by the states of Qin and Jin, and the territory lost was several hundred *li*.[73] This is your military being weak. Zhuang Qiao engages in acts of banditry within our borders, and our officers are unable to stop him. This is your government being in disarray. My king's disarray and weakness is not less than that of Yue, but he desires to attack Yue—this is for his intelligence to be just like his eyes." The king thereupon desisted. And so, in terms of knowledge, the difficult thing does not rest in seeing others, but rather rests in seeing oneself. And so the text says, "To see oneself is called 'sharp-sightedness.'"

Zixia met with Zengzi,[74] and Zengzi said, "How is it that you have so fattened up?"[75] Zixia replied, "In battle I prevailed, and thus I fattened up." Zengzi said, "What are you talking about?" Zixia said, "Upon going in [to Confucius' school], I saw the appropriateness practiced by the former kings and deemed it glorious. Upon going out, I saw the delight belonging to wealth and noble status and also deemed it glorious. The two were battling in my breast, but I did not yet know which would prevail and which would lose, and so I grew scrawny. The appropriateness practiced by the former kings has now prevailed, and so I have fattened up." Thus, in terms of aspirations, the difficult thing does not rest in prevailing over others, but rather rests in prevailing over oneself. And so the text says, "To prevail over oneself is called 'strength.'"

[73] The *li* was an ancient Chinese unit of distance, in the range of roughly 355–416 meters or a bit less than a third of a mile.

[74] Zixia and Zengzi were both disciples of Confucius. Zixia was not known for any martial exploits, and hence Zengzi is puzzled at Zixia's initial answer to his question here.

[75] For modern readers to whom this question might sound rude, it is important to remember that in ancient times, when food could be hard to come by (and especially during the tumultuous historical period in which this story was set), getting "fat" was regarded positively, since it signaled that one's circumstances allowed a good supply of food.

Section Twelve[76]

[Primary Text]

As for one who neither values his teachers,[T]
Nor takes care of his assistants,
Even if he is clever, he is still greatly lost.
This is called the crucial marvel.

[Commentary]

The state of Zhou had a jade tablet. Zhòu ordered Jiao Ge to ask for it, but King Wen would not give it to him. Fei Zhong later came requesting it, and King Wen accordingly gave it to him. This was because Jiao Ge was a worthy man, but Fei Zhong utterly lacked the Way. The Zhou state was averse to that worthy man achieving his aspirations, and so gave the tablet to Fei Zhong.[77] When King Wen raised up the Grand Duke from the bank of the Wei River,[78] it was

[76] This section corresponds to chapter 27 of the *Daodejing* in the Wang Bi arrangement.

[77] This description may seem quite odd to those familiar with typical Confucian depictions of King Wen as a moral paragon who valued worthy men, but the story presented here seems to be following a somewhat different tradition, according to which King Wen schemed to exacerbate Zhòu's failings by bolstering his corrupt ministers such as Fei Zhong and pretending to imitate Zhòu's misrule, and only when Zhòu had reached the extremes of depravity did King Wen and King Wu launch their campaign to overthrow him. For a fairly detailed telling of this version of history, see the "Daoying" chapter of the *Huainanzi* (Major et al. 2010, 465–466). In the present context, the point is that since Jiao Ge was a worthy minister, he was the sort of person who might induce Zhòu to reform himself or—failing that—help him stay in power longer, and hence King Wen was unwilling to assist Jiao Ge.

[78] According to various early accounts, King Wen went hunting and came upon a man named Lü Shang fishing by the side of the Wei River, and after talking with him, realized that he was worthy and wise. So, King Wen brought him into his government, gave him the title "Grand Duke," and established him as a royal teacher. (This last point is especially relevant to how the commentary connects this story to the lines it quotes from the *Laozi*.) In this case, the "Yu Lao" applies the title "Grand Duke" to Lü Shang retrospectively.

a matter of valuing him, and when King Wen assisted Fei Zhong with the jade tablet, this was a matter of taking care of him. And so the text says, "As for one who neither values his teachers, nor takes care of his assistants, even if he is clever, he is still greatly lost. This is called the crucial marvel."[79]

[79] In the Mawangdui B version of the *Laozi* (which is more or less matched by the Beida version), the part of the *Laozi* that is quoted here is preceded by the words 善人善人之師, 不善人善人之資也, which based on the "Yu Lao" commentary (especially its use of *zi* 資, "assist, help") I would translate as "The good person is the teacher of the good person. The bad person is the assistant of the good person." Since the commentary seems to be referencing the idea that the Grand Duke (a good person) was the teacher of King Wen (another good person), while Fei Zhong (a bad person) was an unwitting assistant to King Wen, it may well be that "Yu Lao" author had some such set of lines in mind when writing the commentary.

Textual Notes for Yu Lao

a. Here I follow the gloss of 豐 as 大, as noted in Zhang Jue (2010).
b. I believe that most readers and translators of this line from the primary text do not pay sufficient attention to the explanation offered in the commentary, and hence they construe the line in a way that largely conforms to a fairly common understanding of the line in the *Daodejing* (and so differs substantially from how I translate it). In particular, the commentary specifically singles out Zhufu for criticism on the basis that he handed off the throne *while alive* (*sheng* 生), as opposed to simply letting the succession occur upon his death. Since Zhufu is supposed to be an example of someone who does *not* follow the model proposed in the *Laozi*, that suggests that in the primary text, the phrase 終日 is not being taken as it is nowadays commonly construed, namely as "the whole day," but rather as "to the end of his days."
c. Most scholars seem to agree that the words 故雖有代雲中之樂超然已無趙矣 in the "Yu Lao" seem to be responding to a line in the *Laozi*, which in the received edition reads 雖有榮觀燕處超然. Ōta Hō (2014 [1783]) goes so far as to say of this sentence in "Yu Lao" that it explains *that* line from the *Laozi*. However, such a claim is problematic for two reasons. First, we cannot simply assume that the author of the "Yu Lao" was working from a primary text that exactly matches the received edition. Second, if we read the received version 雖有榮觀燕處超然 along the lines of a fairly straightforward and typical construal (e.g., Ivanhoe (2003), "No matter how magnificent the view or lovely the place, [sages] remain aloof and unaffected"), it is unclear how the remark about Zhufu in the "Yu Lao," especially the part 已無趙矣, is supposed to illustrate *that*. Indeed, since the "Yu Lao" commentary seems to be presenting Zhufu as a negative example, then it appears more likely that the remark 故雖有代雲中之樂超然已無趙矣 about Zhufu is supposed to illustrate how he *failed* to live up to the model presented in the *Laozi*, and in that regard, it seems very hard to make sense of how Zhufu would have failed to do that, if the original line read 雖有榮觀燕處超然. For that reason, in trying to understand the relation of the "Yu Lao" commentary to the primary text, it seems better to think that the "Yu Lao" author was not working from the received version of the line, and to reconstruct the primary text on the basis that it presented a model that Zhufu can be seen as failing. As it so happens, the Mawangdui texts suggest just such a version. For the corresponding line in chapter 26 of the received version, the Mawangdui A text reads 唯有環官燕處若, and the B text reads 雖有環官燕處則昭若. Following other scholars, Henricks (1989, p. 274, n. 144) takes 環 as 闤 and 官 as 館, and produces the following translation combining features of both A and B texts: "When he's safely inside a walled-in [protected] hostel and resting at ease—only then does he transcend all concerns" (brackets in original). While Henricks does not explicitly say how he is combining the two, it appears that his reading is equivalent to 唯有闤館燕處則超然. On that sort of understanding of the *Laozi*, we can see how Zhufu would present a contrast case, namely that even though he was 超然, he failed to have the condition specified in 有闤館燕處, since he had given up his position as king, and so Dai and Yunzhong could not provide the security he needed. For these reasons, my reconstructed translation of the primary text is based on taking it as if it said 唯有闤館燕處則超然 or something close to it. Incidentally, I note that in his 1963 translation of the *Laozi*, D.C. Lau had already proposed reading the line in a similar fashion. He translates it as "It is only when he is safely behind walls and watch-towers/ That he rests peacefully and is above worries." In his notes, Lau explains that he takes 雖 as 唯, and 榮 as 營. Unfortunately, he does not give precise sources for this approach, but a reading like that would also fit with what I take the remark about Zhufu in the "Yu Lao" to be addressing.

d. Here I am persuaded by the arguments of Zhang Jue (2010) to follow those editions that have 勸 instead of 觀.
e. Here I follow those editions that read 處小弱而重自卑謂「損弱勝強」也. However, most scholars seem inclined to take 重 as a verb meaning "to redouble" or "to take seriously," and while that construal is understandable and makes sense grammatically, the problem is that it does not really explain the part about 勝強 in the line from the *Daodejing*. The only way it could do so would be if maintaining humility were itself an act of overcoming a tendency *within oneself* to use force, and while that view makes sense conceptually, it simply does not fit with the character of the commentary, which has been emphasizing how one person overcomes *another* person's strength. In contrast, if we take 重 as a noun that serves as the grammatical subject for 自卑 as I do in the translation, then the two parts 處小弱 and 重自卑 correspond well to the two parts of the quotation, 損弱 and 勝強. (Compare also the preceding sentence 起事於無形而要大功於天下, 是謂「微明」, where the words before the 而 and the words after the 而 explain 微 and 明, respectively.)
f. My understanding of this line and many others in this paragraph mostly follows Zhang Jue (2010).
g. It seems to me that there are two main reasons why scholars who treat 聖人蚤從事焉 as a quotation would be inclined to group it with the preceding discussion of what is now chapter 63 in the Wang Bi edition of the *Laozi*. One is that it would seem somewhat awkward for a chapter to start with a sentence like 聖人蚤從事焉, where the referent of 焉 is not previously specified. The other is that this remark may seem reminiscent of the penultimate line of the received edition, which reads 是以聖人猶難之 (the Guodian version also has this line): Queen (2013, 223), for example, seems to have this view. Neither of those reasons is especially compelling, however. Regarding the former, it is not uncommon for chapters in the received version of the *Daodejing* to begin with lines that have pronouns and the like with no prior explanation for their referents (e.g., chapter 9, which opens with 持而盈之, 不如其已; chapter 36, which starts with 將欲歙之, 必固張之; and chapter 51, which begins with 道生之，德畜之，物形之，勢成之). So, the awkwardness of having a starting line such as 聖人蚤從事焉 is not enough on its own to tilt the scales in favor of treating it as part of the commentary on what is now chapter 63. Regarding the similarity to 是以聖人猶難之, it is important that such similarity is mainly confined to the fact that it is a remark about the sage, since 蚤從事焉 is not very close to 猶難之 in either wording or the thought expressed. On the other hand, it is important to note that 聖人蚤從事焉 *also* has verbal echoes with lines in chapter 64 of the received version. In particular, one line there reads 民之從事常於幾成而敗之, and so the appearance of 從事 in 聖人蚤從事焉 could indicate that it is somehow related to that line (which also appears in the Mawangdui versions). In terms of similarity to other lines in the two chapters, there thus seems to be no especially greater reason to associate 聖人蚤從事焉 with the commentary on the material from chapter 63 than with that on the material from chapter 64. Rather, what does seem to me to be more decisive evidence is that the line 聖人蚤從事焉 appears at the end of the story about Bian Que, and the subsequent commentary on the material from chapter 64 clearly refers back to that story when it says 然則叔瞻、宮之奇亦虞，鄭之扁鵲也. Thus, the "Yu Lao" itself ties the context in which the line 聖人蚤從事焉 appears more closely to the commentary on the material from chapter 64. For that reason, then, I have grouped the Bian Que story and the line 聖人蚤從事 as part of §6 of the translation, rather than as part of §5 (or as an altogether independent section).
h. Here I follow Zhang Taiyan apud Chen Qiyou (2000) in emending 文王 to 武王. I also emend 王門 to 玉門, as most commentators suggest.

PART II
ANALYSES

3

Unraveling and Explicating the *Han Feizi*'s Dissection of the *Laozi*

Eirik Lang Harris

The "Jie Lao" and "Yu Lao" chapters of the *Han Feizi* are undeniably important on many levels. Not only are they arguably the earliest extant commentaries on the *Laozi*,[1] but there are those who have argued that they provide a theoretically sophisticated grounding for the political thought and argumentation that predominates the *Han Feizi*. Indeed, these two sections of the *Han Feizi* have scholars arguing across the board, from those who view them as a ruthless appropriation of Daoist thought for so-called Legalist ends to those who consider them, when coupled with other chapters of the *Han Feizi* with Daoist affinities, to be a correct interpretation of the *Laozi*'s teachings.[2] Finally, important differences not only between the "Jie Lao" and "Yu Lao" chapters on the one hand and the rest of the *Han Feizi* on the other but also between the "Jie Lao" and the "Yu Lao" themselves give rise to heated debates about the authenticity of these two chapters. Some believe that both chapters are the work of Han Fei, others conclude that the "Jie Lao" was an early work by Han Fei, but that the "Yu Lao" predated him, and many argue that Han Fei wrote neither chapter.[3]

[1] For an overview of major commentaries to the *Laozi*, see Chen (2003, 365–408).

[2] For the latter, see Wang and Chang (1986, 108). Other chapters of the *Han Feizi* with clear affinities to the *Laozi* include 5, 8, and 29.

[3] Zhao (1967) and Wang and Chang (1986) argue that Han Fei was the author of both chapters. Lundahl (1992, 218–241) defends claims by Rong (1972) and Hu (1961) that the "Jie Lao" chapter was not written by Han Fei. For a recent systematic analysis

Eirik Lang Harris, *Unraveling and Explicating the* Han Feizi's *Dissection of the* Laozi In: *Explaining and Illustrating the* Laozi. Edited by: Eirik Lang Harris and Eric L. Hutton, Oxford University Press.
 DOI: 10.1093/9780197514948.003.0005

This chapter, however, focuses more on philosophical questions than questions of authorship, though I suggest that it may be a useful heuristic to read these chapters as if they were written by Han Fei. In particular, I ask a set of related philosophical questions: (1) What sort of philosophical vision can we draw out of these two commentaries on the *Laozi*? (2) Is there a reading of these two commentaries that is both internally consistent and consistent with the rest of the *Han Feizi*? And (3) What role does the *Laozi* play for the author(s) of these two commentaries, whoever they were?[4]

I. Brief Overview—The Political Philosophy of the Broader *Han Feizi*

In most chapters, the *Han Feizi* develops an amoral political realism predicated upon views about the realities of the natural world around us and of human nature. The result of the *Han Feizi*'s understanding of these realities is a political philosophy that argues for the development of a strong, stable, and well-organized state bureaucracy, a strong and inviolable legal code, and the rejection of political visions undergirded by substantial moral commitments. The end goal is the development of a political system that is mechanical in nature—one which, once set in motion, would require little in the way of active attention. It would not rely upon the ruler or, indeed, anyone within the political hierarchy, possessing any particular wisdom, talents, character, or characteristics setting them apart from the average individual.

of the authenticity of the *Han Feizi*, see Zheng (1993). Two English-language studies, Sarkissian (2001) and Queen (2013), conclude that Han Fei was not the author of either text, though Hendrischke (2007) argues for Han Fei's authorship of both.

[4] As seen earlier in this volume, the *Laozi* as it has been received did not exist at the time that the "Jie Lao" and "Yu Lao" were written. Thus, references to the *Laozi* in this context should be read as shorthand for "whatever version of the material that became the *Laozi* that the author(s) of these chapters is commenting on."

This approach to political theorizing in the *Han Feizi* arises because, rather than beginning with a conception of an ideal social or political order and then trying to mold people in such a way as to achieve this ideal, the text takes the realities of the world and its various parts as providing constraints both on what is possible and on what should be attempted. Insofar as there is an ideal political organization in the *Han Feizi*, it is conceived as an ideal that is not merely theoretically possible, but realistically viable, given the material available.

This leads the *Han Feizi* to argue that the ruler should "employ what works for the many and abandon what works for the few" (Harris 2023, 376).[5] But how is this to be determined? For the *Han Feizi*, it arises from a deeper understanding of the "Way" (*dao* 道). The text uses this term in both broader and narrower senses. At its broadest, it refers to what we can conceptualize as the cosmic Way. This Way encompasses all that exists, and both provides a standard by which all things can be evaluated and is itself the source of the various patterns and regularities of the natural world (including those of human beings). The term is also used in a range of narrow senses, where the text discusses, among other things, the Way of the ruler, the Way of the minister, and the "political" Way. What ties these Ways together and connects them to the broader cosmic Way is that they each refer to those aspects of the broader cosmic Way that are relevant to ruling, acting as a minister, or creating order within the state. It is essential, argues the *Han Feizi*, to accord with the regularities of the natural world, including the basic dispositions of human beings, if a strong, stable, and flourishing state is to be established and maintained.[6]

Human dispositions, claims the text, consist of a relatively stable set of interests that are primarily self-regarding and not amenable to

[5] Translations of the *Han Feizi* are my own, with references provided to Harris (2023) when available.

[6] For a more expansive discussion of the *Han Feizi*'s conception of the Way outside of the "Jie Lao" and "Yu Lao" chapters, see Harris (2025).

change, development, or cultivation. Additionally, argues the *Han Feizi*, most people are little better than small children at evaluating their actual overall long-term interests, either at the individual level or at the level of how they are impacted by society-wide practices (Harris 2023, 378). Thus, while a well-ordered, stable, and flourishing political organization is actually in the best interests of the people, it cannot be created directly by appealing to people's own understanding of their interests. Rather, a set of external tools must be designed to clearly incentivize the people to work toward this goal.

Three tools come to the forefront: laws (*fa* 法), techniques (*shu* 術), and positional power (*shi* 勢).[7] These tools can be applied to ensure that human societies better accord with the cosmic Way, following its patterns to shape and control the actions of people within society (Harris 2013). However, in most chapters of the *Han Feizi*, unlike in the received *Laozi*, "following," modeling oneself upon, or emulating the Way is not seen as having an intrinsic value. The ethical overtones of the received *Laozi*, keyed to what seems to be the intrinsic goodness of modeling oneself upon the Way, are simply not present in the *Han Feizi*. The reason to follow the Way is purely practical—doing so allows one to achieve a range of goals that would otherwise be unachievable. If one wishes for a strong, stable, and flourishing state, then one must gain an understanding of how the realities of the Way constrain what is possible, detail what will allow for success, and ensure certain tactics result in failure.

Once we understand what is necessary for a strong, stable, and flourishing state, the *Han Feizi* argues, we will realize that laws regulating human activity and channeling it toward achieving such a state must be implemented and that clear rewards and

[7] In his translation of the "Jie Lao" and "Yu Lao," Eric L. Hutton renders this term as "power" or "authoritative power," depending on the context. See his discussion in footnote 29 of the "Jie Lao" translation, p. 45.

punishments must be attached to these laws to ensure that everyone perceives it to be in their interest to help achieve this state. The techniques that the text focuses on provide standards for dealing with the *Han Feizi*'s vast bureaucratic structure. They aim at ensuring that all those in the various positions of this bureaucracy fulfill their assigned responsibilities while not overstepping their bounds. Neither tool, however, can be implemented effectively without a third—the positional power of the ruler. This positional power is the power that the ruler has *qua* ruler, rather than a power attributable to personal characteristics. It bestows upon anyone who holds the position an authority, prestige, leverage, and awesomeness that allow this person to ensure that those below adhere to the political system. These three pillars of the *Han Feizi*'s political theory are interdependent. Laws primarily regulate and manipulate the masses, techniques control the vast bureaucracy, and positional power allows for the effective application of both.

Where, though, does this leave morality? Well, the *Han Feizi* is skeptical of the role that morality can play in the political realm, for the sort of normativity underlying political justification is fundamentally different from the sort of normativity undergirding moral justification, preventing the former from being derived from the latter.[8] Political organization is justified in the *Han Feizi* insofar as it is able to solve pressing problems of the time that would otherwise hinder the survival and effective action of human beings. The ultimate goal for the *Han Feizi* is the creation and sustenance of political order. The fundamental insight here is that political order is necessary for achieving all other goods; to the extent that we wish to achieve any other good, we should do whatever increases political order.

Morality has no role here—indeed, it is seen to be in tension with such a political order. There will be times when

[8] Harris (2013). For an account of the role of morality in the similarly oriented *Shenzi Fragments*, see Harris (2024).

those things leading to political order differ from those things demanded by morality. If we follow the latter in cases where the two diverge, we endanger the security and stability of the state, and thus the security and stability of human beings. The conclusion is clear, thinks the *Han Feizi*—morality offers nothing new or necessary and can play no independent role. With this understanding of the overall philosophy of the *Han Feizi*, let us turn to the "Jie Lao."

II. Unraveling the "Jie Lao"

My aim here is not to provide a full-fledged articulation of the political philosophy of the "Jie Lao" and "Yu Lao" and come to a full conclusion as to how it relates both to the received *Laozi* and to the *Han Feizi*. Rather, in line with the overall aim of this volume—to engage a more general, non-specialist audience—and encourage that audience to grapple with these issues themselves, I will examine these commentaries, highlighting both ways in which they might be read as cohering with the *Han Feizi* as well as potential tensions between these commentaries and the rest of the *Han Feizi*. We may not come to a single "right" reading of these commentaries, but shall, I hope, unravel them a bit, allowing the reader to continue such investigations in a fruitful manner.

Hagop Sarkissian (2001, 67) has argued that "the dominant philosophical orientations of [the 'Jie Lao'] chapter are unmistakably the Daoism of the *Laozi* and the Confucianism of the *Mencius*," while Sarah Queen (2013, 212) contends that "the syncretism of 'Jie Lao' appears to be devoid of influence from what later became identified as 'Legalism,'" and these claims should lead us to wonder why it exists as a chapter of the *Han Feizi*, a text that generally demonstrates a decided antipathy toward the political morality of Confucianism. Sarkissian and Queen's claims cannot be dismissed out of hand—the positions laid out in the "Jie Lao" author's analysis of various parts of the *Laozi* do seem to accord with a range of ideas generally identified as Confucian or Laozian. The latter should not surprise us, since regardless of author, it would be difficult to produce a commentary on a text that was not influenced by that text! The Confucian aspects of the interpretation, however, may leave us wondering not merely whether the "Jie Lao" came from Han Fei himself, but whether its political vision could bear any relation to that found within the rest of the *Han Feizi*.

We can see the reasons for Sarkissian and Queen's interpretations of the "Jie Lao" by examining its opening section, a commentary on a version of the *Laozi* similar to what we see in the received *Laozi* 38. Before doing so, however, it may be useful to quickly review the received version of *Laozi* 38, which reads:

> One with highest virtue does not possess virtue, and thereby has virtue.
> [One with lowest virtue never strays from virtue, and thereby lacks virtue.]
> One with highest virtue takes no action, but leaves nothing undone.
> [One with lowest virtue acts on it, but has something for which he acts.]
> One with highest humaneness acts on it, but has nothing for which he acts.
> One with highest appropriateness acts on it, but has something for which he acts.
> One with highest ritual propriety acts on it, but no one matches him,
> *He then rolls up his sleeves and resorts to force.*
> *And so,*
> *With the loss of the Way comes the rise of virtue.*
> *With the loss of virtue comes the rise of humaneness.*
> *With the loss of humaneness comes the rise of appropriateness.*
> *With the loss of appropriateness comes the rise of ritual propriety.*

Insisting on ritual is the impoverishment of loyalty and good faith, and the start of chaos.
Practicing foreknowledge is a flowery exhibition of the Way, and the start of foolishness.
The great man dwells in what is rich and does not dwell in what is impoverished,
Dwells in what is genuine fruit and does not dwell in what is flowery exhibition,
Discards the latter and chooses the former.[9]

One common reading of this passage is that the person of highest virtue, the sage, lives in complete harmony with the Way. He does not need to strive for virtue, but rather acts in a natural fashion, absent externally inculcated, non-natural desires. However, if this harmony becomes disrupted such that acting in a virtuous manner is no longer completely natural, then the concept of virtue arises as a goal to be pursued—and in pursuing it, one is striving for something lesser, something that is the object of conscious attention. This deviance from the Way continues to unfold and can be represented by the Confucian virtues of humaneness (*ren* 仁), appropriateness (*yi* 義), and ritual propriety (*li* 禮).[10] The humane person on this account acts with a conscious awareness that his actions are "humane," but does not take himself to be better than others because of this and possesses a spontaneous inclination to do so; it is not something imposed externally.

[9] The translation of the received version here is based on the "Jie Lao" author's understanding of the text, except where the "Jie Lao" bases itself on a text that is importantly different from the received version. Italics are used to indicate where the received text varies in important ways from what is in the "Jie Lao," as these instances are important for my analysis. Throughout, [brackets] indicate lines that exist in the received version but are missing from the "Jie Lao" commentary while {braces} indicate lines that exist in the "Jie Lao" version but are missing from the received version.

[10] *Ren* is often translated as "benevolence," while *yi* is often translated as "righteousness" or "rightness."

The decline continues, however, as "appropriateness" becomes a conscious goal. Continuing this common interpretation of *Laozi*, the individual who understands what is appropriate (or right) in any particular situation becomes "self-righteous." As Slingerland (2003b, 81–82) notes, such a sanctimonious individual is guided by standards of "right" and "wrong," of "appropriate" and "inappropriate," with little understanding of what underlies them. This then easily degrades further into blind adherence to rituals—rigid obedience to a code but lacking an understanding of and genuine reverence for the Way—replacing these with empty forms.

I lay out this interpretation not as authoritative, but as a common one that is both plausible and in important ways quite different from the interpretation provided by the "Jie Lao."[11] The "Jie Lao" begins explicating *Laozi* 38 thus:

> Virtue involves what is internal. Possession involves what is external. "One with highest virtue does not possess virtue" means that one's spirit is not drawn out by external things. When one's spirit is not drawn out by external things, then one's self is kept whole. For one's self to be kept whole is called virtue. Thus, virtue is tantamount to possessing one's own self. In every case of virtue, one collects it by means of non-action, completes it by means of non-desiring, secures it by means of non-thinking, and solidifies it by means of non-use. If one acts on it and desires it, then virtue will have no place to lodge. If virtue has no place to lodge, then it will not be whole. If one uses it and thinks about it, then it will not be solid. If it is not solid, then it will lack achievements. This lack of achievements arises from taking virtue as a possession. Thus, if one takes virtue as a possession, then one lacks virtue. And if one does not take virtue as a possession, then one has virtue. And so the text says, "One with highest

[11] This is roughly how Wang Bi seems to read the *Laozi*. See Lynn (1999, esp. 119–127).

> virtue does not possess virtue, and thereby has virtue." (JL §1, pp. 36–37)[12]

This explanation provides a straightforward reading of *Laozi* 38 that focuses on the individual, arguing that virtue is a feature internal to someone. If one turns to the external world to find it, one's efforts necessarily will end in failure. The "Jie Lao" joins the *Laozi* in explicitly cautioning against focusing one's attentions on attainment and desires, for this prevents one from emptying themselves and allowing true virtue to enter. Their virtue will never develop because they are too busy acting; they are too concerned with the external world.

There seems to be no evidence of an instrumentalist, realist reading of the *Laozi* here. If this is Han Fei's commentary, he has not yet begun to interpret the text as promoting the amoral, realist, political philosophy that is developed throughout much of the rest of the *Han Feizi*.[13] To be sure, one of the reasons for the "Jie Lao" author's condemnation of searching for virtue externally may be that this will result in a lack of political power. However, political power itself is neither the focus of this section nor the goal. And, if we take seriously Wang Bo's notion that early Chinese authors placed what they considered to be most important at the beginning (Wang 2001, 19–21), this counsels against the idea that the main purpose of the "Jie Lao" chapter is an instrumentalist one. The author may be concerned with political power, but it does not permeate his entire analysis of the *Laozi*. He has other goals and foci, some of which seem to accord with traditional understandings of the received *Laozi*.

However, while the commentary begins in a way that does not seem foreign to contemporary readers of the received *Laozi*,

[12] Section and page numbers for the "Jie Lao" (JL) and "Yu Lao" (YL) are given according to the translations in Part I of this volume.

[13] Chen (2000, 370–371), however, does try to connect the opening lines of the "Jie Lao" commentary on *Laozi* 38 to chapters 6 and 7 of the *Han Feizi*.

it does not take long for a subtle shift to occur, resulting in an interpretation of *Laozi* 38 that is unique and perhaps even strange. One traditional interpretation of the rest of the received *Laozi* 38, which continues on to discuss humaneness, appropriateness, and ritual propriety, is that it is an attack on these virtues central to the Confucian moral and political project. The "Jie Lao," however, cannot be read in this way. Rather, it proceeds to interpret these virtues and the *Laozi* 38's discussion of them in such a way that they are lauded—in their proper instantiations.

The "Jie Lao" understands humaneness as referring to instances in which "in one's innermost heart one joyfully cares for people" (JL §1, p. 38). It argues that one who is humane delights in the good fortune of others and hates it when others suffer misfortune. Indeed, in a line that recalls *Mencius* 2A6, we are told that this feeling "is born from something that the heart cannot help but feel, and not from seeking for some recompense" (JL §1, p. 38). Thus, for the "Jie Lao," it makes sense to say, as *Laozi* 38 does, that "One with highest humaneness acts on it, but has nothing for which he acts." Such an individual acts from natural empathetic feelings, rather than from an interest in obtaining something beneficial. Unlike what we see in the received *Laozi*, on the "Jie Lao" author's account, the actions that humaneness gives rise to are not actions to be avoided or disparaged—they are to be lauded.

Turning next to appropriateness, the "Jie Lao" argues that it is a concept referring to the proper relations among people in society—between lord and minister, superior and subordinate, father and son, and noble and lowly, as well as connections between acquaintances and friends, divisions between close and distant relatives or insiders and outsiders. It is proper, says the "Jie Lao," that ministers serve lords, subordinates have affection for superiors, sons serve fathers, the base honor the noble, and friends help one another out. As the "Jie Lao" interprets, "Appropriateness means being proper in each of these things.

Because something is proper, one acts on it" (JL §1, pp. 38–39). This then is the text's explanation of the line in *Laozi* 38 that reads, "One with highest appropriateness acts on it, but has something for which he acts."

As with "humaneness," this is an interpretation of "appropriateness" that is anything but disparaging. Such an understanding again differs dramatically from the common interpretation of the received text that, as a concern for appropriateness arises in people, they move further and further from their true selves, increasingly acting in pursuit of selfish desires. On the "Jie Lao" author's account, appropriate actions arise from an understanding of what truly is proper in light of one's particular relationship with someone else rather than from a general (and uncontrollable) sense of caring toward all others. Implicit here is the view that what is appropriate depends on particular social roles.

The "Jie Lao" then turns to a discussion of ritual propriety. As with the case of humaneness and appropriateness, the received *Laozi* 38 traditionally is read as being opposed to ritual propriety, because, as it says,

> One with highest ritual propriety acts on it, but no one matches him;
> He then rolls up his sleeves and *resorts to force*.

The "Jie Lao," however, does not read the discussion of ritual in this negative light. Rather, it tells us,

> Ritual is that by which one provides an exterior display for one's inner essence. It is the ornamentation and adornment of the various things that are appropriate. It is the fitting interaction between lord and minister, father and son. It is that by which noble and lowly, worthy and unworthy are all differentiated. . . . Ritual is that by which external adornment makes understood what is internal. (JL §1, p. 39)

If this is correct and ritual is to be appreciated, what are we to make of the received *Laozi* 38's discussion of ritually correct individuals rolling up their sleeves and resorting to force when others do not match their actions, something that many interpretations take to demonstrate the problem with an adherence to ritual? Here, a subtle change of character arises. Rather than the character *reng* 扔, which appears in the received *Laozi*, the text that the "Jie Lao" cites has *reng* 仍. The former character can mean "to force" or "to destroy," while the latter means "to continue" or "to redouble," leading to an importantly different understanding in which,

> One with highest ritual propriety acts on it, but no one
> matches him;
> He then rolls up his sleeves and **redoubles his efforts.**[14]

The "Jie Lao" focuses on explaining that the masses, because they do not understand that the point of ritual is to give expression to inner feelings, use them instead as a way to venerate others. However, since they see the point of ritual to be outside of themselves, at times their ritual activities will wax, and at times they will wane. This sort of ritual practice is quite different from the way that the *junzi*, the cultivated gentleman, uses ritual. The gentleman employs ritual to express his inner feelings.[15] But, since the masses do not understand what underlies the ritual of the gentleman, they cannot match his ritual actions appropriately. The response to this by the gentleman in the "Jie Lao" is not to attack the common people, but rather to "roll up his sleeves and redouble his efforts" with his ritual activity, redoubling his reverence and respect and exhausting himself in doing so. In all these cases—humane, appropriate, and ritually appropriate actions are taken because these

[14] Note, however, that a change of character is not required for the "Jie Lao" author's reading. Rather, *reng* 扔 can also refer to "continuing," "guiding," or "clarifying."

[15] For more on the communicative aspect of rituals, with a focus on Xunzi, see Berkson (2016).

values have been internalized—acting from them is the virtuous way to behave.

While the preceding may very well provide a coherent interpretation of the first part of *Laozi* 38, demonstrating why these virtues are valuable, one may wonder what to do with the following lines from the received version that seem to indicate that "virtue" arose after people had lost the true Way, and imply that a focus on humaneness marks a further departure, with subsequent focuses on appropriateness and ritual propriety marking ever further steps away from the Way:

> With the loss of the Way comes the rise of virtue.
> With the loss of virtue comes the rise of humaneness.
> With the loss of humaneness comes the rise of appropriateness.
> With the loss of appropriateness comes the rise of ritual propriety.[16]

The "Jie Lao" deals with this by quoting a version of this passage that is importantly different and that could be translated thus:

> With the loss of the Way comes the loss of virtue.
> With the loss of virtue comes the loss of humaneness.
> With the loss of humaneness comes the loss of appropriateness.
> With the loss of appropriateness comes the loss of ritual propriety. (JL §1, p. 40, n. 16)[17]

The addition of the Chinese character *shi* (失, "to lose") a second time in each statement effectively reverses the causal arrow. Rather than implying that an awareness of and focus on virtue, humaneness, appropriateness, and ritual propriety mark ever further steps away from the Way, on the "Jie Lao" author's account, these are all

16 故失道而後德, 失德而後仁, 失仁而後義, 失義而後禮.
17 失道而後失德, 失德而後失仁, 失仁而後失義, 失義而後失禮.

components of this Way. As such, they are lost once the Way is lost rather than arising in response to the loss of the Way. Moreover, as Eric Hutton notes in his translation of these lines, the "Jie Lao" author seems to interpret them as describing a process of decay at the individual level, rather than just at a societal level.

The fundamental problem remains the same as in the received version of the *Laozi*, namely a loss of understanding of the Way. However, unlike the traditional understanding of the received text, the virtues associated with Confucianism are not seen as problematic.[18] What is problematic is merely when they are misunderstood or misapplied. In their proper form, these virtues bolster the Way, rather than appearing in indication that we have departed from it.

The "Jie Lao" thus provides a unique interpretation of *Laozi* 38 that does not seem strained, so long as we accept that it provides an accurate account of the material upon which it comments. Additionally, this interpretation is one that melds together a range of ideas found in both the received *Laozi* and in a range of early Confucian texts. Furthermore, the vision espoused in this commentary is hard to reconcile with important ideas found elsewhere in the *Han Feizi*. It stands in stark tension with discussions of human motivations, the desirability of the ruler focusing on cultivating any virtues, and the role that virtues can play in a well-ordered state. For example, chapter 50 ("On the Illustrious Schools of Thought") says:

> When a sage governs a state, he does not wait for people to do good for his sake. Instead, he ensures that they can do no wrong.

[18] Some excavated versions of the *Laozi* can also be read as less explicitly anti-Confucian. For example, the Guodian version of *Laozi* 19 is missing the line "Cut off sageliness, abandon wisdom, and the people will benefit one-hundred-fold" as well as the line, "Cut off humaneness, abandon appropriateness, and the people will return to being filial and kind" (modified from Ivanhoe 2003, 19). As the "Jie Lao" author was working with a version of the *Laozi* that preceded the received version, what he saw may well have similarly lacked explicit anti-Confucian sentiment. Note, though, discussions by Henricks (2000, 11–15) and Cook (2012, 210–216) about whether the Guodian *Laozi* is actually less anti-Confucian.

> If he waits for people to do good for his sake, within his borders there will be fewer than ten who do so; if he ensures that people can do no wrong, the entire state can be brought into line. Those who govern employ what works for the many and abandon what works for the few. Therefore, they do not work on their kindness [*de* 德, translated above as "virtue"], they work on their laws. (Harris 2023, 376)

In numerous places elsewhere in the *Han Feizi* these ideas are expanded upon, making it clear that it has a vision that conflicts in important ways with that laid out in the "Jie Lao."

With this initial understanding of the "Jie Lao" author's interpretation of *Laozi* in mind, let us next turn to its commentary on what is now *Laozi* 59. The version upon which the "Jie Lao" comments can be translated as follows:

> For ordering human affairs and serving Heavenly affairs, nothing is as good as frugality.
> When one is called frugal, this is due to submitting early.
> As for submitting early, this means repeatedly amassing virtue.
> If one repeatedly amasses virtue, then there is nothing that one does not overcome.
> If there is nothing that one does not overcome, then no one will know where one's limits lie.
> If no one knows where one's limits lie, then one can hold the state.
> By means of the mother of holding a state, one can last long and endure.
> Make deep the root, make solid the base—this is the way to long life and enduring sight. (JL §3, pp. 48–49)

There are at least two possible ways of understanding this. This passage could be a list of the steps one must go through to attain and retain a grasp on political power, or it could simply be a description of what arises out of a focus on frugality. Under the former interpretation, the person addressed has a goal and is given a strategy to attain this goal. In the latter, there is simply a description of what happens as a natural result of cultivating oneself in a certain way. If one is frugal, then one deeply accumulates virtue. And, once this virtue has been accumulated, the rest falls into place, and one naturally attains and retains power. Furthermore, political power itself may be seen merely as being a means to a further end—that of long life.

If we take *Laozi* 59 on its own, without reference to the *Laozi* as a whole, the first reading is plausible. Indeed, it seems to accord with other chapters of the received *Laozi*, including 36, in which we are told that:

> The supple and yielding overcome the hard and strong. A fish must not be separated from its watery abode. The valuable implements of the state must not be presented to others.[19]

Here, the *Laozi* seems to direct rulers to engage in certain counterintuitive actions, as well as actions of secrecy, implying that such actions better allow them to attain and retain power, and this is not the sole instance of apparent sponsorship of purposive action as methods for gaining advantages over others or attaining one's desires.[20]

However, *Laozi* 16 argues that one should embody the Way. If we are to accord with the *Laozi*, we must grasp that all actions to be taken are to be so taken because they accord with the Way, not simply to attain advantages for oneself.[21] This understanding of the *Laozi* provides an inducement to opt for the second interpretation of *Laozi* 59, taking it to describe what happens when one cultivates

[19] Parts of *Laozi* 36 are analyzed in "Yu Lao" §4.

[20] See, for example, *Laozi* 43 and 61. Creel (1970) takes this line in his discussion of a darker "purposive" Daoism that he sees within the *Laozi*.

[21] For more on this, see the Introduction to Ivanhoe (2003).

oneself in a certain way.[22] The *Laozi* embraces "the idea that the elimination of human 'cleverness' and 'scheming' would itself represent an improvement" to the conditions of any society (Ivanhoe 2003, xxiii). The former reading, one that views *Laozi* 59 as putting forth a method for personal benefit, does not seem to fit in with such a vision.

Having addressed these issues arising from *Laozi* 59 itself, we can now turn to the "Jie Lao" author's commentary on this chapter, which includes the following:

> When one amasses virtue, then one's spirit is calm. When one's spirit is calm, then one's harmoniousness increases. When one's harmoniousness increases, then one's plans are successful. When one's plans are successful, then one can harness the power of the ten thousand things. If one can harness the power of the ten thousand things, then it is easy to prevail over one's opponents in battle. When it is easy to prevail over one's opponents in battle, one's proclamations are sure to dominate one's era. One's proclamations are sure to dominate one's era, and so the text says, "There is nothing that one does not overcome." (JL §3, p. 51)

Here, as in the *Laozi* itself, at least two readings are possible. The reading often taken interprets the "Jie Lao" as counseling the ruler to deeply accumulate virtue and adopt a tranquil state of mind, so as to realize his plans, defeat his enemies, and engulf the world with his principles. Essentially, under this interpretation, the "Jie

[22] This claim depends upon an argument that the *Laozi* should be read as containing a coherent, unified vision. Perhaps this is lacking in the *Laozi*, but in interpreting a text, one should search for such a unified vision. If such a vision cannot be found without warping the text, then we can continue and read it as simply a collection of disparate entries. Not allowing for the possibility of the former, however, seems to preclude the possibility of a greater understanding of a text. Additionally, the *Laozi* has been read throughout Chinese history as having a consistent vision. Indeed, if the various passages that came to be compiled together as the *Laozi* were not viewed as presenting a somewhat consistent vision, then it is unclear how or why they would have been brought together into a single text.

Lao" gives the ruler a process allowing him to more effectively engage in means-end reasoning by first calming the self. This reading works well if we desire to fit the "Jie Lao" chapter in with the rest of the *Han Feizi*. Certainly, one might be tempted to say, the author of chapter 7 ("The Two Handles") and chapter 49 ("The Five Vermin") would have employed such an instrumental attitude in writing the "Jie Lao." Nonetheless, it behooves us to examine an alternative reading.

This alternative reading would have the "Jie Lao" explaining to the ruler, in a fashion similar to our second reading of the *Laozi* itself, that the natural result of a deep accumulation of virtue is the ability to defeat one's enemies and to promulgate one's principles. It would not be that the ruler is provided with a set of tools for realizing power but rather that he is being advised that if he focuses on accumulating virtue (and here we are talking about the highest form of virtue, or true virtue—that internal characteristic described in the commentary to *Laozi* 38) as paramount, and acquires it by following the Way, then his rule will naturally be extended.

This reading of the "Jie Lao" author's intentions in this specific passage brings it in line with both the non-instrumentalist reading of the *Laozi* itself and the "Jie Lao" commentary on *Laozi* 38. There are reasons for being skeptical of such a reading, however. Most prominent is that the "Jie Lao" continues its analysis of *Laozi* 59 by arguing that the ability to defeat enemies allows one to take control of the world and become master of the common people. As no one will be able to see the full extent of his power, the people will consider such a ruler to be all-powerful, the natural result of which is acquiescence. Regardless of whether this is read with instrumentalist overtones or not, it seems to push the *Laozi*'s ideas forcefully into the political arena and provide the ruler with direct advice for how to ensure that these political goals will be obtained, even if they are merely a means to the more fundamental end of a long life.

Further evidence for this concern can be seen by moving up a few lines where the "Jie Lao" notes:

> What it means by "serving Heavenly affairs" is to refrain from pushing the powers of acute hearing and clear vision to the extreme and to refrain from exhausting one's intelligence and discernment. If one pushes them to the extreme and exhausts them, then one's expenditure of spirit will be great. If one's expenditure of spirit is great, then the misfortunes of blindness, deafness, and unruly witlessness will arrive. Therefore, one is to be frugal with these things. Being frugal with these things is to use one's energy and spirit sparingly and to use one's intelligence and discernment frugally. And so the text says, "For ordering human affairs and serving Heavenly affairs, nothing is as good as frugality." (JL §3, p. 50)

Here, the "Jie Lao" argues that the ruler must be careful with his spirit, intelligence, and discernment. Wasting these inevitably leads to a diminution in power, resulting in the ruler having no more authority than a commoner. Frugality is a trait that will lead to political power. However, there remains a question of whether political power is a direct goal or merely an outcome of understanding how frugality connects to the Way. Regardless of how we understand it, though, the "Jie Lao" pushes the *Laozi* in a more overtly political direction. Further, there are reasons to think that this aspect of the commentary sits ill with the received *Laozi*'s abhorrence of violence and conquest, evident in *Laozi* 30, and the Confucian focus on moral character rather than infallible planning.

Moving ahead to the "Jie Lao" author's commentary on *Laozi* 46, we see a distinct warning against allowing desires to encompass one's life. The reconstructed version reads as follows:

> When all under Heaven hold to the Way, then swift horses are relegated to carrying dung.
> When all under Heaven lack the Way, then war horses are born from the suburbs.

> {Of crimes, none is greater than approving desires.}[23]
> Of misfortunes, none is greater than being insatiable.
> Of faults, none is more agonizing than desiring *benefit*.
> [Knowing when to be satisfied is truly satisfying.] (JL §5, pp. 56–57)

This section of the *Laozi* is often read as being substantively anti-war. And a reading of the "Jie Lao" author's take on this passage seems to reinforce such an understanding.[24] It commences its interpretation by arguing that,

> As for a ruler who holds to the Way, outside the state he harbors no resentment or enmity against his neighbors and rivals, and inside the state he shows virtue and generosity toward his subjects. (JL §5, p. 57)

It continues by claiming that:

> If when meeting with the feudal lords he follows the rituals and standards for what is appropriate, then the occasions for military conscriptions will be few. If in ordering the affairs of the people he works at what is fundamental, then licentiousness and extravagance will cease. (JL §5, p. 57)

Here, the "Jie Lao" calls upon the ruler to accord with the Way. He is admonished to act in such a way as to preserve harmony both within the state and without. By preserving such a balance, the ruler will benefit his subjects, not alienate his neighbors, and thus have little difficulty retaining power. Such an interpretation accords both with the abhorrence of war generally found in the *Laozi* as well as with a range of Confucian concerns and advice on how to ensure success.

23 While this line is missing in received versions of the *Laozi*, it is included in both the "Jie Lao" and the "Yu Lao" commentaries on *Laozi* 46.

24 So too does the "Yu Lao" author's commentary on *Laozi* 46, as we shall soon see.

Again, however, the skeptic could claim that the "Jie Lao" has left nothing of the purposeful attitude behind in providing this commentary. After all, it is in the ruler's interests to reduce the resentment and enmity of his neighbors. Indeed, one could think that the only reason that the ruler displays virtue and generosity toward his subjects is because he wishes them to be more productive and cease their extravagances, seeing as both actions would be to his direct benefit. The position on warfare expanded upon in the "Jie Lao" is certainly consistent with a concern that runs throughout the rest of the *Han Feizi*—that war is risky and consumes state resources, endangering not only the strength and stability of the state but the ruler's very life. However, such a reason for caution is very different than the reason that arises, for example, in the received *Laozi* 31, which neither the "Jie Lao" nor "Yu Lao" mention, and which reads, in part:

> Peace and quiet are the highest ideals;
> A military victory is not a thing of beauty.
> To beautify victory is to delight in the slaughter of human beings.
> One who delights in the slaughter of human beings will not realize his ambitions in the world. (Ivanhoe 2003, 31)

Here, the concern is not with the dangers of warfare to the ruler, but rather with human life itself, something toward which the *Han Feizi* overall seems to attach no more than instrumental value. Therefore, the skeptic might continue to argue, the "Jie Lao" is still giving the ruler advice on how best to retain power.

Such a purposive view of the "Jie Lao" may, however, be tempered if we continue to analyze its commentary to *Laozi* 46. Toward the end of its analysis, it argues,

> And so as for the sage, if his clothing is enough to withstand the cold and his food is enough to fill his empty stomach, then he has

> no distress. As for the masses, it is not so. Even if at greatest they were to become feudal lords, or if at least they were to have wealth in excess of a thousand pieces of gold, the distress that comes from their desire to possess things would still not be eliminated. . . . And so the text says, "Of misfortunes, none is greater than being insatiable."
>
> And so, if one greatly desires benefit, then one will be distressed. If one is distressed, then anxiety will arise. When anxiety arises, then one's intelligence and wisdom decline. If one's intelligence and wisdom decline, then one will lose the ability to measure and weigh. If one loses the ability to measure and weigh, then one will select actions recklessly. If one selects actions recklessly, then misfortunes and harms will arrive. . . . And so the text says, "Of faults, none is more agonizing than desiring benefit." (JL §5, pp. 59–60)

Here, it becomes clear that the "Jie Lao" advocates a view that shares core commonalities with both the received *Laozi* and aspects of some Confucian texts. The difference between the sage and the ordinary person, whether noble, or commoner, is that the sage is not insatiable and lacks a desire for profit. As such, the "Jie Lao" can be seen as contending that a desire for profit is in and of itself bad, regardless of one's position. This pronouncement is not directed solely at those who are ruled. Rather, it argues that the sage is defined by his lack of desire for profit, indeed, for his lack of desire for anything more than the bare necessities of life. This, then appears to be the goal—a reduction of desires, and an ability to find satisfaction in simplicity, a trend that crops up frequently in the *Laozi*. And while it may initially seem to conflict with my contention that there is much with which Confucians would agree to be found in this claim, it does adhere to the previously discussed role of ritual. It would run counter to Xunzi's arguments that there is a ritual role for accouterments of a manner far beyond what is necessary for material survival, but it may not run counter to the fundamental understanding of the role of ritual. Indeed, it reminds one quite explicitly of *Analects* 7.16 and *Mencius* 7B35, the latter of which reads:[25]

> Mengzi [Mencius] said, "For cultivating the heart, nothing is better than having few desires. If someone has few desires, although there will be times when he does not persevere, they will be few. If someone has many desires, although there will be times when he perseveres, they will be few." (Van Norden 2008, 193)

It should also be noted that comments against desires are not limited to the commentary on *Laozi* 46. We also see such admonitions emerging in the commentary to *Laozi* 60:

> Therefore, the ruler who holds to the Way values emptiness and calmness and views changing the laws as a weighty matter. And so the text says, "Ordering a large state is like cooking a small fish."
>
> When people experience sickness then they value doctors. When they have misfortunes then they fear ghosts. When a sage is in power, the people reduce their desires. If the people reduce their desires, then their blood and *qi* will be well regulated, and their actions and behavior will be well ordered. If their blood and *qi* are well regulated and their actions and behavior are well ordered, then this will reduce their misfortunes and harms. (JL §4, p. 54)

When sages rule by valuing emptiness and calmness, the desires of the people will be minimized, and they will act according to

[25] Note as well that while Xunzi's discussions of ritual do stress the value of accouterments far beyond what is necessary for survival, and while a sage does enjoy luxurious things, he does not need these things (Hutton 2014, 246–247). Though, of course, Xunzi does not advocate reducing or eliminating desires to attain this state.

the natural patterns. Here again, we see the advocacy of a reduction of desires in a manner quite familiar from many chapters of the received *Laozi*, including several the "Jie Lao" does not discuss.[26]

The preceding is just a sample of the sort of analyses that one could engage in to better understand the philosophical vision evident within the "Jie Lao," to more clearly figure out the role that the *Laozi* itself plays for its author, and to ascertain the relationship between the "Jie Lao" and the rest of the *Han Feizi*, and the reader is encouraged to continue in this vein. A few points seem already to emerge from this analysis. First, the "Jie Lao" interprets the *Laozi* as providing a philosophical vision that stresses the importance of virtue and the cultivation of the ruler's internal, psychological state, points also stressed in many historical and contemporary interpretations of the received *Laozi*. However—and this goes against many interpretations of the received *Laozi*, in part because the "Jie Lao" relies upon a different version of the text—the "Jie Lao" also takes the traditional Confucian virtues of humaneness, appropriateness, and ritual propriety as being central components of virtue, and goals for the ruler to strive toward. Further, while many of the points that the "Jie Lao" draws out are explicitly political in nature, and little time is spent dwelling on metaphysical or epistemological concepts unrelated to the political, the message of the *Laozi* is not taken, as it easily could have been, in a hyper-realist direction. The author of the "Jie Lao" does not see his commentary as a venue for pushing an interpretation of the *Laozi* most amenable to the political theory found throughout the majority of the *Han Feizi*, a point to which we shall return in the final section of this essay. For now, let us turn to the "Yu Lao."

[26] Examples include *Laozi* 1, 12, 19, 20, 34, 53, 64, 80, and 81.

III. Explicating the "Yu Lao"

The format of the "Yu Lao" differs substantially from that of the "Jie Lao." Rather than focusing on philosophical analysis to draw out the meaning of the passages of the *Laozi* upon which it comments, the "Yu Lao" uses a range of historical incidents that were likely well known to its audience to illustrate the meaning of the passages from the *Laozi* that it examines. Further, the historical incidents that serve to illustrate the meaning of the *Laozi* are all political in nature, and thus the "Yu Lao," even more so than the "Jie Lao," is almost purely political in nature. The passages cited from the *Laozi* are used to undergird and promote particular political advice that the author of the "Yu Lao" wishes to justify.

Initially, these differences may lead contemporary readers to assume that the "Jie Lao" and "Yu Lao" must have been written by different individuals. However, a difference in style and method of argumentation should not, in and of itself, lead us to this conclusion. As anyone who has read through the entirety of the *Han Feizi* knows, Han Fei often writes deep philosophical analyses to support his views—much as we have seen the author of the "Jie Lao" do.[27] Just as often, though, Han Fei supports his conclusions not by deeper conceptual analysis but by appeal to historical events, implying that the rulers of old to whom he refers failed precisely because they did not do something that Han Fei believed to be central to achieving political order, much as the author of the "Yu Lao" does.[28]

In his analysis of the "Yu Lao," Sarkissian argues that the dominant emotion of the text is fear, with a focus solely on survival. As he notes, the "Yu Lao" author "cites, without exception, stories of disasters that could have been avoided—as opposed to missed opportunities that could have been seized" (Sarkissian 2001,

[27] See *Han Feizi* chapters 5, 6, 7, 27, 29, 40, 49, and 50.

[28] See *Han Feizi* chapters 22–23, 30–35, and 36–39.

38–39). There is a fundamental insight here, though it may be overstated. Fear of disaster is certainly an important theme in the text, though other stories in the "Yu Lao," including that of Sunshu Ao, seem to emphasize the success of those who seize the right opportunity. The focus and implicit arguments that the illustrative stories of the "Yu Lao" draw out might more profitably be described in slightly different terms. The stories of disaster that could have been avoided point out what happens when a ruler forgets what is essential to the survival of the state. Furthermore, throughout the "Yu Lao," the author notes that rulers who listen to his words may well become hegemons or true kings, results that go substantially beyond mere survival.

The "Yu Lao" does not, then, focus solely on survival, but rather warns not to allow one's desires to lead one to forget what is fundamental to survival. To see this, let us begin with the "Yu Lao" author's commentary on *Laozi* 46, which at least initially seems to go against this claim. The particular part of the commentary of interest to us is that which illustrates the following lines from *Laozi* 46:

> {Of crimes, none is greater than being desirable}
> Of misfortunes, none is greater than being insatiable.
> Of faults, none is more agonizing than desiring gain.
> Knowing when to be satisfied is truly satisfying. (YL §1, p. 83)

These lines are illustrated by a story about Earl Zhi, the head of one of the six ministerial families who governed the state of Jin. Dissatisfied with controlling only a sixth of the state, Earl Zhi attempted to usurp power from the other families. While initially successful, he overextended himself and was betrayed, resulting in his death and the desecration of his corpse, illustrating the *Laozi*'s point that there is no misfortune greater than being insatiable nor fault more agonizing than desiring gain. As the "Yu Lao" continues,

> When a state settles for survival as its constant aim, then becoming a hegemon or true king is feasible, and when a person settles for staying alive as his constant aim, then achieving wealth and nobility is feasible. If one does not harm oneself through desiring, then one's state will not be led to perish, and one's person will not be led to die. And so the text says, "Knowing when to be satisfied is truly satisfying." (YL §1, pp. 85–86)

This explication does focus on survival, but not because the author is only concerned with survival or fears destruction. Rather, it is because nothing else is possible if one does not secure one's foundation. If one forgets one's foundation and directly pursues expansionary goals in an attempt to become a hegemon or gain wealth and power, this foundation will crumble and bring one down alongside it. If, however, one never neglects the foundation, but ensures its strength and stability, then it can serve as a platform for a great structure, allowing one to become a wealthy hegemon or a true king.

Perhaps we can clarify things a bit more by moving to the "Yu Lao" author's illustration of *Laozi* 64, another chapter that focuses on desires. The quoted lines read:

> Desire not to be desirous, and do not value goods that are difficult to obtain.
> Learn not to be learned and return back to what the masses pass over.
> Rely upon how the ten thousand things are so of themselves, and do not dare to take action. (YL §8, pp. 98–99)

The "Yu Lao" seems to read the first two lines as describing the results of following the advice of the third line. As the commentary says,

> Things each have their constant features. Accord with and harness these to guide them. By according and following with the features

of things, then when at calm one will be established in virtue, and when on the move one will conform to the Way. (YL §8, p. 100)

Here we see an advocacy of a type of naturalism that is shared in important ways by the received *Laozi*, the *Han Feizi*, the "Jie Lao," and the "Yu Lao." In figuring out what to do and how to act, we must first come to an understanding of the patterns of the Way. Once we understand the patterns of the Way insofar as they impact the lives of human beings, we have two options: accord with these patterns or try to work against them. If we work against them, pursuing things that we cannot achieve, or the achievement of which will leave us vulnerable and destitute, failure is inevitable. If, however, we follow the "Yu Lao" author's advice and accord with the patterns of the Way, it will be possible not only to survive but to thrive.

This is no easy task, though, and the "Yu Lao" is at pains to point out the various ways that we can fail, while also elucidating how to get back on track. It is in this vein that we can understand its illustration of *Laozi* 47, which it quotes as follows:

By not going out the door, one can know all under Heaven.
By not peering out the window, one can know the Way of Heaven.
The farther out one goes, the less one knows.
[For this reason, the sage] does not venture about and yet is knowledgeable,
Does not look about and yet sees sharply,
Does not take action and yet is accomplished. (YL §9, p. 101)[29]

Of particular interest is the illustration of *Laozi* 47 by means of the story about Master Xiang of Zhao learning the art of charioteering from Wang Yuqi. After losing a chariot race to Wang, Master Xiang accuses Wang of not fully teaching the appropriate techniques. Wang responds that it is not that Master Xiang lacks the appropriate

[29] While there are differences in wording between the text the "Yu Lao" comments on and the received *Laozi* 47, the meaning remains the same.

techniques but rather that he is concentrating on the wrong things. He is not honing in on what is fundamental, but rather is focusing on something outside himself—the desire to beat Wang. Being a good charioteer, Wang argues, requires that one's focus be on the horses themselves. It is necessary that one ensure that "the horses' bodies feel at ease with the chariot and that the person's heart is attuned to the horses" (YL §9, p. 102). Focus on what is fundamental to effective charioteering, Wang says, and the winning will come naturally.[30]

Such an interpretation of the central argument of the "Yu Lao" also allows us to make sense of its author's illustration of *Laozi* 26 by means of a story about Zhufu. *Laozi* 26 as cited in the "Yu Lao" reads:

> To be heavy is to be the root for what is light.
> To be still is to be lord over what is restless.
> To the end of his days, a prince, when on the march, does not abandon his heavy-transport wagon.
> [Only when he has a walled-in lodge in which to rest at ease, then he is unconcerned.]
> [Why ever would a ruler who can field ten thousand war chariots make himself a lightweight in the world?]
> If one becomes light, then one loses the role of root.
> If one becomes restless, then one loses the role of lord. (YL §3, p. 87)[31]

As the story goes, Zhufu was primarily interested in military adventures and did not want to spend his time administering his

[30] Note also similarities with chapter 19 of the *Zhuangzi*, which says, "When you're betting for tiles in an archery contest, you shoot with skill. When you're betting for fancy belt buckles, you worry about your aim. And when you're betting for real gold, you're a nervous wreck. Your skill is the same in all three cases—but because one prize means more to you than another, you let outside considerations weigh on your mind. He who looks too hard at the outside gets clumsy on the inside" (Watson 2013, 148).

[31] [Brackets] indicate lines found in the received version of the *Laozi* but not in the "Yu Lao."

state. Thus, he abdicated the throne, giving the responsibilities of administering the state to his son, and focused on military campaigns. But in doing so, Zhufu gave up his authority and abandoned his position, turning away from what was fundamental, the very things that had earlier allowed him to be successful not only at home but on his prior military adventures. The problem with Zhufu's action was not that he engaged in expansionary military campaigns, but that he did so at the expense of the safety and security of his own state, and he paid the ultimate price.

The "Yu Lao" focuses on a range of passages from the *Laozi* that can be illustrated by historical events and stories, with an emphasis on political survival. The *Laozi* is explicated in such a way that it urges rulers to never forget those things that are essential to the survival of the state in the pursuit of goals tangential to this aim. To do this successfully, it is essential to understand and accord with the patterns of the Way. Understanding the patterns of the Way as they manifest themselves in the political world is what ensures that the ruler is able to safeguard internal stability and prevent external takeovers. It is not that this should be the sole aim of the ruler. A ruler can have other goals, and the "Yu Lao" is not opposed to him becoming wealthy or powerful—becoming a hegemon or true king. Rather, the emphasis is on realizing that these goals are only achievable when the ruler maintains a focus on what is fundamental. If he ignores the minor cracks in the dikes that control flooding within his state, concentrating instead on fulfilling his desires, he is sure to come to an untimely end when the dikes burst. If, however, he never loses sight of what is fundamental, this solid foundation will allow achievements that could never have been otherwise obtained.

Throughout, the message is that it is necessary to understand the Way and to focus on the fundamental in order to survive (and thus, in order to flourish). The "Yu Lao" clearly says that insatiable desires lead away from what is fundamental, and that the ruler, if he is to survive and thrive, must focus on understanding and following "the arrangements of the Way and its proper order," as we see in the "Yu Lao" author's illustration of *Laozi* 64. A wide array of fundamental principles that accord with the arrangements of the Way and its proper order in the political realm are explicated throughout the "Yu Lao." The illustration of *Laozi* 26 emphasizes that "authoritative power" (*shi* 勢), sometimes translated as "positional power," is essential for survival, as does the illustration of *Laozi* 36. The latter also interprets the *Laozi*'s discussion of "the valuable implements of the state" as referring to rewards and punishments, tools which the ruler must ensure that he has complete control over if he is to survive and thrive.

These, then, provide an interpretation of the *Laozi* that resonates quite clearly with what we see elsewhere in the *Han Feizi*, particularly in its emphasis on carefully guarding the ruler's positional power, ensuring personal control over rewards and punishments, and preventing ministers and subordinates from appropriating the ruler's authority. However, again, much like we saw in the "Jie Lao," these stories that are used to illustrate the *Laozi* do not push the *Laozi* in directions that seem implausible. Indeed, had the main goal of the author been to draw from the *Laozi* a hyper-realist message that buttressed the overall political message that runs throughout much of the *Han Feizi*, it would not have been difficult to have pushed the text much further in such a direction.

IV. Relating Back to the Rest of the *Han Feizi*

We could continue to examine how the "Jie Lao" and "Yu Lao" unravel and explicate other parts of the *Laozi*, and much more analysis awaits for both chapters. However, what I have sketched above hopefully provides a basis from which to engage in a bit of speculation on the role of these chapters and a way in which they may fit into the *Han Feizi* as a whole.

I shall not argue that what follows is the only, or best, way to understand the role of the "Jie Lao" and "Yu Lao." Rather, I wish merely to see what might fall out of contemplating why Han Fei might have written such commentaries on the *Laozi*. And, while I shall speak in what follows as if Han Fei himself wrote this commentary, it is perhaps more accurate to say that I am conjecturing as to why someone holding the views expressed in much of the *Han Feizi* might have written such commentaries, so take subsequent references to Han Fei as shorthand for this.

This rumination begins by noting that while neither commentary ever devolves into a purposeful misinterpretation of the *Laozi* along Legalist lines,[32] both do, in different ways, push their interpretation directly into the political realm. Additionally, they focus on those aspects of the passages they are interpreting that relate to the sorts of concerns that Han Fei himself has elsewhere in the text, namely those of a political nature: creating order, strengthening the state, consolidating power, and ensuring that one is victorious. This, then, leads to the question whether the author(s) of the "Jie Lao" and "Yu Lao" have as a goal ascertaining what the *Laozi* "really" means, or whether the goal is simply to figure out how to apply the ideas found in the *Laozi* to political matters. Unfortunately, given the material that we have, little can be said about this, though it may be noteworthy that we do not see Han Fei arguing against other interpretations of the *Laozi*.

[32] For an example of what one would be hard pressed to read as anything but a purposeful misinterpretation of the *Laozi*, see the *Xiang'er Commentary*'s explanation of the opening line of *Laozi* 21. As Bokenkamp (1997, 113) translates the line and the subsequent commentary: "The all-encompassing nature of Confucius's virtue came precisely from his following the Dao." The commentary itself then reads: "The Dao is greater than all else. It taught Confucius all that he knew. Those of later generations have not kept faith with the writings of the Dao, but merely revere Confucius's writings, considering them the highest. This is why the Dao clarifies the situation to inform later worries." Here, the *Xiang'er Commentary* reads the character 孔 *kong* as referring to Kongzi (孔子, Confucius), an individual who never appears in the *Laozi*, rather than as meaning "great" or "broad." For a comparison, the traditional understanding of this line can be seen in Ivanhoe (2003, 21): "The outward appearance of great Virtue comes forth from the Way alone."

However, there is another question that might prove more fruitful: whether the goal of the author(s) is merely explaining the text of the *Laozi* or whether it includes displaying a critical distance from the text, and here the difference is both quite clear and quite illuminating. In particular, it may be useful to compare the discussion of the *Laozi* in the "Jie Lao" and "Yu Lao" chapters with the *Han Feizi*'s discussion of Shen Buhai (申不害) and Gongsun Yang (公孫鞅, also known as Shang Yang 商鞅 or Lord Shang) in chapter 43 ("Establishing Methods of Government"). This chapter is an extended discussion of the administrative techniques (*shu* 術) advocated by Shen Buhai[33] versus the laws (*fa* 法) advocated by Gongsun Yang.[34]

> Someone asked, "As for the words of Shen Buhai and Gongsun Yang, between the two, which is more critical for the state?"
>
> In response, I say, "They cannot be measured [against one another]. If someone does not eat, they will die within ten days. But, in the depths of winter, without clothing, one will also die. If one asks whether clothing or food is more critical for people, isn't it that one cannot lack either? They are both tools for nourishing life. Now, Shen Buhai discussed administrative techniques while Gongsun Yang implemented laws. Administrative techniques dictate awarding offices on the basis of qualifications, following proposals in evaluating results, grasping the handles of life and death, and examining the abilities of the assembled ministers. This is what the ruler controls. [Employing] laws means that statutes and decrees are promulgated through the governmental offices and bureaus, punishments and fines are felt as inevitable in the hearts of the people, rewards accrue to those who are scrupulous with respect to the laws, and punishments are conferred

[33] For a translation of the remaining fragments attributed to Shen Buhai, see Creel (1974).

[34] See Pines (2017) for a translation of the work attributed to Gongsun Yang.

> upon those who violate decrees. These are what provide models for the ministers. If rulers lack administrative techniques, they will be blinded above, while if the ministers lack laws, they will be chaotic below. There cannot be a lack of either one—they are the tools of emperors and kings." (Harris 2023, 353–354)

On this account, Shen Buhai and Gongsun Yang focused on the two most fundamental tools for governing, and any state that lacked either one was doomed to failure. However, argues Han Fei, in focusing on one tool to the exclusion of the other, Shen Buhai and Gongsun Yang were each blinded in their pursuit of political order. Indeed, Han Fei's criticism of these thinkers runs even deeper. It was not just that they were blinded by their pursuit of a single tool. Rather, they are criticized for lacking a full understanding of how to correctly employ the tool that they did focus on, as Han Fei's discussion of Gongsun Yang makes clear:

> The laws of Gongsun Yang said, "Someone who chops off one head in battle shall be raised one level in rank, and if this person desires to take office, it will be to a position with a salary of 50 bushels of grain. One who chops off two heads in battle shall be raised two levels in rank, and if this person desires to take office, it will be to a position with a salary of 100 bushels of grain." Position and rank [in this system] corresponded to achievements in beheading. Now, if there were a law that said: "Those who chop off heads are ordered to become doctors and carpenters," houses would not be constructed, and illnesses would not be cured. A carpenter requires skilled hands while a doctor requires a comprehensive understanding of medicine, and if one takes success at beheading as the standard for handing out these positions, positions will not correspond with abilities. Now, managing governmental offices depends upon knowledge and ability. Beheading people depends upon bravery and strength. Employing the brave and the strong to manage governmental

> offices that require knowledge and ability is the same as making success at beheading the criterion for becoming doctors or carpenters. (Harris 2023, 356)

Laws are important, essential, even, to the order of the state, and Gongsun Yang is praised for understanding this. However, order does not arise simply by establishing a set of laws and faithfully implementing them. Rather, it is essential to have the right laws—those that actually lead to order within the state.[35] Laws that give administrative positions to those on the basis of skills that are completely unrelated to administering the state will result in disaster.

So, in his discussion of other figures, even those from whom he wishes to draw in developing his political philosophy, Han Fei maintains a clear critical distance. However, the "Jie Lao" and "Yu Lao" and, indeed, the *Han Feizi* as a whole do not evince a similar explicitly critical eye toward the *Laozi* and its ideas. Indeed, there are only two places in the *Han Feizi* that may be read as making even oblique attacks on the *Laozi*. In chapter 49, we see,

> Moreover, those whom this age describes as worthy are those whose actions are pure and trustworthy. Those whom this age describes as wise are those whose words are abstruse (*wei* 微) and mysterious (*miao* 妙). Abstruse and mysterious words are difficult for even the wisest to understand. Now, if one makes laws for the sake of the masses by using words that even the wisest find difficult to understand, the people will have no way to understand and follow them. So, someone who cannot even get enough dregs and husks to fill their stomach should not pursue the finest of millet and meat. Someone who has only a threadbare short coat of rough cloth should not wait for fine embroidered silk. The work of governing this age is the same: if you cannot deal with what is urgent, do not focus on what is unimportant. The task of

[35] For more on Han Fei's understanding of the law, see Harris (2011).

> government is to put the affairs of the people in order. If you do not employ methods that any man or woman can clearly understand, but rather admire the discussions of the wisest of people, this is at odds with good order. Thus, abstruse and mysterious proposals are not the business of the people. (Harris 2023, 365)

And in chapter 51, Han Fei writes,

> Those whom this age regards as illustrious distance themselves from the masses, act on their own, and have different aims from others. They follow the teachings of tranquility (*tian* 恬) and quietude (*dan* 淡), and set out indistinct (*huang* 恍) and confused (*hu* 惚) proposals. I take tranquility and quietude to be teachings that are unusable and the indistinct and confused to be proposals that provide no model. As for proposals that arise from what lacks standards and teachings that arise from what is useless, the world describes these as brilliant. I take it to be the case that while alive, people should serve their ruler and care for their parents. Those who serve their ruler and serve their parents cannot focus on tranquility and quietude. Those who govern the people must focus on discussions of loyalty, trustworthiness, technique, and law. Discussions of loyalty, trustworthiness, technique, and law cannot focus on the indistinct and confused. Indistinct and confused proposals and teachings of tranquility and quietude are the most misleading techniques in the world. (Chen 1969, 820–821)

In these passages, there is an attack on things that are "abstruse" (*wei* 微), "mysterious" (*miao* 妙), "indistinct" (*huang* 恍), and "confused" (*hu* 惚) as well as on "tranquility" (*tian* 恬) and "quietude" (*dan* 淡), all of which have positive connotations in the received *Laozi*, as we can see by looking at the received *Laozi* 14 and 15:[36]

[36] Note as well the use of "mysterious" (*miao* 妙) in *Laozi* 1.

Laozi 14

Looked for but not seen, its name is "minute."
Listened for but not heard, its name is "rarified."
Grabbed for but not gotten, its name is "abstruse" (*wei* 微).
These three cannot be perfectly explained, and so are confused and regarded as one.
Its top is not clear or bright,
Its bottom is not obscure or dark.
Trailing off without end, it cannot be named.
It returns to its home, back before there were things.
This is called the formless form, the image of no thing.
This is called the "confused" (*hu* 惚) and "indistinct" (*huang* 恍).
Greet it and you will not see its head;
Follow it and you will not see its tail.
Hold fast to the Way of old, in order to control what is here today.
The ability to know the ancient beginnings, this is called the thread of the Way. (Ivanhoe 2003, 14, modified)

Laozi 15

In ancient times, the best and most accomplished scholars;
Were abstruse (*wei* 微), mysterious (*miao* 妙), enigmatic, and far-reaching.
Their profundity was beyond understanding.
Because they were beyond understanding, only with difficulty can we try to describe them:
Poised, like one who must ford a stream in winter.
Cautious, like one who fears his neighbors on every side.
Reserved, like a visitor.
Opening up, like ice about to break.
Honest, like unhewn wood.
Broad, like a valley.
Turbid, like muddy water.

> Who can, through stillness, gradually make muddied water clear?
> Who can, through movement, gradually stir to life what has long been still?
> Those who preserve this Way do not desire fullness.
> And, because they are not full, they have no need for renewal.
> (Ivanhoe 2003, 15, modified)

Regardless of whether Han Fei had these passages from the *Laozi* in mind, or indeed, whether he was thinking of the *Laozi* at all when writing Chapters 49 and 51, he seems clearly to attack views very similar to the ones advocated in *Laozi* 14 and 15, at least insofar as they are applied as advice for how to rule.[37] That is to say, the discussion in chapter 51 against indistinct and confused proposals and in chapter 49 against abstruse and mysterious ones clearly shows an antipathy against using the ideas of those whom the *Laozi* regards as the "best and most accomplished scholars" of ancient times in the political realm. Enacting such proposals in law would be counter-productive precisely because they are difficult for the average person to understand.

But note that the discussion of these concepts in *Laozi* 14 and 15 is not a discussion of how to employ these ideas in the political arena. Neither chapter needs to be read as providing advice either on how to govern or about what sorts of rules, regulations, techniques, or laws to implement. To the extent that Han Fei does criticize ideas from the *Laozi*, he may be doing so only insofar as its ideas are applied in arenas where he thinks they are not applicable.

Further, even if we take these criticisms seriously, the text leaves open the possibility that these ideas from the *Laozi* may well be useful for the ruler *himself* to employ. After all, the *Han Feizi* advises the ruler to be but a shadowy figure, who is incomprehensible to his ministers,

[37] While the "Jie Lao" quotes a line from *Laozi* 14, it does not quote or discuss those lines speaking of the "abstruse," "confused," or "indistinct."

and to use such an air of mystery to prevent his ministers from taking advantage of him.[38] And, as noted above, unlike virtually every other thinker Han Fei discusses, from Confucians to Mohists to Gongsun Yang and Shen Buhai, we see no direct attack on the *Laozi*.

Returning to the commentaries themselves, then, it is very tempting to read them as an attempt on the part of Han Fei to examine the implications of the ideas of the *Laozi* on the task of political philosophy. While perhaps anachronistic, we might see this as an act of intellectual honesty—attempting to understand what is going on in a particular text—though, of course, with an eye on the sort of implications that are most relevant to Han Fei's own interests. On such an interpretation, Han Fei does not back away from or try to hide the fact that the *Laozi* advocates a range of activities on the part of the ruler that Han Fei himself does not believe will work. Indeed, it may even be that this analysis of the *Laozi* underlies certain of the positive arguments that Han Fei makes.

Take for example the "Jie Lao" author's commentary on *Laozi* 46 and the "Yu Lao" author's commentary on *Laozi* 46 and 64, which note that ruling the state effectively requires that one understand sufficiency and not continue striving for more and more. This is an aspect of ruling that Han Fei has much sympathy for. He counsels the ruler against acting based upon his likes and dislikes and notes numerous times the hazards that arise when rulers allow others to know their preferences and thus give such people the power to manipulate the ruler. It would certainly make sense for Han Fei to promote a scenario in which the ruler is not swayed by these excessive and extraneous desires.

Or take the discussion of *Laozi* 38 with which we began. If the ruler were to achieve the sort of virtue advocated therein, or if the ruler were able to instantiate in his people the virtues of humaneness, appropriateness, and ritual advocated therein, and thus achieve the political benefits that such achievements and instantiations would allow for,

[38] For more on this point, see Ivanhoe (2011), Galvany (2013), and Pines (2013).

then Han Fei would, I believe, find such a path quite attractive. After all, as we saw in the beginning of this chapter, Han Fei's political vision is in important ways predicated on the Way, on according with both the broader cosmic Way and the narrower Ways regulating what sort of activities will be successful in the social and political realms and the Way regulating human activity. The worry Han Fei would have with the broader vision laid out in the received *Laozi* is not necessarily that its goals are problematic, but rather that they are simply unachievable. And this arises because of how Han Fei's conceptions of human nature and the Way differ from those of the *Laozi*.

In brief, he argues that individuals are born with relatively stable interest sets that do not change in any appreciable manner throughout their lives. As such, they are not amenable to cultivation, moral or otherwise.[39] There may be instances in which it appears that one's interest set has changed. However, in reality, what has happened is that the individual has re-evaluated what actions will best allow her to achieve her interests. In addition, for the vast majority of individuals, these interest sets are mostly self-regarding, with people generally acting in ways that they perceive to be in their own best interest. Han Fei does not deny that we have other-regarding feelings and that these give rise to actions, but he is quite suspicious of the strength of these feelings in relation to our self-regarding ones.[40]

So, Han Fei believes that it is fruitless to attempt to change the primarily self-interested dispositions that he thinks most human beings were born with. The *Laozi*, on the other hand, seems to see the original dispositions of human beings in a much more benign

[39] See Flanagan and Hu (2011), Bárcenas (2012), Harris (2013), and Sato (2013).

[40] Han Fei does discuss a range of individuals whose natures were extremely humane as well as those whose natures were extremely violent, but he makes two points about them. First, they are very rare, and second, their natures are still fairly stable. The extremely humane did not become that way through a process of cultivation; they were always that way. Thus, it makes no sense to try to cultivate others so that they have a comparable level of humaneness.

light, implying that our current dispositions reflect a warping of our original dispositions, and that the solution is to return to how we naturally were. For the *Laozi*, this means returning to a point in which our desires are much more limited in scope. Both Han Fei and the *Laozi* then agree on one fundamental point, a point brought out in both the "Jie Lao" and the "Yu Lao": in order to be successful, it is necessary to accord with the patterns of the world including, importantly, the natural dispositions of human beings. Where they disagree is on what the patterns of the Way actually tell us, and particularly, what they convey about human beings. So, while Han Fei might agree with the *Laozi* on the desirability of restricting desires, he would likely not see this as a viable solution to the problem of excess desires, given how the Way actually manifests itself in the world.

And this is a second point of divergence—the Way itself. Throughout the received *Laozi*, discussions of the Way go far beyond the practical and political, and the text is concerned with gaining a deeper insight into a range of metaphysical and epistemological questions of the sort that Han Fei is supremely unconcerned with. Indeed, an analogy of the difference between a scientist and an engineer may be useful in comparing the two texts. Physicists wish to come to a deeper, and, ideally, a comprehensive understanding of how the universe works. Engineers, on the other hand, care about how the universe works insofar as that is relevant to their particular task. So, while the physicist may be excited by the potential for the James Webb Space Telescope to expand our understanding of the universe, the engineer would say that such an understanding is irrelevant to her task of building a dam across the Three Gorges. It is not that physics is irrelevant to engineering; parts of it are supremely relevant, but its scope is much broader than that of engineering. In the same way, the scope of the *Laozi* in its pursuit of understanding of the Way is much more comprehensive than what we see in the *Han Feizi*. As we saw in the beginning of this chapter, insofar as Han Fei is interested in the Way, he is interested in understanding those aspects of the Way that are directly relevant to the political task of ordering the state and ensuring that this order leads to strength, stability, and flourishing. He is not saying that this is all there is to the Way, merely that this is all that is relevant to his task of social and political engineering.

Given this, I wonder whether it may be profitable to read the "Jie Lao" and "Yu Lao" chapters as, in part at least, laying out what Han Fei genuinely believes to be the most plausible account of a *Laozian* political philosophy. We might even think that part of what underlies his doing so as a commentary as opposed to simply taking those aspects he thinks fit in well with his own view and attacking the rest is because he finds himself quite attracted to many of the values found in the *Laozi*—according with the Way, modeling the social and the political on the natural, among others. As such, he may want to ensure that he understands the views of the text as fully as possible, utilizing the commentary format in order to elucidate more fully its views and develop his own understanding of them.

And, even if one does not buy into this sort of psychologizing of Han Fei and thinks that I am attributing to him motivations that we have absolutely no evidence to think that he ever had, it may still be profitable to use the understanding of the political aspects of the *Laozi* as they appear in the "Jie Lao" and "Yu Lao" in an attempt to more fully understand why Han Fei makes the various arguments, both positive and negative, in support of his political vision elsewhere in the *Han Feizi*.

These two commentaries on the *Laozi*, then, appear to be earnest attempts to elucidate the meaning of those chapters (or parts thereof) upon which they comment. And, while they do so primarily by explicating the political implications of the *Laozi*, neither chapter pushes their interpretation of the text as far as they could had the goal been to use the *Laozi* to defend the more substantial amoral political realism that appears throughout much of the *Han Feizi*. Thus, we end up, particularly in the "Jie Lao," with a political vision that is not a fully comfortable fit with the rest of the *Han Feizi*, primarily because Han Fei cannot quite accept either the *Laozi*'s view of the possibility of thoroughgoing change in human nature or its conception of a Way that allows for non-coercive methods of changing the actions of the populace.

4

The Interiority of Virtue and Its Logical Entailments

The "Jie Lao" in Comparison with Other Early *Laozi* Commentaries

Alan K. L. Chan

Whether or not the "Jie Lao" came from the hands of Han Feizi, it aimed to explain the *Laozi* material that was at its disposal. It might have selected the passages it discussed from a larger corpus, or it had access to only the passages it analyzed. This chapter is only concerned with what it took them to mean and how it went about interpreting them. Comparisons with Wang Bi's (226–249 CE) *Laozi* commentary and the commentaries attributed to Yan Zun 嚴遵 and Heshang Gong 河上公, both traditionally traced to the Han period, should provide a thicker context for engaging the "Jie Lao" (abbreviated as JL hereafter).[1]

JL references the *Laozi* as a written work, introducing several quotations with the remark, "What the book [or document] calls

[1] The editions of these commentaries cited here are: for Wang Bi, Lou (1980); for Yan Zun, Wang (2004); and for Heshang Gong, Zheng (1971). References to these commentaries will be cited by the corresponding chapter number of the *Laozi*. All translations of them given here are my own, but those who wish to read a complete translation of Wang Bi's commentary may consult Lynn (1999). Quotations from JL are taken from the "Translations" of the present book and will be indicated by their section number and page numbers in this volume. In some instances, I will provide a literal rendering, so as to heighten the differences in interpretation on certain passages. These will be indicated separately.

Alan K. L. Chan, *The Interiority of Virtue and Its Logical Entailments* In: *Explaining and Illustrating the* Laozi. Edited by: Eirik Lang Harris and Eric L. Hutton, Oxford University Press. © Oxford University Press 2026. DOI: 10.1093/9780197514948.003.0006 [and means by]" (書之所謂).[2] On that basis, it can be assumed that it has a certain interpretive aim and strategy. Understanding the *Laozi* requires careful delineation, cutting it up, and untying the hermeneutic knots that may give rise to erroneous interpretation. This is what "explaining" (*jie* 解) entails, extending the root meaning of the verb *jie*, which suggests graphically separating the horns of an ox with a knife, and that is what JL sets out to do.[3]

There is a clear logic to the *Laozi*, reflecting a deep understanding of the human condition. This underlies JL's interpretation of the *Laozi*. As this is not immediately apparent, it thus requires exposition, which defines the task of the interpreter. Specifically, there is pronounced emphasis on the need to bring order to the human heart-mind (*xin* 心), which can easily be confused and consumed by desire. To realize the kind of fulfillment envisaged in the *Laozi*, it is vital that the heart-mind attains calmness and clarity, which enables it to discern the proper order of things and affairs and set the right direction. This in essence captures the perceived meaning of "virtue" (*de* 德), the embodiment of the Dao. Moreover, the insight derived from the *Laozi* forms the basis of certain practices of leadership and governance, which the wise ruler would do well to take to heart.

The first section of JL covers a great deal of interpretive ground and will be examined in detail. Next, Sections 2–4 will be presented in turn. This will afford a better understanding of how JL approaches the *Laozi* and will facilitate comparison with other early *Laozi* commentaries. There is a logical flow to JL's argument that merits attention, notwithstanding occasional overlaps between the sections.

[2] JL §3, pp. 50 and 53, and §11, p. 74.

[3] See Y. K. Lo's chapter on this form of commentarial writing. The "Yu Lao" chapter serves a different interpretive aim and should be treated separately. Comparisons will be offered when its reading bears on the interpretation of JL. Lo also discusses the genre of "illustrative stories" in his chapter.

I. The Interiority of Virtue

JL begins with an extensive commentary on what corresponds to chapter 38 of the current 81-chapter version of the *Laozi* that accompanies the Wang Bi and Heshang Gong commentaries. Perhaps the *Laozi* material it was trying to decipher began with it, which is the sequence we find in the *Laozi* commentary ascribed to Yan Zun and the Mawangdui *Laozi* silk manuscripts.[4] However, what is of concern remains the substantive interpretation that JL offers, which should also give a good sense of its overall approach to the *Laozi*.

Laozi 38 opens with what appears to be a paradox: "High virtue (*shang de* 上德) (is) not virtuous (*bu de* 不德); thereby (*shi yi* 是以), (it) has virtue (*you de* 有德)." This is a "bare bone" interpretation, and the challenge is to understand how commentators flesh out its perceived meaning.

The meaning of *de*, "virtue," is rich, as noted in the Introduction and translation in this volume, encompassing senses of moral excellence, potency, and life-force (JL §1, p. 36, n. 2). In explaining *Laozi* 38, it seems reasonable to focus on the meaning of *de*/virtue. Alternatively, one may assume that the meaning of *de* is well understood and direct attention to the noun phrase "high virtue" (*shang de*) instead. This latter is the approach taken in the Heshang Gong commentary (abbrev. HSG).

What does *shang de* signify? To HSG, it is not a general reference to superior virtue but refers specifically to the lords of distant antiquity who were without titles or fame. Their virtue was peerless nonetheless, and this is the reason why the *Laozi* speaks of *shang de*, which should be understood in this context as virtue that cannot be surpassed, that is, not merely superior but in fact, virtue of the highest order (上德, 謂太古無名號之君, 德大無上, 故言上德也).

[4] See Henricks (1989).

Identifying the subject of *shang de* and the meaning of *shang* itself requires interpretive judgment. Precisely because *shang de* could be understood generally in the sense of superior virtue, which to HSG would be missing the point of the *Laozi*, commentarial intervention is needed. Still, if *shang de* means the "highest virtue" that is embodied and exemplified by the ideal ruler, why is it said to be "not virtuous"? It is not posing a paradox, as HSG explains, but indicates that these sage rulers did not teach the people with doctrines of moral excellence, the assumed meaning of *de* here; rather, they followed the course of what is "naturally so" and devoted themselves to providing for the people. As such, "their virtue is not visible, and this is why it is said to be 'not virtuous'" (不德者,言其不以德教民,因循自然,養人性命,其德不見,故言不德也). Thus framed, *Laozi* 38 is not so much about the meaning or nature of virtue, as the way in which the sage governs and brings benefits to the people, which is also to say, how the present-day ruler ought to govern.

To Yan Zun, too, *shang de* is not an abstract concept, but refers to "the lords with the highest virtue" (上德之君). However, to an interpreter, is it enough to simply mark the reference and draw out the implications for governance? Would the intended audience not want to understand what makes someone come to possess the highest or most superior virtue?

This is the approach that Yan Zun took. What needs to be explained further is that human beings are endowed with a measure of vital *qi* 氣, which defines their sphere of accomplishment and its limits.[5] The noun phrase *shang de* thus essentially refers to the rulers whose inborn nature is blessed with the finest *qi* that issues from the Dao, which accounts for their incomparable virtue (上德之君,性受道之纖妙). Without going into Yan Zun's detailed argument, the point is that with their exceptional endowment, these ideal leaders are able to realize munificent

[5] On the concept of *qi*, see JL §3, p. 51, n. 39.

transformations and bring peace and prosperity to the people, without the latter knowing that their good fortune is due to the unsung virtue of their lords. In this respect, Yan Zun and HSG converge in explaining the sense in which the ruler with the highest virtue is "not virtuous."

JL also takes *shang de* to refer to a subject who embodies the highest virtue. This is indicated by the use of the possessive pronoun *qi* 其 ("one's") in its explanation. However, the focus of *Laozi* 38 is not about any extraordinary ruler of the remote past, but the concept of virtue and how it may be embodied in a person. To JL, these are the hermeneutic knots that need to be untied in explaining the *Laozi*.

Virtue (*de* 德) is internal; possessing something (*de* 得) is external (德者,内也.得者,外也), according to JL. The close semantic link between *de*/virtue and *de*/obtaining something or having something in one's possession (see JL §1, p. 36, n. 3) seems to have been assumed; otherwise, this would have been a rather abrupt way to begin an exposition on *de*/virtue.

Possession or ownership generally connotes beneficial outcomes and is to be welcomed. This is an important point. There are counterexamples, to be sure—for example, *de zui* 得罪, acquiring culpability due to having offended someone or committing an offense, is clearly to be avoided. *De*/possession as such is also to be distinguished from acquisitiveness or rapacity, which one must guard against, especially in one's old age, as the *Analects* famously warns (16.7). The potential for abuse is evident and informs JL's discussion here; nevertheless, possession is typically understood to be a positive value. Rulers possess wealth in all its forms, and benevolent rulers share what they possess with the people. In a sense, rulers come to lord over their subjects by virtue of what they own. According to Wang Bi (abbrev. WB), *de*/virtue means precisely *de*/possession, in the sense that it presupposes full ownership, a perpetual state of abundance that yields benefits and produces no harm. Because of the value that *de*/possession dispenses, the *Laozi* therefore calls it *de*/virtue (德者得也.常得而無喪,利而無害,故以德為名焉) (commentary to *Laozi* 38).

More succinctly, as Wang Bi puts it elsewhere, "Virtue is what things come to possess (from Dao) (德者物之所得也)" (commentary to *Laozi* 51), which is a good thing. There is more to WB's interpretation, as we will see shortly, but the point is that although JL recognizes the close link between *de*/virtue and *de*/possession, it introduces a further distinction, that between what is "internal" and "external," for it sees a deeper meaning in *Laozi* 38.

What, then, does virtue mean? If *de*/virtue is internal and possessing something is external, presumably in the sense that it involves interaction with people and things, what does it mean to say that the highest virtue is not virtuous?

The deeper point the *Laozi* is making here, according to JL, is that the "spirit" (*shen* 神) of the person who possesses the highest virtue does not leach out and become steeped in external strivings (言其神不淫於外也), which is to say that it is not "drawn out" (JL §1, p. 36) or perhaps "enticed," in the older sense of the word as being excited, stirred, set on fire, as it were, by external stimuli. Not being drawn out or enticed means that the "self" (*shen* 身), which encompasses both spirit and body, will be "kept whole" (*quan* 全). This, then, is how *de*/virtue should be properly understood, as being in full possession of one's own self (德者,得身也).

If that is the case, how does one come to be in possession of virtue, that is, able to keep body and spirit in perfect condition? In a kind of sequential reasoning and rhetorical display common in early Chinese philosophical texts, as is evident from the translation in this volume, JL argues that virtue in the sense defined here is the result of "non-action" (*wuwei* 無為) and "non-desiring" (*wuyu* 無欲) (JL §1, p. 37). Both these concepts require explanation.

Thinking and applying oneself under the influence of desire will only lead to a depleted self, consumed by the unquenchable thirst for external *de*/possessions. More will be said on the concept of desire later, but in this light, in asserting that "*shang de* is not virtuous," the *Laozi* is not saying that such virtue is not visible but rather that "one with highest virtue does not possess virtue." Whereas the former, "highest virtue," is a kind of internal fullness, the latter, "possessing virtue" as a result of willful exertion, reflects external transactions that can only be harmful to the self. Though not fully spelled out at this juncture, the implication is that such transactions will inevitably tax the vital *qi* and disturb the heart-mind. "Thus, if one takes virtue as a possession, then one lacks virtue." Conversely, for good measure, JL adds, "if one does not take virtue as a possession, then one has virtue." "And so the text [the *Laozi*] says, 'One with highest virtue does not possess virtue, and thereby has virtue'" (JL §1, p. 37).

If the distinction between what is internal and external is not made clear, the meaning of virtue will remain elusive. The relationship between the two will still need to be worked out, but this is a decisive first step in explaining *Laozi* 38.

For WB, to provide a fuller comparison, the key question is how one comes to "possess virtue" (*de de* 得德) and realizes it fully (*jin de* 盡德). Virtue ultimately stems from Dao and can be realized only through non-action. On this argument, "emptiness" (*xu* 虛) is essential to embodying non-action and the Way, which finds expression in virtue.

Emptiness in WB signals the absence of self-interest or partiality (*si* 私), which is detrimental to the well-being of both self and others. From this perspective, those with superior virtue naturally will not apply themselves to deliberately bring about beneficial outcomes for themselves or society, as intentionality harbors self-regard. This is attested by the beneficent ways in which "Heaven and earth," as well as the sage rulers, provide for all, without any conscious striving to achieve the kind of perpetual abundance that defines a state of virtue. Without intending to benefit others, they nonetheless bring about harmony and prosperity. As WB concludes, "Therefore, though they (truly) have virtue, they do not have the name of being virtuous" (故雖有德而無德名也) (commentary to *Laozi* 38).

There are only so many ways one can explain the sense in which a person with extraordinary virtue can be said to be "not virtuous." WB and HSG agree that this is because genuine virtue is never deliberate or artificial and as such leaves no trace for recognition and thus fame, despite their very different interpretation of *Laozi* 38.

Alternatively, one might suppose, as the *Shuoyuan* 說苑 (*Garden of Persuasions*, compiled 17 BCE) does, "Those who dispense virtue value not being repaid, whereas those who receive kindness or largesse cherish the opportunity to return the favor" (施德者貴不德，受恩者尚必報).[6] "Not being repaid" translates the phrase "*bu de* 不德," which in this interpretation is not to be understood literally as being "not virtuous," but in the sense of not obtaining anything in return.

With a different interpretive focus, and the analysis here is particularly concerned with highlighting the different options available to an interpreter, JL seeks to illuminate the distinction between the fullness of the spirit within and the spirit-sapping effect of seeking possessions in the external environment. This alleviates the need to pin the sense of "not virtuous" to a sage ruler who does not have the reputation of being virtuous or does not seek anything in return for his beneficence, both of which, to JL, fail to appreciate the deeper philosophical meaning of *Laozi* 38. Once "not being virtuous" is understood in the sense of not possessing virtue acquired through deliberate effort, the apparent paradox is resolved.

However, on this reading, the meaning of non-action and how that connects with a state of being empty of desire become crucial to understanding the *Laozi*. Put differently, given the premise,

[6] Liu Xiang 劉向, *Shuoyuan*, ch. 6, "Fu'en pian" (復恩篇), in Lu and Chen (1988, 158). Cf. Henry (2021, 283), which takes *bu de* here in the sense of "doing so unostentatiously." On this work, see Loewe (1993, 443).

certain entailments follow that would determine the course of JL's interpretation.

II. The Meaning of Emptiness

The extant versions of *Laozi* 38 go on to contrast "highest virtue" with "inferior virtue" (*xia de* 下德). This is not cited in JL. While opinions abound as to whether this additional line formed a part of the *Laozi* that JL had worked from, they do not affect the discussion at hand. The next line that JL does cite reads, "One with highest virtue takes no action, but leaves nothing undone" (上德無為而無不為也).[7] The sustained focus on "highest virtue" allows the interpreter to draw out more fully the perceived meaning of the *Laozi*.

No interpreter of the *Laozi* can afford not to come to terms with the concepts of emptiness and non-action. These concepts, however, are hermeneutically porous, open to diverse interpretation. In JL, they are viewed primarily as a function of the heart-mind.

Xu/emptiness "achieved through non-action and no-thought" is to be valued, JL asserts (JL §1, p. 37). This marks out emptiness as the goal of non-action and "no-thought" (*wusi* 無思). The reason why emptiness thus achieved is to be valued is that it entails a pristine state of the heart-mind, in which its movement or intentionality is not bound, controlled, or prescribed (*zhi* 制) by any preconceived ideas, prejudices, or other thoughts and feelings it may harbor (所以貴無為無思為虛者, 謂其意無所制也).

[7] The textual quotation here agrees with that of Yan Zun, except for the absence of the final particle *ye* 也 in the latter. However, it differs from the *Laozi* text we find in WB and HSG. In place of "leaving nothing undone" (*wu bu wei* 無不為), the latter both read, "does not have any basis or purpose for so doing" (*wu yi wei* 無以為), which according to HSG means that the sage ruler does not practice non-action to make a name for himself or gain fame (言無以名號為也), and for WB, without partiality or self-interest (無所偏為也). It has been suggested that "leaving nothing undone" in JL is itself a scribal error—e.g., Liu (2006, 395). Leaving the textual issues aside, to JL this statement is important because it signals the centrality of non-action and being "empty" (*xu* 虛) in realizing virtue.

Few in early China would question that the heart-mind is the "master" of the physical body, which is to say it powers all physiological and mental functions. As the seat of both cognition and affects, animated by vital *qi*, the heart-mind is constantly stirring, moving in certain directions, forming thoughts, feelings and emotions, and other expressions. Its movement or intentionality (*yi* 意) is typically driven by self-regarding interests, preconceptions, and external influences. Drawn hither and thither, succumbing to the pull of desire, the heart-mind easily becomes confused, lost, resulting in an enervated self and spirit. The antidote to this sorry state of affairs, then, lies in cultivating an "empty" heart-mind. Yet, what does "emptiness" of the heart-mind mean?

According to the *Xunzi*,

> How do people know the Way? I say: with the heart. How does the heart know the Way? I say: it is through emptiness, single-mindedness, and stillness. The heart is always holding something. Yet, there is what is called being "empty". . . . The heart is always moving. Yet, there is what is called being "still."[8]

JL appears to be thinking along similar lines, taking the idea of emptiness not in the sense of a heart-mind that is devoid of movement or content, but rather a kind of perfect clarity or clear-mindedness, absent any interference from whatever that is held, even deep in the subconscious heart-mind, or disturbance brought about by external stimuli, that is, "no-thought," which enables the heart-mind to become perspicacious, see things as they are, and make sound judgments.

If emptiness so defined is attained, "then one's virtue flourishes." The full flourishing of virtue, as JL concludes, is precisely what the *Laozi* means by "highest virtue" (虛則德盛, 德盛之謂上德) (JL §1, p. 38).

[8] Hutton (2014, 228).

However, there are those who would then suppose that they must strive to effect non-action and no-thought through certain techniques in order to achieve emptiness of the heart-mind. They are but on a fool's errand, as JL is blunt in calling them out. They are exactly those "who lack the right technique" (*wu shu zhe* 無術者), that is, who lack understanding of the heart-mind and the human condition and are thus doing things in totally the wrong way, for in deliberately trying to still the heart-mind, they fill it with the desire to possess emptiness, constraining it with the very thought of attaining an unconfined heart-mind, which can only lead to undesirable outcomes.

In sum, for JL, *Laozi* 38 is important because it shows the true meaning of virtue and how it may be realized, and for this reason, it has been given extensive treatment here. Fundamentally, virtue depicts a perfect "internal" mode of being, which cannot be "possessed" through any mental machination or active striving. On the contrary, any such striving will only act to weaken one's vitality and spirit. However, the reason for this must be made clear. The *Zhuangzi* also states at one point, "Supreme virtue does not obtain/possess anything" (至德不得),[9] but the reason remains difficult to fathom, which is the work of interpretation.

Non-action is a key concept in the *Laozi*, and in JL it is shown to be grounded in a heart-mind that is unmoved by desire, not bound by any prejudgment or predilection, and not enticed or beguiled by external influences, and in that sense, empty. Emptiness ensures wellness within and clear discernment of people and affairs, with which there is nothing that cannot be accomplished. For this reason, *Laozi* 38 states, "One with highest virtue takes no action, but leaves nothing undone." To the undiscerning reader, indeed, this may appear perplexing, but with clear explanation disclosing the logic of the argument, it emerges that the *Laozi* is above all

[9] See *Zhuangzi*, chapter 17, "Autumn Floods," in Guo (1985, 574). Cf. Watson (2013, 129).

concerned with the interiority of virtue and the emptiness of the heart-mind.

JL next turns attention to the concepts of *ren* 仁, *yi* 義, and *li* 禮 in *Laozi* 38, with special attention to the last. As these concepts have been addressed at some length in the translation (JL §1, pp. 38–41) and Eirik Harris' chapter in this volume, I will only highlight that JL's interpretation is consistent with its focus on an unburdened, and thus untainted and perfectly functioning heart-mind.

Ren, "humaneness," is defined as a natural and irrepressible tendency to joyfully care for people that arises from the "innermost heart-mind," which aligns well with the explanation of "highest virtue." As such, humaneness at the highest level is never about seeking "recompense," which is to say, not to gain or possess anything in return.

The concept of *yi*, "appropriateness," is taken to mean what is naturally appropriate, fitting, and proper to the ordering of human relationships, which encompasses roles, attitudes, and responsibilities. For example, according to JL, it is proper for ministers to "serve" (*shi* 事) their lord, and for subordinates "to cherish" (*huai* 懷) their superiors. Given that the heart-mind is seen to be pivotal to realizing virtue, which JL also defines in this section as "the achievement that comes from following the Way," *ren* and *yi*, as ingredients of that perfect state, should be interpreted in the same light. In contrast, working with different interpretive assumptions, HSG and WB locate the meaning of *yi* in the righteous actions taken to rectify injustice and wrongdoings.

The discussion on *li*, "ritual," is considerably more extensive, and there should be a reason for it. *Li* is a structured behavior that gives expression to kindness, JL explains, and the presentation of appropriate conduct regulating human relationships. *Li* is "that by which external adornment makes understood what is internal," or in other words, the "exterior display for one's inner essence" (JL §1, p. 39). How does this fit with the emphasis on cultivating emptiness? Is *li* a positive value in the field of *de*/virtue?

Although *li* is external, JL argues, its true purpose is for self-cultivation. This is easily missed, and most people perform *li* not for their own fulfillment but out of extrinsic motivation. This is how JL connects *li* with the overall emphasis on the "internal" that it sees as central to the meaning of *de*/virtue articulated in *Laozi* 38. *De*/virtue, *ren*, *yi*, and *li* are shown to form a value chain, and this is why the *Laozi* traces the loss of *li* in the sense defined here to the loss of *yi*, and the latter to the loss of *ren*, and ultimately to the loss of virtue and the Way.

The *Laozi* text that accompanies HSG and WB has a different wording, which predisposes the interpreter to seeing *ren*, *yi*, and *li* as arising only after the decline of the Dao (see Eirik Harris' analysis in this volume). For our purposes, we need only to concern ourselves with JL's interpretation. There is certainly no reason to suspect that JL had changed the wording of the *Laozi* here to suit its interpretation. Still, *Laozi* 38 also states that "*li* is the impoverishment of loyalty and good faith, and the start of chaos." Would that not throw doubt on JL's interpretation?

The value of *li* seems suspect to many readers of the *Laozi*, for it evokes images of rituals that are artificial, against the very grain of non-action and naturalness. However, in view of the perceived divide between a perfectly clear heart-mind within and its corruption as it seeks possessions without, it is not difficult to imagine how JL would navigate this part of *Laozi* 38 differently. When *li*/ritual does not serve the project of self-cultivation, it impoverishes *de*/virtue. Thus, the *Laozi* is entirely right to point out that *li* could become a liability in a world where virtue is overwhelmed by the desire to gain possessions.

This is reinforced by the further claim in *Laozi* 38 that "the great man dwells in what is rich and does not dwell in what is impoverished." JL specifically defines "greatness" as referring to superior "intelligence" (*zhi* 智) (JL §1, p. 43). What this means is that the "great man" stays focused on enriching the internal and eschews any intellectual trickery or calculated display of propriety that will only take one further away from "the proper order and the actuality of what is essential." In this way, JL is able to provide a consistent interpretation of *de*/virtue and its key components. This has little to do with reconciling "Daoism" with "Confucianism," which are later constructs, but everything to do with discerning the inner logic of the *Laozi*.

III. Minding the Heart-Mind

The assumption in this analysis is that interpretation proceeds on the basis of certain lead ideas and is guided by their logical entailments. As the interpreters are being drawn into the world of a text, they seize on certain perceived key insights and seek to draw out their conceptual underpinnings and implications. To JL, the *Laozi* brings to light the profound truth of virtue and the Dao, and the practical significance of emptiness and non-action. The real issue is that emptiness and non-action must be properly understood. In other words, the interiority of virtue raises the question of the meaning of emptiness, which leads directly to the workings of the heart-mind. Once it is clear that the attainment of virtue hinges on the heart-mind, the different intellectual pieces fall into place.

Arguably, there is a certain intellectual bias to JL's interpretation, finding the meaning of non-action especially in a state of clear-mindedness that makes possible perfect discernment, optimal response to the complexity of sociopolitical life, and sage rulership. The "great man," as we have seen, is marked not by *ren* or *yi* but by "the greatness of his intelligence." Commenting on a passage that corresponds to chapter 67 of the current *Laozi*, JL similarly privileges the role of intelligence, matching a person of intelligence (*zhi shi* 智士) with the sage and the ruler (JL §10, p. 71). This is not casual interpretation—nor does it reflect any self-interested intervention to elevate the worth of the scholar, I would argue—but is the result of a thorough engagement with the *Laozi*.

The same basic understanding is reflected in the other sections of the commentary, though they address more fully the workings of the heart-mind and the "governing order" (*li* 理) of things and affairs. JL next discusses *Laozi* 58–60, in that order. Comparisons with HSG and WB should help bring out JL's key emphasis in explaining the *Laozi*.

"Misfortune, indeed, is what good fortune rests upon," *Laozi* 58 declares (JL §2, p. 44). To HSG, this can only mean that if people can repent when met with misfortune and perform good deeds, fortune would smile on them once more. To JL, however, the point the *Laozi* is trying to make is that "misfortune" would induce "fear and caution" in the heart-mind, which in turn would cause one's "thoughts and deliberations" (*silü* 思慮) to be "thorough" and one's conduct, "correct and upright." With the heart-mind in full command, functioning without interference or confusion, the person will be able to "grasp the proper order for affairs," which is a prerequisite to having a pack of blessings, as it were, light upon one's back.

Laozi 58 also decries that people have been "lost" (*mi* 迷) for a long time. As HSG understands it, the *Laozi* is referring specifically to the rulers here, who are confused or deluded (*mi huo* 迷惑) and have lost their sense of rectitude (*shi zheng* 失正). WB similarly, albeit in a more general vein, explains that this means the people have long become deluded and lost the Way (*mi huo shi dao* 迷惑失道). Since the *Laozi* immediately goes on to discuss the rectitude or uprightness (*fang* 方) of the sage, it would seem to make sense to pursue an ethical reading. Nevertheless, there is every reason to probe more deeply into the root cause of this regrettable state of affairs. According to JL, the reason why the people are lost must be traced to the workings of desire (*yu* 欲).

"Whenever a person misses the road to where he desires (*yu*) to go and recklessly wanders off, this is called being lost," JL writes, making use of an analogy (JL §2, p. 46). Whereas HSG and WB did not see any need to go beyond defining what the *Laozi* means by *mi* 迷, dictionary-like, as *huo* 惑, a state of confusion or being deluded, and the same is true of Yan Zun's interpretation in this instance, JL brought more to the interpretive table. "If one is lost, then one will simply never be able to go where one desires (*yu*) to go. Now the masses are thus unable to go where they desire (*yu*) to go, and so the text says that they are 'lost'" (JL §2, p. 46.).

Yu/desire is a function of the heart-mind, setting it in motion, always tending toward certain ends, such as wealth, honor, or long life. These latter are of course much coveted. Nevertheless, they remain objects of desire and should be distinguished from the movement and intentionality of the heart-mind itself. This is not a trivial point, because the *Laozi* may be seen to be advocating a kind of "emptiness" that takes the cessation of desire as its final objective. Even the idea of having few desires needs to be interpreted carefully, for while it may contribute to the project of virtue, it is not by extinguishing certain desires, with deliberate effort, that the self may be kept whole. Rather, it is by ensuring that the heart-mind is able to set the course of desire with calmness and clarity that virtue may be attained.

With the heart-mind thus in command, having few desires can be expected, which is a consequence of virtue flourishing within, as opposed to a task to be accomplished. Indeed, on the concept of *fang* 方 in *Laozi* 58, which denotes a square and is usually understood in the sense of uprightness, JL takes pain to explain that it connotes perfect correspondence between "one's inner states and outer performances" (JL §2, p. 47). Coming at the *Laozi* from a different angle, HSG simply glosses it as "rectitude" (*zheng* 正), whereas to WB, all that needs to be said is that the sage leads the people with uprightness to make them shed their perverted ways (cf. WB's commentary to *Laozi* 41).

Calmness and clarity require careful tending. The logic of the interiority of virtue, which shapes JL's interpretation of the *Laozi*, leads directly to this point. This is also what JL takes to be the focus of *Laozi* 59, which opens with a sweeping statement, "For ordering human affairs and serving Heavenly affairs, nothing is as good as frugality" (JL §3, p. 48).

JL explains in some detail that "acuteness, clarity and sharp intelligence" are endowed by Heaven, on the basis of which human beings come to see, hear, and think and deliberate. Overexertion of the senses and the heart-mind inevitably invites ruin. On this premise, what the *Laozi* means by "ordering human affairs" (*zhi ren* 治人) is not so much about managing the affairs of the people, important as that may be (and which is WB's reading, for example), but is more about regulating the activity of the heart-mind and the senses, in particular avoiding excesses and preserving their clarity and sharpness. Being "frugal" with one's endowed resources and capacity is thus crucial, which is also what is meant by "serving Heaven's affairs" (*shi tian* 事天) in the *Laozi*.

Sensory perception and cognitive functions exact a measure of "expenditure of spirit." Exhaustion in this context will bring dire consequences indeed. This, to JL, explains the emphasis on "frugality," which should be understood as consuming "one's energy and spirit sparingly" and applying "one's intelligence and discernment frugally." Unlike the common people, the sage exercises his spirit calmly, conserving the inner *qi* essence that animates and sustains life. As a form of practice or technique (*shu* 術), being frugal in this sense is ultimately "born from the proper order of the Way" (JL §3, p. 50).

JL provides extensive commentary to *Laozi* 59, because it sees the text as shedding light on the management of the heart-mind. To most commentators, the *Laozi* here is concerned with the proper way for both governing a state (*zhi guo* 治國) and governing the self (*zhi shen* 治身). According to HSG, for example, there is nothing more important than managing the wealth of the people with care, as opposed to squandering it for the ruler's own gratification. At the same time, treasuring one's essential *qi* so that it does not dissipate is necessary to ensuring the well-being of the self. JL's focus is clearly on preserving the integrity of the self, extending the argument from the interiority of virtue and the centrality of the heart-mind to cultivating calmness and clarity, although it does bring government into the interpretive frame later in its commentary on *Laozi* 59.

JL goes on to elaborate how someone whose "thoughts and deliberations are calm," which can only issue from an "empty" heart-mind, will be able to preserve their "original virtue" (JL §3, p. 51). This refocuses attention on the interiority of virtue, but it also provides additional insight into the cultivation of the heart-mind.

With calmness within, the sensory organs, which are defined as "the 'doors' and 'windows' for one's spirit and intellect" in the "Yu Lao" (YL §9, p. 101), will remain clear and unobstructed, rendering them receptive to the inflow of "harmonious *qi*."[10] In this way, the person will be able to "amass virtue repeatedly" and grow in calmness and clarity, which of course would enable one to overcome all challenges and for the ruler, to enjoy a vastly successful reign. This is why the *Laozi* says, "If one repeatedly amasses virtue, then there is nothing that one does not overcome." The promised results are certainly appealing, but the important point is that they have their roots "in repeatedly amassing virtue" (*Laozi* 59, JL §3, p. 51), which is possible only if the heart-mind is clear and properly nourished, and this is what the interpreter of the *Laozi* must make clear.

Laozi 60 clearly directs the interpreter to issues of government, for it begins with the oft-quoted remark, "Ordering a large state is like cooking a small fish" (JL §4, p. 53). JL explains how, with the help of several analogies and reasoning "from the perspective of proper order" (以理觀之), "the ruler who holds to the Way" cherishes "emptiness and calmness" and does not disturb the people with frequent and presumably arbitrary changes to the laws and standards. This attests that policy and public administration cannot be divorced from minding the heart-mind within. In comparison, Yan Zun and WB both focus on the way to manage a large

[10] See JL §3, p. 51, n. 39, for a discussion of this concept.

state in this instance, with the former situating the insight of the *Laozi* in a broader cosmological context, whereas HSG emphasizes that taxing and troublesome practices will only bring disturbance, whether in government or self-cultivation.

The outcome of holding to the Way in ruling a state is that "the people reduce their desires," JL affirms (JL §4, p. 54). The calmness of the sage ruler will have a direct impact on the populace. This requires further clarification, but at this point it should be clear that with their desire in check, people will enjoy good health and behave well ethically, or in the language of JL, in accordance with "proper order."

Laozi 60 goes on to invoke an ideal state in which "ghosts and spirits" do not harm the people, and vice versa. Leaving aside the reference to the supernatural as agents of disease and misfortune, which is not out of the ordinary in the context of early China, JL's point remains that arising from the wealth of *de*/virtue of the sage ruler, exemplified by a heart-mind of calmness and clarity, people will prosper and multiply, which is surely an indication of abundance of *de*/possessions obtained in the right way. Otherwise, their essential *qi* and spirit will be in disorder, and the loss of virtue and possessions can be expected.

IV. Managing Desire

The distinction between the "internal" and "external," with which JL introduces its exposition of the *Laozi*, points to an opposition in one sense, but ideally, the two should form a continuum. While deliberate and assertive striving for *de*/possessions, which reflects an unruly heart-mind at work, is counterproductive, *de*/virtue naturally brings riches and fulfillment.

This is fundamental to JL's interpretive project, although it does not mean that it disregards the importance of good governance. JL's interpretation of *Laozi* 46 is a good example in this regard: "As for a ruler who holds to the Way, outside the state he harbors no resentment or enmity against his neighbors and rivals, and inside the state he shows virtue and generosity toward his subjects" (JL §5, p. 57). The attention to governance is unambiguous, and the same may be said for JL's treatment of *Laozi* 53 (JL §11), although this does not detract from the need to attend to the more basic issue of the interiority of virtue.

At the most basic level, *de*/virtue is "that by which a person establishes his life" (JL §3, p. 53, commentary to *Laozi* 59). This should refer to the vital *qi* energy that forms the basis of existence and connects *de*/virtue with *de*/possession. "In the case of a person, virtue consists in accumulated energy," JL also writes (JL §12, p. 77, commentary to *Laozi* 54), which brings into view the developmental function of virtue in human life. If individuals follow the proper order of things and affairs, naturally, the benefits will extend beyond them to their clan, which "will have an abundance of wealth." While wealth is "external," here it grows out of *de*/virtue. Following the same logic, JL could therefore understand Laozi's confidence in asserting how the cultivation of virtue would result in the flourishing of not only the self and the extended family but also the village, state, and empire (JL §12). However, all this is predicated on the assumption that the heart-mind is able to achieve calmness and clarity.

Human beings, after all, depend on external sustenance to survive. This should be recognized. As such, the heart-mind cannot but be "desirous of benefit." There is thus inherent potential danger for the heart-mind to go astray, become lost, in lusting after endless objects of desire. Unlike the sage, whose desire does not exceed satisfying basic needs, the common people may be drawn to "licentiousness and extravagance" (JL §5, p. 57, commentary to *Laozi* 46). As desire intensifies, "one's intelligence and wisdom decline," impairing judgment and leading to heedless actions that will only invite pain and suffering. The emphasis on cognitive clarity driving affective calmness and blameless conduct seems unmistakable.

Commenting on *Laozi* 46, JL also states, "If people have desires, then their plans and calculations will become chaotic" (JL §5, p. 58). If unchecked, this will fuel greater desire for more possessions, which in the end will certainly corrupt the heart-mind.

The emphasis on clarity of mind, a heart-mind that is capable of "measuring and weighing" (*du liang* 度量) things properly, that is, discerning the proper order of things and affairs, is consistent with JL's overall understanding of the *Laozi*. However, what is equally noteworthy is that JL recognizes that there is a supply side to the calculus of desire.

The heart-mind may easily turn "deviant" (*xie* 邪), as it succumbs to the lure of desirable things. This harks back to the key idea that the person with "highest virtue" is not enticed by external influences (JL §1, commentary to *Laozi* 38). One of the reasons why "swift horses" are "relegated to carrying dung" when "all under Heaven hold to the Way," as *Laozi* 46 so graphically puts it, according to JL, is that the horses will not be used "to transport licentious goods" but returned to cultivating the fields (JL §5, p. 57).[11] Whereas both WB and HSG point straight to agriculture, JL alone senses the need to explain more clearly the logic of consumption.

The impact of objects of desire on the heart-mind, in other words, cannot be underestimated in the cultivation of virtue. They can make good people do terrible things and bring calamities to the community, as JL emphasizes. "Therefore, a sage is neither led on by the five colors nor enticed by lovely sounds and music, and an intelligent ruler despises frivolous enjoyments and gets rid of enticing beauties" (JL §5, p. 59). This may imply that people are generally incapable of withstanding such temptations, and thus it is necessary to restrict supply. Be that as it may, there are different aspects to the distinction between *de*/virtue and *de*/possessions and they need to be distinguished.

[11] The "Yu Lao" (§1, p. 83) offers a different reading: "In the case where all under Heaven hold to the Way, there are no urgent troubles, and hence there is no use for rapid communications. And so the text says that 'swift horses are relegated to carrying dung.'"

Commenting on *Laozi* 54, JL explains,

> Whether intelligent or foolish, nobody fails to have predilections and aversions. When reposed and calm, none fail to know the origins of misfortune and good fortune. But when they are in the grip of likes and dislikes or aroused by licentious things, then they become confused. (JL §12, p. 76)[12]

This should serve as a succinct reminder of the need to cultivate calmness and clarity of mind. Both the supply and demand side of desire must be taken into account, so that one's heart-mind and spirit will not be "uprooted," lost in a sea of unbridled desire. In the end, what is envisaged is that "in bringing order to one's person, external things cannot confuse one's energy and spirit" (JL §12,

[12] *Laozi* 54 begins by stating that those who are firmly established "will not be uprooted" and those who have a firm grip "will not be thrown off." It continues, "As son and grandson, one uses this so that one's familial sacrifices will not be cut off." To JL (§12), this can only be talking about the ideal sage who firmly "establishes his predilections and aversions" and is thus able to resist the lure of desirable objects. As such, he will not be uprooted from his existential ground. "Unified in his essence," "his spirit will not be moved," which is what the *Laozi* means by "not being thrown off" by coveted possessions. Furthermore, "In being a person's son or grandson, he embodies this Way in order to preserve his ancestral temple. When one's ancestral temple is not destroyed, this is called 'familial sacrifices not being cut off'" (JL §12, p. 77). In contrast, the "Yu Lao" relates:

> After King Zhuang of Chu had prevailed over the state of Jin . . . he went home and rewarded Sunshu Ao. . . . [who] asked for some territory in . . . a place of sand and rocks. According to the laws of the Chu state, ministers with heritable emoluments were to have their territory taken back after the second generation, but only Sunshu Ao stands apart from this. The reason why his enfeoffment was not taken back is that it was unproductive, and so after nine generations, the familial sacrifices conducted there have not broken off. And so when the text says, 'One who is established well will not be uprooted. One who has taken a good grip will not be thrown off. His sons and grandsons will take up the familial sacrifices and go on for generation upon generation without cease,' it is referring to a Sunshu Ao. (YL §2, pp. 86–87)

On this evidence, it would seem difficult to entertain that the two interpretations came from the same source. However, on *Laozi* 47, which asserts that "By not going out the door, one can know all under Heaven. By not peering out the window, one can know the Way of Heaven," the "Yu Lao" does draw attention to the centrality of the "spirit and intellect," the ruinous consequences of having one's sensory functions overwhelmed by external influences, and the need for one's "center" to have a master (YL §9, p. 101).

p. 77). "No-thought" is thus crucial, but it is now shown to entail thoroughness of thinking and deliberations (*silü shu* 思慮熟). Only then will one be able to appropriate, make it one's own, the "proper order for affairs" (*de shili* 得事理). This point is repeated in both Sections 2 and 12 of JL, with the further assurance that every accomplishment would follow.[13]

V. Following the Order of Things and Affairs

This is not a utilitarian argument that arises from concerns for optimization. Although favorable outcomes are assured, to JL, the *Laozi* is fundamentally concerned with the very order of things and affairs.

Mind and body are always in motion, which means they consume the vital *qi* allotment a person is endowed with. Premature death is certain to follow from excessive activity, for which reason "the sage uses his energy and spirit sparingly and values dwelling in calmness" (JL §9, p. 66, commentary to *Laozi* 50). With calmness and clarity, one is able to command the course of desire and consequently one's spirit will not be moved by objects that may inflame desire (JL §12). The notion of "spirit" (*shen* 神) or "energy and spirit" (*jing shen* 精神) may have a specific reference, but it is inextricably tied to the heart-mind, and in the final analysis, spirit and body are constituted by vital *qi*. The concept of *de*/virtue represents an integral view of an idealized self. What is now further shown is that the argument on clarity stems from insight into the *li* 理 or governing order of things and affairs.[14]

All things have forms and dimensions, which give them certain qualities: "Short and long, small and big, square and round, hard

[13] The need for deep thinking and deliberation is also emphasized in JL's commentary to *Laozi* 59 (JL §3), as mentioned previously, though the particular focus there is on calmness.

[14] On the concept of *li*/order, see JL §1, p. 41, n. 20.

and brittle, light and heavy, illumination and shadow are called governing orders" (JL §10, p. 71). JL sees fit to repeat the point in another part of the commentary: "In every case, the governing orders [of things] are what divide square from round, short from long, coarse from fine, and hard from brittle. And so, when there is a fixed governing order [for something], only then can it be delineated" (JL §8, p. 64). However, the point is not only that there are set principles or patterns inherent in things and affairs, but more importantly, that it is through careful thinking and deliberations that one can come to understand them and bring about successful outcomes. For this reason, according to JL, *Laozi* 67 states, "One who does not dare to be ahead of anything under Heaven is thereby able to be a leader in completing affairs" (JL §10, p. 69).

Tracing the idea of "not daring to be ahead" to an intellectual foundation is probably not the most intuitive reading—HSG, for example, emphasizes humility and deference in this instance—but it follows from an interpretation that privileges the role of the heart-mind in discerning the principles and patterns that underlie natural phenomena and human endeavors. "To anticipate the state of affairs and to anticipate the order of things in one's movements" is "to baselessly and recklessly use one's thoughts to measure things," the JL also states (*Laozi* 38, JL §1, p. 42). In contrast, the sage always "follows after the compasses and squares of the ten thousand things" (JL §10, p. 71). The advice to follow the *li*/order of things is unlikely to strike any reader at the time as particularly novel, but the more significant insight is that it presupposes understanding, which in turn requires calmness and clarity, a heart-mind firmly in control.

JL Section 6 gives a more detailed exposition on the concept of *li*/order:

> The Way is that to which the ten thousand things conform, and that wherein their ten thousand governing orders unite. These governing orders are the patterns of completed things. The Way

> is that by which the ten thousand things are brought to completion. And so the text says, "The Way is that which orders them." (JL §6, p. 61)

There is one more important point that needs to be made. Things and affairs may be unique with their own governing order or principle, but they form an integral whole in the larger scheme of things. This, to JL, is what the *Laozi* means by Dao, which "comprehensively unites the governing orders of the ten thousand things" (JL §6, p. 61). As such, in the context of a dynamic order, change and transformation emerges as the universal governing principle, following which "the *qi* associated with life and death are received from it, the ten thousand intelligences pour in lesser or greater measure from it, and the ten thousand affairs arise from and cease in it" (JL §6, p. 61).[15]

"In every case, opposed things cannot simultaneously flourish; *yin* and *yang* are an example of this"; individuated ordering principles "take from and yield to each other," such as the application of force and benevolent policies in managing state affairs (JL §1, p. 41). The element of change, which encompasses "preservation and loss ... death and birth ... and flourishing and decay" (JL §8, p. 64), renders the discernment of *li*/order all the more critical. The specific mention of "intelligence" in the passage cited above seems unlikely to be accidental. Although things and affairs are governed by fixed principles, which are open to inspection and deliberation, they are by no means static. "In every case, the essence of the Way has no limit, has no form, is supple and yielding, flows with the times, and matches the governing orders of things" (JL §6, p. 63). This is also the reason, according to JL, that the *Laozi* says, "A way that can be delineated is not the constant Way" (JL §8, p. 65).

[15] Cf. *Hanfeizi* 8, "Brandishing Authority" or "Wielding Power" ("Yangquan" 揚權). For an English translation, see Watson (2003, 35–42).

VI. Concluding Remarks

The *Laozi* is of course about the Way and *de*/virtue. Anyone who has come across it, as a text or reported sayings, would be keen to learn more about them. Perhaps these formed the intended audience of JL, as opposed to those totally unfamiliar with the *Laozi.* The reality of the Dao, as it is not bound by any category that would allow delineation, has to be sought through *de*/virtue. This defines the basic interpretive orientation of JL.

In dissecting the *Laozi*, it becomes clear that *de*/virtue is to be understood as the embodiment of the Dao. Yet, this immediately raises the question, "How would we know?" From the outset, it has to be assumed that the "achievement" of the Dao is discernible (JL §1, p. 40). JL devotes considerable effort to explaining the interiority of *de*/virtue, which by way of a horticultural metaphor should be understood as the "tap roots" and "spreading roots" of human existence (JL §3, p. 53). Whereas the former constitutes life, which grounds the meaning of *de*/virtue in a theory of vital *qi*, the latter extends its meaning to the world of human affairs. In either case, it follows that one should "make deep the root," which can be achieved only if one is able to understand and follow the governing order of things and affairs.

If one is able to embody the Dao, of course, "one's intelligence will be profound," and "if one's intelligence is profound, then one's comprehension will be far-reaching" (JL §3, p. 52). However, it is by no means certain that one can come to embody the Dao, possess genuine virtue, and perceive clearly the *li*/order of things. The complex workings of the heart-mind must therefore be investigated.

Although desire as the movement of the heart-mind cannot be denied, it is essential to avoid the situation where it "recklessly wanders off" (JL §2, p. 46), or "go[es] off" and becomes "uprooted" (JL §12, p. 77). This must be why the *Laozi* focuses on emptiness and non-action. At every turn, one may be "led on by external things and confused by frivolous likes" (JL §12, p. 76). It is only with calmness and clarity of mind that one may "grasp what is appropriate among predilections and aversions" (JL §12, p. 76), which is to say, understand the governing order of things and the complexity of human life.

"In every case of virtue, one collects it by means of non-action, completes it by means of non-desiring, secures it by means of non-thinking, and solidifies it by means of non-use. If one acts on it and desires it, then virtue will have no place to lodge. If virtue has no place to lodge, then it will not be whole" (JL §1, p. 37).[16] There is thus every reason to elucidate the way to realizing emptiness of the heart-mind. Desire is in a sense a kind of seeing, and it is imperative that the heart-mind is able to see right. The assumption that this is possible when the heart-mind is free of the influence of prejudgments and objects of desire may seem unsubstantiated, but this is supported by a *qi* theory that promises nurturance and renewal. Nevertheless, the heart-mind must first become calm so that it is able to prevail against the onslaught of enticements and benefit from the influence of "harmonious *qi*." Whereas a "deviant heart" will spiral toward an injurious end, the accumulative effect of emptiness and renewal will strengthen the *de*/virtue within.

Compared with the other *Laozi* commentaries cited here, JL stands out in its attention to the workings of the heart-mind, and specifically the management of desire. Although a full comparison cannot be pursued in this chapter, Yan Zun's commentary seeks to draw out especially the cosmological underpinnings of the Dao and *de*/virtue. The cosmos and all living beings are constituted by *qi*, and interpretation of the *Laozi* cannot but proceed from that premise. To HSG, the task of the interpreter is to identify the concrete referents of the sayings of the *Laozi*. The meaning of

[16] Cf. *Guanzi*, "Art of the Mind, Part I" ("Xin shu shang" 心術上), which also likens *de*/virtue to where the Dao "lodges" (*she* 舍). Rickett (1998, 77) translates: "Power [*de*/virtue] is a dwelling of the Way. Things must obtain [*de*/possess] it in order to live. The living must know how to obtain it in order to grasp the essence of the Way. Therefore, Power is obtainment" (德者, 道之舍, 物得以生, 生知得以職道之精. 故德者得也).

de/virtue, for example, cannot be sought in the abstract. *Laozi* 38, as we have seen, is concerned with the ideal sage ruler who embodies the height of virtue, which is defined elsewhere in the commentary as the "one" (*yi* 一), that is, the original vital *qi* that engenders all living things (commentary to *Laozi* 51). The *Laozi* also intimates in several places that the truth of the Dao is deeply profound and mysteriously wondrous (*xuan* 玄) (e.g., chs. 1, 6, 15, 56). To HSG, *xuan* refers specifically to "Heaven" (*tian* 天), and it is only by unmasking these referents that the meaning of the *Laozi*, with its dual focus on sage governance and self-cultivation, can be fully understood.

In contrast, to WB, identifying the textual referents at best scratches the surface meaning and risks misinterpreting the *Laozi* altogether. A single idea runs through the *Laozi*, which is fundamentally about embodying a mode of being marked by naturalness and non-action. In some respects, WB shares JL's emphasis on returning to and safeguarding the "roots" of existence, understood as grounded in an ideal mode of being free of the dictates of desire, but the latter's attention to the interiority of virtue and management of desire reflects a keener interest in the workings of the heart-mind. Perhaps this should not come as a surprise. The *Han Feizi* displays a deep concern with laws and standards. If we assume that JL came from the hands of Han Feizi or was associated with his teachings, we should find the same concern in its interpretation of the *Laozi*. Like everything else, there are basic patterns of operation that govern the heart-mind; as JL emphasizes, "One who cares for his own person does not dare to deviate from the law and its measures" (JL §10, p. 72), and the "law" in question should be understood as that which ensures proper governance of the heart-mind.

In this chapter, we hope to have shown how JL locks its interpretive lens on the interiority of virtue and follows through on the logical commitments to arrive at an explanation of the *Laozi*. In engaging JL, or any other *Laozi* commentary for that matter, it is important not only to bring across its interpretation but also to delineate the interpretive options at its disposal and how it comes to rest on a particular reading. While the former may yield rich philosophical dividend, understanding the process of interpretation itself provides insight into the complexity and contested nature of the intellectual arena of early China that promises equally handsome returns.

5

Situating the "Jie Lao" and "Yu Lao" among the Practices of Commentary in Early China

Yuet Keung Lo

I. Introduction

When scholars speak of commentary, it is usually used in a loose sense to mean "something that serves for illustration or explanation" (defined by *Merriam-Webster Online Dictionary*), and it applies to virtually all explanatory comments or critical remarks on texts regardless of their differences in form, structure, and intent. But what constituted commentary in early China was not determined once and for all; it evolved over time along with the various texts explained for particular considerations and purposes. A nuanced understanding of Chinese commentary needs to appreciate its various names as well as styles and modes of explanation, which appeared at different junctures of history; not all commentaries are the same. In modern scholarship, the "Jie Lao" 解老 ("Explaining *Laozi*") and "Yu Lao" 喻老 ("Illustrating *Laozi*") chapters in the *Han Feizi* 韓非子 are invariably, if loosely, viewed as commentaries on the *Laozi* 老子. Yet, the two chapters are largely dissimilar in their style and mode of explanation, which was integral to how interpretation was crafted and advanced. Moreover, since "explaining" and "illustrating" were two different styles of

Yuet Keung Lo, *Situating the "Jie Lao" and "Yu Lao" among the Practices of Commentary in Early China*
In: *Explaining and Illustrating the* Laozi. Edited by: Eirik Lang Harris and Eric L. Hutton, Oxford University Press. DOI: 10.1093/9780197514948.003.0007

exegesis as their names indicated, they should each have a specific name, even though they can be collapsed into one generic kind of commentary. To gain a refined understanding of Chinese commentary, it is worthwhile to compare how the two chapters attempt to fathom the meanings of the *Laozi*, respectively. Furthermore, through an analysis of early commentarial forms such as *zhuan* 傳 (commentary), *shuo* 說 (explanation), *jie* 解 (expository essay), and *yu* 喻 (illustrative story), this essay also situates the craft of interpretation in the two chapters in the larger context of the Chinese commentarial tradition in early China and traces its impact on the practices of commentary in Han times.

II. What Is a Chinese "Commentary"?

The meanings of words change over time. According to the *Oxford English Dictionary*, commentary meant "a collection of notes or memoranda; a notebook" or "memoir; historical records" from the sixteenth to the nineteenth century. These meanings are now obsolete. During the same period, commentary could also mean "a treatise consisting of a systematic series of comments or annotations on the text of a literary work; an expository treatise following the order of the work explained."[1] These denotations are usually what scholars mean in their usage.[2] Still, commentary may be used in a "*transferred* and *figurative*" *sense*, as is also common nowadays, *to mean* "anything that serves for exposition or illustration; a comment, remark." *A critical question may be asked if there was an equivalent term for "commentary" in early China.*

[1] *The Compact Edition of the Oxford English Dictionary*, 22nd printing in the United States, under "commentary."

[2] As will be shown, the "Jie Lao" and "Yu Lao" do not fit these definitions, as they were not intended to produce a "systematic series of comments or annotations" on the *Laozi*, nor did their explanations follow its order as a text, at least in our received version.

In the field of Chinese studies, "commentary" usually, if unthinkingly, refers to the indigenous Chinese term *zhuan* 傳, as if they meant the same thing.[3] In fact, this may not be the case. Pronounced as *chuan*, the same graph literally means "a horse that delivers messages or mail for the government" or "what is thus delivered,"[4] and a verbal sense of transmitting was developed later. Still, another derivative meaning subsequently came to mean "transmission; dissemination" (pronounced in this sense as *zhuan*). This could refer to the transmission of knowledge; hence, the act of transmitting and the product of transmission were also called *chuan* and *zhuan*, respectively. As the metaphor suggests, *zhuan* meant to deliver intact what was entrusted, thus it aimed to preserve and express the original meaning or intent of the text explained. This, however, is not necessarily the purpose of a commentary as *OED* defines it. In actual interpretive practices, as will be shown, *zhuan* was not always faithful to the letter.

There were only three known commentarial works known as *zhuan* from the Warring States period: the *Zuo zhuan* 左傳, *Gongyang zhuan* 公羊傳 and *Guliang zhuan* 穀梁傳, and they allegedly explicated the *Spring and Autumn Annals* 春秋 attributed to Confucius. Traditionally, they were called the *Three Commentaries on the Spring and Autumn Annals*.[5] The *Spring and Autumn Annals* records events spanning 722 to 481 BCE. In the commentary on the year 718 BCE, Master Guliang 穀梁子 was mentioned apparently by his disciple, who addressed him with the honorific "Master" (*zi* 子). Similarly, in the commentary on the years 706 BCE and 604 BCE, Master Gongyang 子公羊子 was also cited with a similar

[3] Though *zhu* 注 would immediately come to mind to most scholars in Chinese studies when we ask for a Chinese counterpart for the term commentary, it did not come into use until at least after the year of 136 BCE when the Five Confucian Classics were officially recognized as the curriculum for civil examinations. The earliest record of its appearance in the title of a work of commentarial nature appears in the mid-second century. For further discussion, see Lo (2020a, 189–193, esp. 192).

[4] Duan (2000, 377).

[5] See chapter 6 of Nylan (2001, 253–306).

form of honorific address. Thus, it seems that originally, commentary as a form of textual explication was orally transmitted from master to disciple, and this explains why it was called *zhuan*.[6] In fact, the *Gongyang* and *Guliang* were possibly written down only in the early Han dynasty (second century BCE), though their oral transmission might have begun three hundred years earlier.[7] Both commentaries attempted, among other considerations, to tease out the motivation and intent that informed and determined the exhortative diction and didactic rhetoric that defined the historiographic craft of the sage Confucius in his *Spring and Autumn Annals*.

Yet, the *Zuo zhuan* presents a controversial case. Unlike the other two commentaries that end with the final entry of the *Spring and Autumn Annals*, it records an important event from 453 BCE. That year, the powerful state of Jin was finally partitioned into three successor states: Han, Zhao, Wei, and this, according to later historians, marks the end of the Spring and Autumn period and the beginning of the Warring States period. Scholars argue that such oddities suggest that the *Zuo zhuan* was not meant to be a commentary on the *Spring and Autumn Annals*. Similarly, the *Zuo zhuan* has extensive comments where there was no entry in the *Spring and Autumn Annals*. Neither does it comment at all on many entries. However, such a challenge presupposes what the formal characteristics of a commentary should be, even as the genre was just about

[6] As tradition has it, Confucius orally transmitted the authorial meaning of the *Spring and Autumn Annals* to his disciples, who continued the transmission, and subsequently it was passed onto Masters Gongyang and Guliang. The "Treatise on Literature" in the *Hanshu* 漢書 (Han History) explicitly stated that the *Gongyang* and *Guliang* along with [Sire] Zou and [Sire] Jia were transmitted orally (及末世口說流行, 故有公羊、穀梁、鄒、夾之傳. 公羊、穀梁立於學官, 鄒氏無師, 夾氏未有書). See Ban (2002, 3:1715). Whether the *Three Commentaries* were originally called *zhuan* may be debatable. See below.

[7] For the nature of the *Gongyang* and *Guliang* texts, see Cheng (1993). The *Gongyang zhuan* was recently translated in full: see Miller (2015). The *Gongyang* was alluded to twice without the title in the late Warring States text *Xunzi* 荀子 as we have it today. See the "Dalüe" 大略 chapter in Wang (1988, 498, 506–507); see also Chapter 27 in Hutton (2014, 299, 308).

to develop in its earliest stage. There is no reason why a commentator could not refer to events from his own lifetime in commenting on the *Spring and Autumn Annals*, particularly given the enormous significance of the partitioning of Jin, even if it might have occurred well before the *Zuo zhuan* was composed. Nor must a commentary remark on every sentence or event recorded in the work it explains. This is certainly not the case with later commentaries, including the "Jie Lao" and "Yu Lao."

The *Gongyang* and *Guliang* presented their explanations of the *Spring and Autumn Annals* text in the format of question and answer. In contrast, the *Zuo zhuan* is primarily written in narrative form, and much of it elaborates the skeletal records of events in the *Spring and Autumn Annals* with details about their historical backgrounds, rather than commenting on the events themselves. The author of the *Zuo zhuan* is not mentioned in the text, much less addressed in honorific terms, and this might indicate that this text of 180,000 words in its received version was not orally transmitted, at least not from one single source at one time. Indeed, the *Zuo zhuan* as a text is composite in nature, comprising exegetical materials from different sources probably accreted over time. Professor Newell Ann Van Auken has identified 185 passages in the *Zuo zhuan* that explicitly explain the text of the *Spring and Autumn Annals*, and she calls them "direct commentary passages."[8]

Unlike the *Gongyang* and *Guliang*, whose exegetical purpose was to fathom how praise or blame was subtly expressed in the *Spring and Autumn Annals* in its hierarchies of naming and ranking,[9] the *Zuo zhuan*, according to Van Auken, aims to show that the purpose of the *Spring and Autumn Annals* "was not to evaluate events, but simply to register judgments already made and reported," and these judgments were "neither subtle nor concealed

[8] Van Auken (2016, 39).

[9] For one example of the *Gongyang*'s commentarial style, see Csikszentmihalyi (2006, 84–88).

but on full display."[10] Nevertheless, the *Zuo zhuan*'s "direct commentary passages" all share one thing in common: they are not as interested in the semantics of words as in the moral and political implications of their usage. These differing formal features and exegetical purposes of the *Three Commentaries on the Spring and Autumn Annals* show that the very idea of *zhuan* itself was fluid and had yet to develop into a stable form of exegesis in the Warring States period. It is not clear that the three commentaries were necessarily faithful to the authorial intent of the *Spring and Autumn Annals*. In fact, many *Zuo zhuan* narratives were written independently of the annals of the *Spring and Autumn Annals*, as there are no records at all in the latter about the partitioning of the Jin and the death of Confucius (in 479 BCE). Moreover, as Van Auken correctly observes, the *Zuo zhuan* contains remarks attributed to "the gentleman" (君子曰) and Confucius/Kongzi (孔子曰) that do not actually comment on the events recorded in the *Spring and Autumn*.[11]

The *Three Commentaries* are not intent on making arguments per se; rather, they aim to elucidate the (hidden) meanings embedded in the vocabulary and historiography of the *Spring and Autumn Annals* or elaborate on the historical episodes in them. Chronologically, they began to appear over time during the Warring States period. As mentioned, the *Gongyang* and *Guliang* were probably transmitted orally at first and only written down in the early Han. It is reasonable that the two traditions of oral transmission might not bear a title until they became written texts, so strictly speaking, the *Gongyang* and *Guliang* did not exist as commentaries in pre-Han times, if commentary required a written form. In fact, they were not called *zhuan* until the early Han,

[10] Van Auken (2016, 82, 87).

[11] Van Auken (2016, 121–24). There are eighty-nine and twenty-nine remarks ascribed to "the gentleman" and Confucius, respectively.

insofar as extant literature testifies.[12] Similarly, the *Zuo zhuan* was constituted of different sources in the Warring States period, but its title does not appear in pre-Han sources, and we do not even know how it was labeled then. In fact, it was formally called *Zuoshi zhuan* 左氏傳 (Commentary by Sire Zuo) instead during the Han, with *Zuo zhuan* only being its contracted form. It is then fair to say that the *Gongyang*, *Guliang*, and *Zuo* were not identified as *zhuan* until the Han dynasty. Even then, the meaning and significance of *zhuan* changed between the early Han in the third century BCE, when it was considered a form of orally transmitted explanation of the *Spring and Autumn Annals*, and a century later, when the Five Confucian Classics were adopted by the imperial government as the official curriculum for civil examinations. The *Gongyang* and *Guliang* were then recognized as the two official commentaries on the *Spring and Autumn Annals*, which comprised one of the Five Classics, and they themselves generated multiple sub-commentaries of various names, each trying to explain the tradition they followed. Although the *Zuo zhuan* did not enjoy the same privilege as the *Gongyang* and *Guliang*, it also inspired its admirers to write sub-commentaries as they did.

While the *Gongyang* and *Guliang* were not called by *zhuan* during the Warring States era, *zhuan* itself functioned as a rhetorical device in a completely different way and it was not bound or associated with any particular texts. Nearly all early Chinese philosophical texts contain citations of transmitted sayings prefixed with the expression *zhuan yue* 傳曰 ("It was said in the transmitted saying"), except the so-called Legalist writings such as

[12] It is noteworthy that the so-called *Shi yi* 十翼 (*Ten Wings*), a set of seven commentaries of different interpretive strategies on the *Book of Changes* dated to the late Warring States period, were not originally called *zhuan*, but were formally recognized as such by the mid-second century BCE; eight of them had the word *zhuan* suffixed to their original titles while the *Xici* 繫辭 ("Appended Words"), in two parts, was now also esteemed as the *Da zhuan* 大傳 ("Great Commentary") because it was considered the most important one in the set, owing to the authority of its alleged author Confucius/Kongzi.

the *Shangjun shu* 商君書 (Book of Lord of Shang), *Shenzi* 慎子 (Master Shen), and the *Han Feizi* 韓非子. This might not be accidental, because transmitted sayings were invariably quoted to defend a philosophical position or legitimize a recommended course of action, but the Legalists usually had little respect for much of the received wisdom from earlier times. Of course, this does not mean they were in principle against any received wisdom; Han Fei apparently confessed that "no ancient proverbs were empty of truth" and that "we could not afford not to pay them attention" (古無虛諺，不可不察).[13] Occasionally, other Legalists, too, would cite maxims to justify their views with the prefatory remark *chen wen zhi* 臣聞之 ("I have heard").[14] Han Fei, for instance, appeals (once each) to the authority of the legendary Yellow Emperor and the Duke of Zhou, or quotes (once) a written work from the Zhou dynasty (Zhou *shu* 周書) without a title.[15] Moreover, he often derives lessons from recent history to drive his arguments home. Similarly, Daoist works such as the *Laozi* and the *Zhuangzi* are also free of *zhuan yue* quotations, as both hardly draw from historical insights. As the extant sources show, the earliest Warring States text citing transmitted sayings is the Mohist work *Mozi* 墨子, though only twice. Later, we find them in the Confucian texts *Mencius* 孟子 and *Xunzi* 荀子; both are argumentatively oriented despite the fact that the former is constructed mainly of dialogues[16] while the latter is largely written in discursive essays.

[13] The "Jianjie shichen" 姦劫弑臣 chapter. See Chen (1974, 251).

[14] The prefatory remark is cited three times in the *Book of Lord Shang* and ten times in the *Han Feizi*.

[15] The citations appear in "Yang quan" 揚權, "Jie Lao," and "Shuo lin shang" 說林上, respectively. See Chen (1974, 123, 377, 422). Another titleless book of the Zhou dynasty is cited in a story in the *Han Feizi*. Moreover, there are two more citations of a written work without specifying it came from the Zhou, and they also appear in a chapter that assembles stories. Whether or not Han Fei himself gave credence to the facticity of the legendary or "historical" figures he cited might be irrelevant, it seems clear that he believed their alleged authority was useful for his arguments.

[16] For Mencius's hermeneutical approach to reading the *Odes* and the *Documents*, see Lao (2010, 22–26). More recently, Wiebke Denecke has a brief discussion of Mencius as an exegete on the *Odes*, but she does not focus on Mencius's mode of exegesis. See Denecke (2011, 164–166).

There are still several thousand *zhuan yue* quotations extant, and the majority appear in Han texts of different genres. The contents of transmitted sayings vary from allegedly historical anecdotes to moral lessons to philosophical insights. Yet, none of them, in their excerpted form, appears to be commentary of any kind in a strict sense. Rather, they are often used to support an argument or illustrate a point. For instance, when Zhou Xiao asked Mencius if the gentlemen in ancient times took office, Mencius replied:

> "Yes. The *Records* (*zhuan yue*/transmitted saying) say, 'When Confucius was not in the service of a lord for three months, he became agitated. When he left for another state, he always took a present for the first audience with him.' Gongming Yi said, 'In ancient times when a man was not in the service of a lord for three months he was offered condolences.'"
>
> "Does this not show an unseemly haste?"
>
> "A Gentleman losing his position is like a feudal lord losing his state. The *Rites* say, 'A feudal lord takes part in the ploughing to supply the grain for sacrificial offerings. His wife takes part in sericulture to provide the material for sacrificial dresses. When the sacrificial animals are not fat, the grain not clean and the items of dress not ready, he dare not perform the sacrifice. In the case of a Gentleman, if he has no land, he does not offer sacrifice.' When the vessels used for killing the animals and the items of dress are not ready, he dare neither offer sacrifices nor hold banquets. Is this not serious enough for condolences to be offered?" (*Mencius* 3B3)[17]

Evidently, Mencius quotes the transmitted saying to substantiate his view in the same way he refers to the *Rites* and a well-known contemporary figure. In a sense, the quotations function like a footnote to what Mencius says; they are effectively his self-annotations.

[17] Lau (1984, 107–108). I have modified Lau's translation of *zhuan* as "The Records."

Mencius, in fact, is wont to annotate himself in his disputations with popular sayings and authoritative texts such as the *Odes* and the *Documents*, though he quotes transmitted sayings only once. When arguing elsewhere for the governance of sage-kings Yao and Shun as the model of rulership, Mencius cited a popular saying and the *Odes*, and he would continue to develop his argument with quotations from another popular saying *in tandem with* another song from the *Odes*.[18]

While this kind of self-annotation does not formally constitute a commentary as an independent genre, its illustrative purpose and mode of explication are worth noting, as it would gain popularity and become even common practice toward the end of the Warring States period. In "Cultivating Oneself" 修身 in the *Xunzi*, it says:

> If one's intentions are cultivated, then one will disregard wealth and nobility. If one's concern for the Way and *yi* is great, then one will take kings and dukes lightly. It is simply that one examines oneself on the inside, and thus external goods carry little weight. A transmitted saying goes, "The gentleman makes things his servants. The petty man is servant to things." This expresses my meaning.[19]

Xunzi uses the transmitted saying to endorse his own view rather than the other way around. As such, transmitted sayings virtually function as a running commentary to the author's position or philosophical arguments. A total of twenty transmitted sayings in fifteen of the thirty-two chapters in the received *Xunzi* are cited for such purpose, in contrast with only once in the *Mencius*. Like Mencius, Xunzi sometimes cites a transmitted saying *and* a song from the *Odes* or a line from the *Documents* to argue for the same point.[20]

[18] *Mencius* 4A1, Lau (1984, 117). See further explanation below.
[19] Hutton (2014, 12). I modified the original translation from "saying" to "transmitted saying." For another example, see Hutton (2014, 196–197).
[20] See "The Way to Be a Minister" and "Correct Judgments" in Hutton (2014, 133–140, 183–200).

As far as his particular purpose is concerned, they carry the same weight. In fact, at least in one citation, the unidentified transmitted saying also appears in the received *Documents*.[21] The quotation of *zhuan yue* sayings was not a genre of formal commentary in the Warring States period, but it became so in the Han, and we still have a fortunate example in Han Ying's 韓嬰 (fl. mid-second century BCE) *Hanshi waizhuan* 韓詩外傳 (*Outer Commentary on the Han* Odes).[22] Meanwhile, *zhuan* as a mode of exegesis exemplified in the *Three Commentaries on the Spring and Autumn* continued to develop into diverse forms of interpretive commentary in the Han dynasty, including the *Hanshi waizhuan* (see below).

A final note is in order. Although *zhuan yue* sayings are not found in the received *Laozi* and *Zhuangzi*, they do appear in a different guise. For instance, Chapter 41 of the *Laozi* says:

> When the best student hears about the way
> He practices it assiduously;
> When the average student hears about the way
> It seems to him one moment there and gone the next;
> When the worst student hears about the way
> He laughs out loud.
> If he did not laugh
> It would be unworthy of being the way.
> Hence the established saying has it:
> "The way that is bright seems dull;
> The way that leads forward seems to lead backward;
> The way that is even seems rough.
> The highest virtue is like the valley;
> The sheerest whiteness seems sullied;
> Ample virtue seems defective;

[21] The same text is also quoted as sourced from the *Documents* in both the *Classic of Filial Devotion* (*Xiaojing*) and the "Ziyi" 緇衣 chapter in the *Book of Rites* (*Liji* 禮記). See Wang (1988, 451); see "The Gentleman" in Hutton (2014, 259).

[22] See Hightower (1952).

Vigorous virtue seems indolent;
Plain virtue seems soiled;
The great square has no corners.
The great vessel takes long to complete;
The great note is rarefied in sound;
The great image has no shape."
The way conceals itself in being nameless.
It is the way alone that excels in bestowing and in accomplishing.[23]

The term *jian yan* 建言 ("established sayings") literally suggests that the author was quoting from a supposedly well-known source, although it might very well be a fabrication intended to be rhetorical camouflage. Still, even if the author fabricated the source, it nevertheless functioned as a transmitted saying. This chapter starts off with an indirect intimation of the way, then describes it in intelligible particulars, and ends with a summation in the final two lines about the way as the author understands it. The "established sayings" are quoted to support the initial pronouncement in the chapter and elaborate the way in graphic detail. However, it is conceivable to take the "established sayings" as the real crux of the chapter, as all modern scholars do, thus rendering the opening remarks and the concluding summation as their commentary. Viewed this way, Chapter 41 of the *Laozi* presents a form of explanation, which, as will be shown, seems to foreshadow the practice of exegesis in the "Jie Lao" chapter of the *Han Feizi*.[24]

[23] Modified from Lau (1963, 102). Lau takes *jian yan* (literally, "established words") to mean the title of a work, which I do not find likely because, among other things, there were not many works that came with a title in the Warring States period as far as we know. Lau also thinks quotation ends with the chapter, but I believe it stops at the third to last line, so I added quotation marks accordingly.

[24] Purportedly ancient wisdom and popular sayings are also cited for support or affirmation in the *Laozi*. See, for instance, chapters 22 and 50.

In fact, at least the source of one such ancient saying quoted in the *Laozi* that remained popular in Warring States times can be identified. Chapter 36 reads:

If you would have a thing shrink,	將欲歙之
You must first stretch it;	必固張之
If you would have a thing weakened,	將欲弱之
You must first strengthen it;	必固強之
If you would have a thing laid aside,	將欲廢之
You would first set it up;	必固興之
If you would take from a thing,	將欲奪之
You must first give to it.	必固與之

> This is called subtle discernment:
> The submissive and weak will overcome the hard and strong.
> The fish must not be allowed to leave the deep;
> The instruments of power in a state must not be revealed to anyone.[25]

Before the summation of "subtle discernment," the four conditional statements were either verbatim quotations or adaptations from a work called the *Book of Zhou* (*Zhou shu* 周書), which apparently was circulated quite widely in the Warring States. In the *Stratagems of the Warring States* (*Zhanguo ce* 戰國策), there is an account from the state of Wei as follows:

> Viscount Huan yields Earl Zhi land to feed his arrogance. Earl Zhi demanded territory from Viscount Huan of Wei and he refused.
>
> "What is your reason for not giving it to him?" asked Ren Zhang.
>
> "The unreasonableness of the demand is the reason I refuse to give," replied Viscount Huan of Wei.

[25] Lau (1963, 95).

"Unreasonable demands for land make neighbouring states fearful," replied Ren Zhang. "Doubled desire cannot be satisfied, so the empire is alarmed. Give Earl Zhi land, my lord, and he will become arrogant; being arrogant he will scorn his enemies. The states around him will become alarmed and draw closer together. If the troops of countries which are close deal with a country that scorns its enemies, then the destiny of the Zhi clan will not be a long one. As it is said in the *Book of Zhou*, 'If I would destroy, I must first support; if I would gain I must first give' (將欲敗之，必姑輔之；將欲取之，必姑與之). The best thing you could do would be to yield land to Earl Zhi and make him arrogant. Can my lord let slip this chance to use the whole empire in a scheme against Earl Zhi and instead cause him to single out our country for his target?"

"You are right," said Viscount Huan of Wei, and ceded one town of ten thousand families. Earl Zhi was delighted. He immediately demanded Cai and Gaoliang from Zhao, and Zhao refused to yield them. Earl Zhi then surrounded Jinyang. When Han and Wei turned against him on the outside, Zhao responded from within the city and the Zhi clan perished.[26]

It is noteworthy that the "Shuo lin" 說林 ("Forest of Stories") chapter of the *Han Feizi* copied this account virtually verbatim.[27] As the chapter was meant to be a mere repository of historical tales, no moral lesson was attached to the Earl Zhi story. Viscount Huan of Wei reigned from 455 to 447 BCE, and the *Laozi* text was still in the process of formation around 300 BCE, as evidenced in the excavated Guodian bamboo text of *Laozi*, which contains in part or in full only 31 of the 81 chapters of the standard received version. Thus, it is conceivable that the *Laozi* text was quoting directly

[26] Crump (1970, 370). Wade-Giles romanization is converted to *pinyin*.
[27] Chen (1974, 422). For a recent study of the philosophy in the "Shuo lin," see Reeve (2003).

from the *Book of Zhou*.[28] The concluding statements in Chapter 41 should be original to the *Laozi*, which evidently is an extrapolative interpretation of the preceding quotation.[29]

Unlike the *Laozi* example, Zhuangzi often names the transmitted sayings he cites. For instance, in the first chapter of the eponymous work, he introduces an extraordinary gigantic Peng bird to symbolize the exemplary Daoist who aspires to carefree wandering across the stratosphere. To support his claim, he cites a written work entitled *Qixie* 齊諧,[30] though some traditional commentators take the term to refer to a person's name instead. It seems clear that Zhuangzi is keen on playing with the subtle significance of the term, which literally means "equality in doctrinal harmony," and viewed in such light, he probably invented the coinage. He wants to say that in spite of his imaginary, outrageously ridiculous creation of the Peng bird, it was meant to open up our philosophical vision about the inconceivable yet nameless enormity of self-transformation. Regardless, Zhuangzi, at least on the surface, is quoting from a transmitted saying, and in this case, to verify the enormous Peng bird and its transformation in his allegory. In this sense, this mode of substantiation resembles Mencius' self-annotation. In another chapter, Zhuangzi twice cites another source called *fayan* 法言 ("maxim," literally, "words about norms").[31] On both occasions, the quotation is intended to strengthen his own views with established authority in the same fashion transmitted sayings operated in the *Mozi*, *Mencius*, *Xunzi*, and *Laozi*. Moreover, Zhuangzi is

[28] Indeed, the *Annals of Sire Lü* (*Lüshi Chunqiu* 吕氏春秋) recounted a somewhat similar historical incident and cited the *Odes* to draw an identical moral lesson in slightly different wording—"If you wish to destroy it, You must first pile it up. If you wish to topple it, You must first raise it high" (將欲毀之, 必重累之; 將欲踣之, 必高舉之). See "Proper Conduct and Assessing the Situation," 20/6.4, in Knoblock and Riegel (2000, 532–534). The *Annals* was completed in 239 BCE.

[29] The concluding statement was quoted in the "Yu Lao" chapter of the *Han Feizi* and referenced in the "Neichu shuo xia" chapter. See Chen (1974, 570, 577).

[30] Guo (1985, 4).

[31] Guo (1985, 157, 160). I think it is problematic to take *fayan* to mean the title of a book, as some modern scholars do. The *fayan* is cited in the text by Confucius, who is at that point speaking from common experience.

also known for using so-called reputed words (*zhongyan* 重言) to lend credibility to his discourse; when appreciated as a form of self-exegesis, they were effectively identical to transmitted sayings.

III. *Shuo*: Explanations

Another early form of exegesis that might have begun to appear in the Warring States period is called *shuo* 說 (explanation). As early as Confucius' time, *shuo* as a noun connoted the sense of interpretation and comment,[32] and this continued into the Warring States period;[33] Mencius even talks about "explaining the *Odes*" (*shuo shi* 說詩), and the connotations of exegesis and persuasion (belief/doctrine) are evident.[34] Indeed, Mencius himself warns that literalism should be avoided in explaining the *Odes*: "[I]n explaining an ode, one should not allow the words to obscure the sentence, nor the sentence to obscure the intended meaning. The right way is to meet the intention of the poet with sympathetic understanding."[35] Thus, *shuo* clearly meant the practice of interpretation, which was evidently quite prevalent in Mencius' time. In the case of Mencius, he no doubt aimed at fathoming authorial intent when that was the intended goal, even though he appeared to dismiss literalism and even went so far as to proclaim that "if one believed in everything in the *Book of History*, it would have been better for the *Book* not to have existed at all."[36]

[32] See, for example, *Analects* 3.11, 3.21, and 12.8.

[33] *Mencius* 4B15, 5B4.

[34] See, for example, *Mencius* 3B9 (where the expression *xie shuo* 邪說, "deviant doctrine," is used).

[35] *Mencius* 5A4. Translation borrowed from Lau (1984, 142). For a recent study of Mencius' interpretation of the *Odes*, see Huang (2001). See also Goldin (2005).

[36] *Mencius* 7B3, Lau (1984, 194). It is true that Mencius occasionally would extrapolate from an ode for his extratextual purpose (e.g., 1B5, 2A4), but that should not be deemed against his fundamental concern in understanding authorial intent and the intrinsic meaning of an ode. For a detailed argument, see Lao (2010, 26–29).

In order that the authorial meaning would not be misconstrued, particularly in philosophical disputations, the *Explanations on the Mohist Canon* 墨經說 in the *Mozi* was composed, and it might be the earliest example of the kind. In our received version of the *Mozi*, there are two chapters called "Jing shang" 經上 (Canon, first half) and "Jing xia" 經下 (Canon, second half) that define the technical meanings of philosophical vocabulary the Mohists employed in their argumentation, and each is accompanied by a chapter that explains the terminological definitions in the Canon. The explanation of each of the technical terms is prefixed with the word *shuo*. For instance, the first two definitions and their explanations are as follows:

> 故，所得而後成也.
> 說故：小故，有之不必然，無之必不然，體也，若有端.
> 大故，有之必然，無之必不然，若見之成見也.
> [Canon:] A cause is that which obtains before something comes about.
> Explanation: Cause: When there is a minor cause, something is not necessarily so; when there is not, something is necessarily not so. It is a part—like a point. When there is a major cause, something is necessarily so; when there is not, something is necessarily not so. Like seeing something completes seeing.
> 體，分於兼也.
> 說體：若二之一，尺之端也.
> [Canon:] A part is a division in the whole.
> Explanation: Part: For example, one is a part of two; a point is a part of a *chi* (measured length).[37]

[37] Wu (2006, 460). I borrow Ian Johnston's translation but add back the word *shuo* that prefixes the explanations. See Johnston (2010, 374).

The definitions of *gu* 故 (cause) and *ti* 體 (part) are technical, as they are not what the two terms normally meant beyond the parameters of Mohist discourse. In its ordinary usage, *gu* could mean a reason or cause,[38] and *ti* a limb of a human being or the entire human body. On the purely formal level, the Mohist explanation is essentially an exegetical gloss independent of any particular syntactical context but equally applicable to all Mohist discourse. As such, it is no different from ordinary, non-technical glosses on texts whose meanings could be found in a lexicon in later times.[39] Furthermore, a short remark without a clear context makes it difficult to understand. One can easily imagine that even with the aid of *shuo*, it remains challenging to decipher what is actually said in a Mohist argument in discursive form. The same is true of Han Fei's numerous stories, which require an interpretive framework to make it speak for the storyteller. As will be clear, this is also the commentarial motivation of Hei Fei's explanation of the *Laozi*.

As mentioned earlier, self-annotation in support of an argument was quite common in the *Mencius*; in fact, sometimes Mencius even glosses uncommon words in the texts he quotes. For instance, he glosses the word *xiexie* 泄泄 ("chatter") in the *Odes* with its equivalent *tata* 沓沓 ("talk too much") in Warring States times (*Mencius* 4A1), as its meaning was presumably obscure to his audience. This is a semantic gloss not intended to draw out any moral and political significance of the word explained, unlike the *Three Commentaries on the Spring and Autumn Annals*. Indeed, interlinear glossing was not uncommon in Warring States times, though it was not always semantic. In the *Great Learning* 大學, for instance, the author quotes the *Odes* and says:

[38] Fung (2020, 181–187). In Guo Xiang's (d. 312) reinterpretation of the *Zhuangzi*, he differentiated *gu* (immediate or efficient cause) as opposed to *yuan* 原 (original cause). See Lo (2020b, 376–377).

[39] There were no dictionaries in the Warring States period; a compendium dating to this time was preserved in the received version of *Erya* 爾雅 from the early Han dynasty (third century BCE), which is often considered the earliest Chinese dictionary. See Loewe (1993, 94–99).

> The *Book of Odes* says, "Look at that curve in the Qi River. How luxuriant and green are the bamboo trees there! Here is our elegant and accomplished prince. [His personal life is cultivated] as a thing is cut and filed and as a thing is carved and polished. How grave and dignified! How majestic and distinguished! Here is our elegant and accomplished prince. We can never forget him!" "As a thing is cut and filed" refers to the pursuit of learning. "As a thing is carved and polished" refers to self-cultivation. "How grave and how dignified" indicates precaution. "How majestic and distinguished" expresses awe-inspiring appearance. "Here is our elegant and accomplished prince. We can never forget him" means that the people cannot forget his eminent character and perfect virtue.[40]

It is clear that the author was not simply adding semantic glosses on the quoted *Odes*; he was offering a line-by-line commentary. While interpretations of parts of a stanza in an ode abound in the *Mozi*, *Mencius*, *Xunzi*, and the *Doctrine of the Mean* 中庸,[41] this example of line-by-line exegesis is rare in extant literature,[42] but

[40] Translation borrowed from Chan (1963, 88). Wade-Giles romanization is converted to *pinyin*.

[41] As Martin Kern recently observes, "Simply put, for the *Xunzi* and other early Chinese texts, to speak in verse is to speak in the voice of traditional authority and of an emphatic claim for truth" (Kern 2016, 4). For Xunzi's appeal to the past as authority, see Cua (2005). For a detailed study of the Mohist use of ancient texts to claim authority, see Brown (2013).

[42] The *Wu Xing* 五行 (Five Conducts), a Warring States silk text excavated from a Han tomb in Mawangdui dated to 168 BCE, was accompanied by an explanation of virtually the entirety of the main text. Neither the main text itself nor the explanation came with any title, but scholars usually identify them as *jing* (base text, translated as "Canon" in the case of the *Mozi*) and *shuo*, respectively. It is uncertain whether the *shuo* was original to the main text as an auto-commentary or added to it later. Still, the proposed nomenclature for the two sections makes good sense as the bipartite structure of the *Wu Xing* text itself and the structure of the explanation are identical with what we find in the example of the *Great Learning* discussed above. When the *Odes* is cited in the *Wu Xing*, some of its explanations are also presented as a line-by-line commentary. For a summary of the excavation of the *Wu Xing* text, see Csikszentmihalyi (2004, 62–67). For a complete annotated translation of the *Wu Xing*, see Cook (2012, 485–520); the *Odes* are cited in passages 9, 10, 18, 19, 25, and 29 in that translation.

it presaged the full development of interlinear commentary in the Han dynasty.

Other than exegetical glosses, there was another kind of *shuo*-explanation. Storytelling was an important and, indeed, popular art of persuasion in the Warring States period. Typically, it took advantage of moral lessons and strategic wisdom from legends, recent events and purportedly historical anecdotes, but creative stories, even with animals and imaginary creatures as protagonists, were also commonly employed. The *Zhuangzi*, for instance, is not only celebrated for its many legendary fables but teems with historical episodes often at variance with competing versions in other contemporaneous texts.[43] The *Stratagems of the Warring States*, mentioned above, is another excellent example that is often overlooked in this regard.[44] Much like these two exemplary works of storytelling, the *Han Feizi* is also famous for its plethora of tales that morphed into proverbs still in use today. Though the logic of Han Fei's arguments did not rely on his stories to stand, their persuasive power would be seriously compromised if he was not allowed to cite them for support. Han Fei's alleged tales about recent history function much the same way as other thinkers' appeal to transmitted sayings and ancient texts.

Han Fei's rhetorical strategy was indeed one of his modes of commentary. In order to have effective stories at his disposal when arguing even in ink, he must have had a full arsenal of them. In the *Han Feizi*, there is one chapter entitled "Shuo lin" divided into two separate scrolls, and together they include seventy-two stories of various lengths.[45] It seems certain that

[43] For a study of Zhuangzi's use of animal metaphors to expound his philosophy, see Lo (2019).
[44] For an excellent translation, see Crump (1970).
[45] Again, for a recent study of the philosophy in the "Shuo lin," see Reeve (2003). As the author says in the abstract, his study aims to provide "a clear account of the content, rhetorical presentation, historical trajectory of the Shuo Lin. . . . [and] seeks to re-establish a lost pedagogical link between the Shuo Lin and its readers. . . ." (Reeve 2003, iii). The study includes a translation of the "Shuo lin" chapter.

they were meant to be employed whenever the appropriate occasion arose. Remarkably, there is another chapter entitled "Nan" 難 ("Rebuttals"), which is divided into four sub-chapters in our received version of the *Han Feizi*. Altogether, the "Nan" consists of thirty historical anecdotes about the permissive behaviors and judgments of the ruler-protagonists, with each tagged with a rebuttal in defense of authoritarian conduct befitting the ruler. This is virtually a record of rehearsals. Conceivably, the rebuttals themselves could be deemed as a form of commentary. As mentioned above, the *Gongyang* and *Guliang* are preoccupied with the praise and blame embedded in the subtle words of the historical accounts in the *Spring and Autumn Annals*; the "Nan" is not far off from this concern, although it was interested in neither rhetoric nor historiography.

Still, there is yet another chapter in the *Han Feizi* which was called "Chu shuo" 儲說 ("Repository of Stories"), but due to its inordinately large size (much longer than any other chapter in the book), our current editions of the text have six chapters all labeled "Chu Shuo" that contain 318 stories, with the vast majority being historical anecdotes. Interestingly, many of the stories are recorded in two or more variant versions. Such an archive of materials intended for disputation, while similar to the Mohist Canon documenting philosophical jargons for the same purpose, is certainly unique in the extant works from pre-Han times and betrays Han Fei's strategy of argumentation and mode of commentary. Indeed, all six chapters on "repositories of stories" share a bipartite structure of *jing* 經 (base text) and *shuo* (explanation). Han Fei's views on the art and craft of rulership are spelled out in the base text, and for every point made therein, one or more stories are referenced in the explanations, which were meant to be auto-commentary or self-annotation.[46] Evidently, Han Fei was

[46] Earlier, we have seen the citation of *Laozi*'s metaphor of the fish not leaving the deep and its interpretation in one of the chapters.

conscious of his role as a commentator. The base text (as few as only four words) is clear in meaning but too terse to reveal its full significance; moreover, its language is dull and lacks the punch to deliver a powerful impact on the audience. The illustrative stories often aim to strike fear into his supposed audience, as Han Fei is ever apt to warn them of the disastrous consequences of flouting his lessons. We may compare the bipartite structure in processual terms. The basic philosophical view is comparable to the structural sketch of a drawing of the subject with basic lines, while the illustrative stories are similar to the values added to the sketch that enliven the subject. The structure of the chapter is unique in the entire *Han Feizi* and should be deliberate in highlighting the points in the *jing*, which serves as an overview at the outset, and then justifying the succinct advice in the *shuo* in a separate section.

Apart from the chapters with storytelling as a mode of commentary, Han Fei actually put this art of persuasion into practice in the remaining chapters written in discursive essays. For instance, the "Er bing" 二柄 chapter ("Two Handles") begins with a gloss of *xing* 刑 (punishments) and *de* 德 (rewards), namely, the "two handles," and continues with a methodical analysis of their benefits and dire consequences, depending on whether the ruler or his subordinate is in control of them. Then it illustrates the disastrous regicide and loss of power of two rulers in recent history who had delegated the charge of the two handles to their ministers. The same structure of argumentation is repeated two more times to present a full account of the importance of the two handles in the charge of the ruler. Clearly, this is Han Fei's typical *modus operandi* in the majority of his argumentative essays, and its prototype can be found in the six chapters on a repository of stories that demonstrates the art of storytelling as argumentation.

IV. *Jie*: Expository Essays

While *jie* 解 gradually became one of the most common names for commentary after Han times, no commentaries or works of any genre in the Han were thus entitled, even as scholasticism began to surge after the second century BCE, insofar as extant literature shows. Prior to the Han, however, some form of exegesis was self-identified as *jie*, and the "Jie Lao" chapter in the *Han Feizi* is solid proof, but it was probably not the lone example. In the received version of the *Guanzi* 管子 from the Warring States, there are four chapters, each of which is paired with an explanatory chapter titled *jie*.[47] They are "Xingshi" 形勢 ("Conditions and Circumstances") and "Xingshi jie" 形勢解 ("Analysis of 'Xingshi'"),[48] "Lizheng" 立政 ("On Overseeing the Government"), and "Lizheng jiubai jie" 立政九敗解 ("Analysis of the Section on Nine Ways to Failure"),[49] "Banfa" 版法 and "Banfa jie" 版法解 ("Analysis of 'Banfa'"),[50] "Mingfa" 明法, and "Mingfa jie" 明法解 ("Analysis of 'Mingfa'").[51] Assuming that the "Xingshi," "Lizheng," "Banfa," and "Mingfa" were each composed by a single author during the Warring States, we do not know whether he also penned the explanatory chapters or someone else did. Nor is it certain when these explanatory chapters were included in the received *Guanzi*, if they were not original to the chapters they explained.[52] The four explanatory chapters share

[47] According to the original table of contents in the received *Guanzi*, there was yet another explanatory chapter called "Mumin jie" 牧民解 ("Analysis of 'Shepherding the People'"), but it was long lost.

[48] Rickett (1985, 58–90).

[49] Rickett (1985, 99–113).

[50] Rickett (1985, 136–147).

[51] Rickett (1998, 152–169).

[52] It is possible that Liu Xiang 劉向 (77–6 BCE) was responsible for pairing up the chapters when he edited the *Guanzi* around 26 BCE. It may be suspected that the term *jie* was not original to the "Jie Lao" chapter and/or the titles in *Guanzi* chapters. However, since there were not any written works of any kind in Han times that bore

a similar structure; they follow the order of the text in the chapter analyzed and typically break it down into meaningful segments of two or more lines, which are usually quoted at the end of the analysis. The full texts of the original chapters are analyzed except for the "Lizheng jiubai jie," which explicates only one of the "nine ways to failure" ("Jiubai" 九敗) in the "Lizheng." No semantic glosses are given, and the analyses are faithful to the original texts. Notably, most of the analyses are comparable in length to and often longer than the stories found in the *Han Feizi*. Indeed, they may be considered short essays. Since the analyses follow the order of the original texts, they share their coherent logic as well, if it is present

the title of *jie*, it does not make sense for Liu Xiang to make it up and attribute it to the *Han Feizi* and *Guanzi* chapters in question. He simply did not have a model to make up a new genre of commentary presented in these chapters. On the other hand, in the "Treatise on Literature" in the *Hanshu* Liu Xiang listed a work called *Zhou shu* (*Book of Zhou*) in 71 *pian*, which is mentioned earlier in this chapter. Fifty-nine of those *pian* are still extant, and in each one the title ends with the term *jie* 解. They are not commentary at all, and their narrative structure is completely different from those of the *Han Feizi* and *Guanzi* chapters. The date and composition of the *Zhou shu*, which is now called *Yi Zhou shu* 逸周書, is rather complicated. Edward Shaughnessy summarizes scholarly consensus:

> Although there is no discernible organisation of the text, in which there is a considerable number of lacunae, it has been demonstrated that 32 of these *pian* are remarkably consistent in both language and thought, and should be regarded as the basic core of the text . . . The first of these was the composition, probably by a single hand, in the late 4th or early 3rd century B.C. of the 32 "core" *pian*. Not only do these *pian* display linguistic and intellectual features that are characteristic of this period; but the extant *Zhou shu* is also quoted in texts such as the *Zuo zhuan*, *Han Feizi*, *Lüshi chunqiu* and *Zhanguo ce*. Two important considerations are that all the passages that are thus quoted derive from the "core" *pian*, and that at least the last three works uniformly attribute the passages to a *Zhou shu*. This demonstrates both that the texts were already in existence by the third century B.C., and also that they had already been collected into an integral unit. (Loewe 1993, 229–230. Wade-Giles romanization is converted to *pinyin*.)

Insofar as we know, Liu Xiang's knowledge of *jie* as a writing strategy from Warring States times would come from works such as the *Zhou shu* if we eliminate the possibility of the *Han Feizi* and *Guanzi* chapters. If he had to rely on the Warring States commentaries to make up a name, his best candidate would be *shuo*, as it resembles *jie* in some aspects but is too short to look like an essay. Moreover, it does not make sense that Liu Xiang did not add *jie* to the title of other *Guanzi* chapters such as "Xinshu" which share the same expository structure (see below). In fine, there is good reason to believe that the term *jie* was original to the *Han Feizi* and *Guanzi* chapters.

in the first place.[53] Thus, the short essays together naturally form an essay of considerable length. In this peculiar sense, *jie* may be rightfully called expository essays. This is markedly different from the story-based explanation in the *Han Feizi.* In this connection, the "Banfa jie" chapter is different from the other three chapters because it concludes its elucidation with an interpretive lesson that includes a dialogue between Duke Huan of Qi and Guan Zhong 管仲 (the putative author of *Guanzi*). The dialogue itself resembles the illustrative stories in the *Han Feizi* chapters discussed above.

The four explanatory chapters in the *Guanzi* have not received much attention for their philosophical contents or their format of expression in modern scholarship. In contrast, another chapter titled "Xinshu" 心術 ("Art of the Mind") has been a focus for scholars of early Daoism, as it offers important insights into self-cultivation.[54] However, its expository structure is usually overlooked. Although there is no explicit marker, the chapter clearly contains a bipartite structure of base text and expository essay. Let us examine a sample from the text in Rickett's translation ("Statement" refers to what I call the "base text"):

[Statement I]

In the body, the mind holds the position of prince. The
functions of the nine apertures resemble the separate officials.
If the mind is at rest in the Way,
The nine apertures will function properly.
Should lust and desire occupy it to the full,
The eyes will not see colors; the ears will not hear sounds.
Therefore it is said:
"If the person on high departs from the Way,
Those below will be lax in their work."[55]

[53] The nine ways to failure do not follow any particular order; there is no inherent logic.
[54] See Reid (2019).
[55] Rickett (1998, 71).

[Explanation I]

> "In the body, the mind holds the position of prince. The functions of the nine apertures resemble the separate officials." The ears and eyes are the sense organs for seeing and hearing. If the mind does not interfere with the activities of seeing and hearing, the sense organs will be able to maintain their separate functions. Now if a person's mind is filled with desires, his eyes will not see when things pass by, nor will his ears hear when there are sounds. Therefore the statement says: "If the person on high departs from the Way, those below will be lax in their work." Hence it is said: "The art of mind lies in controlling the apertures through nonassertiveness." Consequently, the statement refers to it as "prince."[56]

Again, we do not know if the base text and the explanations came from the same hand, but since the explanations quote the base text, there is good reason to believe that they were penned by someone other than the author of the base text, or at least that the two parts were originally separate entities. As this bipartite structure is identical to the four explanatory chapters of the *Guanzi*—the explanations follow the order of the base text and elucidate the key terms in each segment and their philosophical significance to form a brief essay—the explanation embedded in the "Art of the Mind" should be recognized as *jie* (expository essay) as well. *Jie* seeks to understand a text without reference to matters beyond its parameters; it aims at the intrinsic meaning of a text and represents an intratextual mode of explanation much like what Mencius called "meeting the intention of the poet with sympathetic understanding," neither is intent on extrapolating from the text explained.

Although the exact date of *Guanzi*'s composition is unknown, scholarly consensus considers it a collection of works on Huang-Lao Daoism by various thinkers at the Jixia Academy in the state of Qi in the mid-Warring States period (350–256 BCE).[57] In

[56] Rickett (1998, 75).
[57] See Rickett (1993) and Roth (2004, 18–22).

comparison, Han Fei, who allegedly died in 235 BCE, came later, and indeed much of the *Han Feizi* text was heavily influenced by Huang-Lao Daoism.[58] Yet, it should be noted that the well-known "Jie Lao" chapter explaining the *Laozi* might even have borrowed its format of expression, including its title, from texts like the explanatory chapters of the *Guanzi*. The explanation of the first line of Chapter 38 of the *Laozi* in the "Jie Lao," for instance, reads as follows:

> Virtue involves what is internal. Possession involves what is external. "One with highest virtue does not possess virtue" means that one's spirit is not drawn out by external things. When one's spirit is not drawn out by external things, then one's self is kept whole. For one's self to be kept whole is called virtue. Thus, virtue is tantamount to possessing one's own self. In every case of virtue, one collects it by means of non-action, completes it by means of non-desiring, secures it by means of non-thinking, and solidifies it by means of non-use. If one acts on it and desires it, then virtue will have no place to lodge. If virtue has no place to lodge, then it will not be whole. If one uses it and thinks about it, then it will not be solid. If it is not solid, then it will lack achievements. This lack of achievements arises from taking virtue as a possession. Thus, if one takes virtue as a possession, then one lacks virtue. And if one does not take virtue as a possession, then one has virtue. And so the text says, "One with highest virtue does not possess virtue, and thereby has virtue."
>
> The reason to value non-action and no-thought for achieving emptiness is that in such conditions one's considerations are unconfined. A person who lacks the right technique will intentionally try to use non-action and no-thought in order to become empty. If one intentionally tries to use non-action and no-thought in order to become empty, then in one's considerations one never

[58] Goldin (2013, 14–18).

> forgets emptiness, and so one winds up confined by trying to be empty. Emptiness means that one's considerations are unconfined. So now if one is confined by trying to be empty, then this is not true emptiness. In the non-action involved in becoming empty, one does not take non-action as a constant tenet. If one does not take non-action as a constant tenet, then one becomes empty, and if one is empty, then one's virtue flourishes. When one's virtue flourishes, this is called the highest virtue. And so the text says, "One with highest virtue takes no action, but leaves nothing undone." (JL §1, pp. 36–38, in this volume)

This is one of the best examples of *jie*-exegesis as an expository essay. Here, not only is the explanation for each of the lines a standalone short essay that is logical and coherent in itself, but the two essays are seamlessly integrated into one, relating the ideas in each line philosophically in a way that is immediately apparent in the *Laozi*. It should be noted that the opening explanation of "virtue" is philosophical rather than philological (as in Mencius' glossing of ancient words). Indeed, the entire commentary is philosophical and analytical in nature. Like the *Guanzi*'s *jie*-analyses, the "Jie Lao" also employs the intratextual mode of interpretation.

None of the expository essays in the *Guanzi* cites any historical tales or refers to any transmitted sayings, and the "Jie Lao" chapter overall is faithful to this characteristic but with a slight variation (see below). The "Jie Lao" chapter contains thirty-two citations from the *Laozi* along with the author's explanations, and they are grouped into twelve sections in this volume. The explanations mainly aim at a philosophical analysis of the concepts and keywords in the *Laozi* citations, as shown in the example above. While purely semantic gloss is absent, occasionally philosophical annotations are added to remarks on semantics. In Section 3, for instance, the explanation first focuses on the semantic meaning of the word *di* 柢 ("base") in the *Laozi* text but then elaborates on its significance for self-cultivation.

V. *Yu*: Illustrative Stories

The mode of exegesis was not unitary in the "Jie Lao"; the story of Zhan He (JL §1, pp. 42–43) and a mythical account (JL §6, pp. 61–63) were used for illustration. Still, there is another exception of a different nature (JL §10, p. 70) that comprises only a single quotation from the Duke of Zhou to help elaborate the *Laozi* text. As such, it resembles the quotation of transmitted sayings. Few as they were, these exceptions show that either *jie* as a mode of exegesis was not yet carved in stone or Han Fei was not interested in abiding by the customary practice.

In contrast, illustrative stories characterize the mode of expression in the "Yu Lao." Originally, *yu* 喻 was used as a verb that means "to make it clear" or "to be clear about," and only much later did it also become a noun that means "analogy." Thus, the title of the chapter literally means "to make the [meanings] of the *Laozi* clear"; it is only because most of the *Laozi* quotations were explained with an illustrative story that *yu* may be considered a figure of speech in this context. Divided into twelve sections in the translation in this volume, the "Yu Lao" chapter explicates twenty-two quotations from the *Laozi* and all but three use historical stories for illustration (the beginning and the end of YL Section 1 and the beginning of YL Section 9). YL Section 6 presents a typical example which features two historical lessons, but only one of them is cited below, due to space constraints:

> Duke Xian of Jin was trying to use the jade disk of Chuiji to borrow passage through the state of Yu to attack the state of Guo. Grand minister Gong Zhiqi remonstrated with the ruler, saying, "This is not to be allowed. If the lips perish, the teeth will grow cold. For Yu and Guo to save each other is not a matter of treating one another virtuously. If Jin destroys Guo today, then tomorrow Yu will surely follow it in perishing." The lord of Yu did not heed him, but rather accepted the jade disk and lent them

> passage. After Jin had already taken Guo, then on the way back it destroyed Yu. [Gong Zhiqi was] struggling against what was still "in the pores of the skin," but [Duke Xian] disregarded [him]. That being the case, . . . Gong Zhiqi [was] the Bian Que for . . . Yu, but [Duke Xian] did not heed [him] . . . and Yu thereby perished. And so the text says, "That which is secure is easy to maintain. That which has not yet become manifest is easy to strategize against." (YL §6, p. 95–96)

Evidently, the story itself had nothing to do with *Laozi* 64 cited in our example, but read through Han Fei's interpretive lens, it was charmed with the extrapolative power to enliven a piece of mundane advice. The interpretation, extratextual as it is, was not about the intrinsic meaning of *Laozi* 64. It has a bipartite structure of story and quotation, and the two illustrative stories, which are compared to the story of the physician Bian Que that immediately precedes them, are the interpretation itself. There are thirteen similar cases in the "Yu Lao" chapter. The clarifications in the remainder of the chapter contain a tripartite structure of three kinds: (1) story + explanation of story + quote (2 cases); (2) thesis statement + quote + story (3 cases); (3) thesis statement + story + quote (1 case). In all cases, although the thesis statements clarify the *Laozi* quotations, they by no means constitute a continuous narrative, even if they are not broken up by illustrative stories. Moreover, some of the clarifications do not even have a thesis statement at all, while the majority of the individual clarifications were too short to form even a mini essay. Section 1 presents a good example:

> The lord of Yu desired the horse team of Quchan and the jade disk of Chuiji, but did not listen to Gong Zhiqi, and so his state perished and he himself died. And so the text says, "Of faults, none is more agonizing than desiring gain." (YL §1, p. 85)

Thus, the clarifications in the "Yu Lao" are not expository essays such as discussed above regarding the "Jie Lao," but they resembled *shuo* in that they also employed illustrative stories. In this regard, the "Yu Lao" aligns itself with the six *Han Feizi* chapters constituting a repository of stories and differentiates its mode of explanation from the philosophical exegesis in the "Jie Lao."

VI. Concluding Remarks

As an expression of opinion or explanation about an event or a situation, commentary must have been part of humanity since time immemorial. It need not take on any definite form, nor must it be written down. As early as the *Odes*, voices from different strata of society were preserved in writing; many of the songs in the collection reflected grievances about the cruelty of government and lamentations over the adversities of life. They were commentaries of sorts voiced without the conscious notion of commentary. The conscious practice of commentary probably began in the Spring and Autumn period and became diversified during the Warring States era. Naturally, no definitive form or mode of expression had yet to emerge then. Indeed, there was not yet a consensual notion of commentary. Quoting from received wisdom and historical lessons in the form of transmitted sayings was one of the earliest and most popular ways of justifying personal persuasions or illustrating arguments. Quotations could be deployed freely and placed anywhere in a text as its author saw fit; there was no particular convention for appropriation. In comparison, *shuo* (explanation) and *jie* (expository essay) came later and apparently were not as widely employed. Both were distinct modes of *textual* exegesis and could be considered as a genre in their own right. This suggests that their practitioners were keenly aware of a meta-concept of commentary. Indeed, *shuo*/*yu* and *jie* should be considered two prototypes for various types of commentary developed in later times. On the micro-level of semantics, textual glosses and self-annotations were in use during the Warring States; they were predecessors of interlinear commentary with philological glosses common in the Han dynasty.

As far as terminology is concerned, it appears that few commentaries if any in the Former Han period were called *jie* in extant sources. The only known, albeit no longer extant, examples were two commentaries on the *Documents* called *jiegu* (*Shangshu jiegu* 尚書解故, "Adjudicating Ancient Words in the *Documents*") composed by Xiahou Sheng 夏侯勝 and his cousin Xiahou Jian 夏侯建 from the early first century BCE. But *jiegu* is not the same as *jie* per se. While *jie* denotes the sense of dissecting, it also connotes the idea of differentiation, analysis, and adjudication, and in the practice of commentary during Han times, adjudication was instrumental. For instance, *jiegu*, literally, "to adjudicate the meaning of ancient words with contemporary ones," was predicated on multiple possible readings of the same word—a practice already evident in the *Mencius*. This partly explains why the same word in the same context could be understood differently by Han exegetes as they were trying to decipher ancient-style graphs no longer in use in their times.[59] The title *jiegu* suggests that the commentary was not philosophical in nature, unlike the "Jie Lao" chapter of the *Han Feizi*. This seems to be characteristic of *jiegu* exegesis in the Han; unfortunately, no such work is extant today. However, in He Yan's 何晏 (d. 249) *Lunyu jijie* 論語集解 (*Collected Explanations on the Analects*), hundreds of snippets of commentaries by Han exegetes are quoted, and the vast majority are philological glosses. Except for Bao Xian's 包咸 (6 BCE–65 CE) *Lunyu zhangju* 論語章句 (*The Analects in Sections and Sentences*),[60] we only know the names of

[59] Lo (2020a, 194).

[60] For a comparison between the *jie* commentary and *zhangju* commentary, see Lo (2020a, 189, 193–194).

the exegetes but not the titles of their quoted commentaries. Thus, we cannot ascertain if the quoted commentaries were entitled *jie*, but their mode of exegesis was definitely intratextual. Meanwhile, Wang Su 王肅 (195–256), a contemporary of He Yan, composed a *jie* commentary on the *Classic of Filial Devotion*. There were also *jie* commentaries on the *Spring and Autumn Annals* and even one brief *jie* (*lüejie* 略解) on a lexicon called *Xiao Erya* 小爾雅 (*Little Erya*) in the next few centuries after the Han. None of these is extant. It seems that the nature of *jie* had changed over time. It should be noted, however, Su Zhe 蘇轍 (1039–1112) wrote a well-known *Laozi jie* 老子解 (*Explanations of Laozi*), the first of several *Laozi* commentaries that self-identified as *jie* since the Han dynasty; it resembles the "Jie Lao" in some respects with philosophical glosses and creative interpretations that attempt to integrate the Confucian doctrine of the Mean and Chan Buddhist idea of Buddha nature with the Daoist Way.

Based on extant records, *shuo* was clearly a popular mode of interpretation in the Han. Except for the *Spring and Autumn Annals*, the Five Confucian Classics as well as the *Analects* and the *Classic of Filial Devotion* all had *shuo* commentaries. Even the *Laozi* also boasted three; two were called *jingshuo* 經說 ("base text and explanations") and one simply *shuo*.[61] Unfortunately, none survives today. But it is probable that the bipartite structure of *jingshuo* was identical to the Mohist Canon and the *Guanzi* explanatory chapters. As mentioned, no later than Mencius, *shuo* was already a common practice of interpretive poetics and there were at least two *shuo* commentaries on the *Odes*, one each from the Qi tradition and Lu tradition, two of the three major traditions of *Odes* in the early Han. It seems evident that *shuo* was distinct from philological exegesis of the *Odes*. Apart from the vast majority of philological exegesis, He Yan's *Lunyu jijie* also included a small number of philosophical explanations and remarks, which he collectively

[61] See the "Treatise on Literature" in the *Hanshu*: Ban (2002, 3:1729).

called *yishuo* 義說 ("elucidation of significance"), and many of them came from his own hands.[62] As He called his work "collected explanations," philological exegesis and philosophical interpretation were, in effect, conflated together into *jie* commentary. Indeed, this had become the standard mode of interpretation ever since.

The influence of the "Jie Lao" and "Yu Lao" in the *Han Feizi* on the commentarial practice in early Han times was profound yet hidden from modern scholarship. To begin with, Han Fei's repositories of illustrative stories offer an important clue to the evolution of *shuo* commentary in the Han. Plausibly, it inspired Liu Xiang's 劉向 (77–6 BCE) compilation of his famous *Shuoyuan* 說苑 (Garden of Persuasions) consisting of nearly 700 stories, whose purpose was to edify and warn the emperor of foolish and unethical actions. The stories are classified under twenty different topics, but two of them, respectively titled "Tancong" 談叢 ("Clusters of Talks") and "Zayan" 雜言 ("Miscellaneous Aphorisms"), were actually mere collections of stories and sayings with little in common. These exceptional chapters appear to be a cache of aphorisms, tales, and anecdotes that had yet to be designated for a particular purpose and thus resemble the "Forest of Stories" in the *Han Feizi*. In fact, some of the stories in the *Shuoyuan* were similar to those in Han Fei's repositories and might even share the same source with them (see below). As is well known, Warring States philosophical works were classified into ten schools of thought in the "Treatise on Literature" in the *Hanshu*, and one of them, deemed of least significance, was called "Xiaoshuo jia" 小說家 ("School of Small Talks"). The person responsible for such classification was none other than Liu Xiang himself. Whether or not the classification reflected historical reality, the identification of "philosophers of small talks" betrayed Liu's insight into the common practice of making arguments by way of storytelling in the Warring States. Last

[62] For a discussion of He Yan's philosophical interpretation of the *Analects*, see Lo (2020a, 197–205) and Makeham (2004, 23–75).

but not least, Liu Xiang was also the author of one of the three *shuo* commentaries on the *Laozi* mentioned above.

As discussed at the outset, *zhuan* was probably not a proper name for commentary in the Warring States period and only became so in the early Han. In fact, it was further differentiated into *neizhuan* 內傳 ("inner commentary") and *waizhuan* 外傳 ("outer commentary"), its new development. In essence, the former was philological while the latter was interpretive.[63] Han Ying had written an inner commentary and an outer commentary on the *Odes*, which were meant to complement each other. While only fragments of the former survive, the latter still exists in ten scrolls. Typically, each of the chapters in the *Outer Commentary* comprises a transmitted saying and/or an illustrative story as well as two or more lines from one or more songs from the *Odes*. The transmitted saying might come from a titled work or might be identifiable today such as the *Laozi*. It is natural to assume that the *Outer Commentary* aims to interpret the *Odes* as its companion did;[64] thus, the illustrative stories naturally were meant to tease out the intrinsic meanings of the quoted odes. In some cases, this assumption could indeed be sustained. However, it should be noted that the odes were routinely quoted out of context and only in excerpts. Moreover, some of the quoted lines were identical and appeared in different chapters in the *Outer Commentary*, yet they were interpreted differently and illustrated with different stories. It is hard to imagine that the *Outer Commentary*, on the whole, intends to explicate the *Odes* itself. On the other hand, it makes good sense to read it fundamentally as a reverse commentary such that the quoted odes were actually meant to capture the essence or spirit of the accompanying stories

[63] Outer Commentaries were also written for the *Gongyang* and *Guliang*. This seems to suggest that the *Gongyang zhuan* and *Guliang zhuan* were meant to be inner commentaries that aimed to fathom the intrinsic meanings of the *Spring and Autumn Annals*.

[64] For a brief comparison of the *Inner Commentary* and the *Outer Commentary*, see Lao (2010, 37–40).

or transmitted sayings, but it was not uniformly so, much like the aberrations in the "Jie Lao" and "Yu Lao" chapters. Let us read one example from the *Outer Commentary*:

> Of old Sicheng Zihan was minister to [the ruler] of Song. He said to the Prince of Song, "Now the peace of a state and the governance of its people depend on the conduct of the ruler. Titles and rewards are what people like. May your Highness take charge of them. Executions and punishments are what the people hate. Let me be responsible for them."
>
> The Prince said, "Agreed. I will get the approval and you will receive their hatred. I am convinced that I will not be the laughing-stock of the feudal lords."
>
> When the people of the state knew that the punishments of death and decapitation were entirely in the hands of Zihan, the great ministers were friendly with him and the common people feared him. Before the year was out, Zihan had driven out the Prince of Song and taken over the government himself. Just as the *Laozi* says,
>
> "It is best to leave the fish down in the pool;
> Best to leave the State's sharpest weapons where none can see them."
>
> The Ode says,
>
> "But why does he call to action.
> Without coming and consulting with us?"[65]

Interestingly, the story of Zihan also appears as a *shuo* commentary in the "Outer Repository" chapter ("Waichu shuo you xia") of the *Han Feizi* to exemplify the warning in the *jing* ("Statements") that

[65] Translation from Hightower (1952, 234). Wade-Giles romanization is converted to *pinyin*. The same story was also recorded in the "Jundao" 君道 ("The Way of the Ruler") chapter of the *Shuoyuan*.

precedes it, rather than illustrate any text.[66] The warning says: "[If the ruler] shares [the power of] giving rewards and penalties with his ministers, proscriptions and orders will not be observed." Clearly, the story explains the same idea. In comparison, the *Outer Commentary* shares the same bipartite *jing-shuo* structure, only in reverse order.

Here in the *Outer Commentary*, both the *Laozi* (Chapter 36) and the *Odes* are cited, and the story can be said to illustrate either text in the mode of extratextual interpretation. However, it is also possible to argue that both texts serve to illuminate the essence of the story in the mode of intratextual interpretation. To be sure, it is entirely convincing to interpret *Laozi* 36 as the *Outer Commentary* does, but reading the same interpretation into the lines of the ode certainly requires a stretch of imagination. It is this kind of extratextual interpretation that characterizes the *Outer Commentary* on the whole—the same mode of explanation in the "Yu Lao" chapter of the *Han Feizi*. On the other hand, the intratextual mode of exegesis that characterizes inner commentary was consistent with the analytical explanations of the "Jie Lao" chapter that aimed at the intrinsic meanings of the *Laozi*. Viewed in such light, we may conclude that the "Jie Lao" and "Yu Lao" foreshadowed the full-fledged development of the modes of intratextual and extratextual interpretation in the early Han.[67] Perhaps this is how the human psyche is always equipped to map out the unknown world and make the best of it for self-interest.

[66] In two other explanatory chapters on the repository ("Waichu shuo xia"), *Laozi* 36 was cited to substantiate the idea that the ruler cannot afford to delegate power and authority to the ministers.

[67] *Yu* was never used again in the title of native Chinese commentary since the *Han Feizi* although stories continued to be used in Confucian teaching and lectures. It was routinely practiced in Buddhist sermons, and many translated Buddhist scriptures had *yu* or *piyu* 譬喻 (parables) in their titles such as *Bai yu jing* 百喻經 (Scripture on One Hundred Parables) and *Piyu jing* 譬喻經 (Scriptures of Parables).

Glossary

In order to assist readers in understanding how the terminology of the present translations relates to that of other translations (both for the "Jie Lao" and "Yu Lao," as well as other Chinese texts), below is a list of some of the most important concepts that appear in the "Jie Lao" and "Yu Lao," the translations that are used for them here, and renderings that readers may encounter elsewhere.

Chinese term		Translation here	Alternate translations
dao	道	(the) Way	path, course
de	德	virtue	excellence, favor, force, power, potency
jing	精	energy	(vital) essence, semen
junzi	君子	gentleman, prince	noble man, superior person
li	理	governing order, proper order	pattern, principle, coherence
li	禮	ritual	courtesy, manners, propriety, rites
qi	氣	[left untranslated]	energy, ether, pneuma
qing	情	essence	dispositions, emotions, feelings, (natural) inclinations
ren	仁	humaneness	authoritative conduct/person, benevolence, goodness, (co-) humanity, kind-heartedness
shen	神	spirit(s)	divinity/divinities, god(s), miraculous
sheng	聖	sage	saint, saintly man

Chinese term		Translation here	Alternate translations
shi	勢	authoritative power	circumstances, positional advantage/power
shi	士	well-bred man	knight, scholar, scholar-official
shu	術	technique(s)	art(s), craft(s), method(s), skill(s)
tian	天	Heaven	Nature, sky
wuwei	無為	non-action	effortless/non-assertive/non-purposive action, not striving
xin	心	heart	heart-mind, mind
xu	虛	emptiness	openness, receptiveness, vacuity
yi	義	appropriateness	duty, justice, morality, norms, righteousness
ziran	自然	so of itself/themselves	natural, naturally so, naturalness, spontaneous

References

Allan, Sarah. 1997. *The Way of Water and Sprouts of Virtue*. Albany: SUNY Press.

Ban, Gu 班固. 2002 (2nd century CE). *Hanshu* 漢書. Beijing: Zhonghua shuju.

Bárcenas, Alejandro. 2012. "Xunzi and Han Fei on Human Nature." *International Philosophical Quarterly* 52 (2): 135–148.

Berkson, Mark. 2016. "Xunzi as a Theorist and Defender of Ritual." In *Dao Companion to the Philosophy of Xunzi*, edited by Eric L. Hutton, 229–267. Dordrecht: Springer.

Bokenkamp, Stephen R., ed. 1997. *Early Daoist Scriptures*. Berkeley: University of California Press.

Brown, Miranda. 2013. "Mozi's Remaking of Ancient Authority." In *The Mozi as an Evolving Text: Different Voices in Early Chinese Thought*, edited by Carine Defoort and Nicolas Standaert, 143–174. Leiden and Boston: Brill.

Chan, Alan K. L. 1991a. "The Formation of the Heshang Gong Legend." In *Sages and Filial Sons: Mythology and Archaeology in Ancient China*, edited by Julia Ching and R. W. L. Guisso, 101–134. Hong Kong: Chinese University Press.

Chan, Alan K. L. 1991b. *Two Visions of the Way: A Study of the Wang Pi and Ho-shang Kung Commentaries on the Lao-tzu*. Albany: SUNY Press.

Chan, Wing-tsit. 1963. *A Source Book in Chinese Philosophy*. Princeton: Princeton University Press.

Chen, Guying 陳鼓應, ed. 2003. *Laozi zhuyi ji pingjie* 老子注譯及評介. Beijing: Zhonghua shuju.

Chen, Ming 陈明, and Wang Qing王青. 2008. *Hanfeizi quanyi* 韩非子全译. Chengdu: Bashu shushe.

Chen, Qitian 陳啟天. 1969. *Zengding Hanfeizi jiaoshi* 增訂韓非子校釋. Taibei: Taiwan shangwu yinshuguan.

Chen, Qiyou 陳奇猷. 1974. *Han Feizi jishi* 韓非子集釋. Shanghai: Shanghai renmin chubanshe.

Chen, Qiyou. 2000. *Hanfeizi xin jiaozhu* 韓非子新校注. Shanghai: Shanghai guji chubanshe.

Cheng, Anne. 1993. "*Ch'un ch'iu* 春秋, *Kung yang* 公羊, *Ku liang* 穀梁 and *Tso chuan* 左傳." In *Early Chinese Texts: A Bibliographical Guide*, edited by Michael Loewe, 67–76. Berkeley: Society for the Study of Early China and Institute of East Asian Studies.

Cleary, Thomas. 2009. *The Way of the World: Readings in Chinese Philosophy*. Boston: Shambhala Publications.

Cook, Scott, tr. 2012. *The Bamboo Texts of Guodian: A Study and Complete Translation*. Ithaca: Cornell University Press.

Creel, Herrlee G. 1970. "On Two Aspects in Early Taoism." In *What Is Taoism? And Other Studies in Chinese Cultural History*, 37–47. Chicago: University of Chicago Press.

Creel, Herrlee G. 1974. *Shen Pu-Hai: A Chinese Political Philosopher of the Fourth Century B. C.* Chicago: University of Chicago Press.

Crump, J. I., tr. 1970. *Chan-Kuo T'se*. Oxford: Clarendon Press.

Csikszentmihalyi, Mark. 2004. *Material Virtue: Ethics and the Body in Early China*. Leiden and Boston: Brill.

Csikszentmihalyi, Mark, ed. and tr. 2006. *Readings in Han Chinese Thought*. Indianapolis: Hackett Publishing.

Csikszentmihalyi, Mark. 2015. "Thematic Analyses of the *Laozi*." In *Dao Companion to Daoist Philosophy*, edited by Xiaogan Liu, 47–70. Dordrecht: Springer.

Cua, Antonio S. 2005 (1984). "Ethical Uses of the Past." In *Human Nature, Ritual, and History: Studies in Xunzi and Chinese Philosophy*, 73–98. Washington, DC: The Catholic University of America Press.

Denecke, Wiebke. 2011. *The Dynamics of Masters Literature: Early Chinese Thought from Confucius to Han Feizi*. Cambridge, MA: Harvard University Press.

Duan, Yucai 段玉裁. 2000 (1815). *Shuowenjiezi zhu* 說文解字注. Shanghai: Shanghai guji chubanshe.

Durrant, Stephen, Wai-yee Li, and David Schaberg, trans. 2016. *Zuo Tradition/Zuozhuan: Commentary on the "Spring and Autumn Annals."* Seattle: University of Washington Press.

Flanagan, Owen, and Jing Hu. 2011. "Han Fei Zi's Philosophical Psychology: Human Nature, Scarcity, and the Neo-Darwinian Consensus." *Journal of Chinese Philosophy* 38 (2): 293–316.

Fung, Yiu-ming 馮耀明. 2020. "Reason (*Gu* 故) and Principle (*Li* 理)." In *Dao Companion to Chinese Philosophy of Logic*, edited by Yiu-ming Fung, 181–202. Cham, Switzerland: Springer.

Galvany, Albert. 2013. "Beyond the Rule of Rules: The Foundations of Sovereign Power in the *Han Feizi*." In *Dao Companion to the Philosophy of Han Fei*, edited by Paul R. Goldin, 87–106. Dordrecht: Springer.

Gao, Huaping 高华平, Qizhou Wang 王齐洲, and Sanxi Zhang 张三夕. 2015. *Hanfeizi* 韩非子. Beijing: Zhonghua shuju.

Goldin, Paul R. 2005. "The Reception of the *Odes* in the Warring States Era." In *After Confucius: Studies in Early Chinese Philosophy*, 19–35. Honolulu: University of Hawaii Press.

Goldin, Paul R. 2013. "Introduction: Han Fei and the *Han Feizi*." In *Dao Companion to the Philosophy of Han Fei*, edited by Paul R. Goldin, 1–21. Dordrecht: Springer.

Guo, Qingfan 郭慶藩. 1985 (1894). *Zhuangzi jishi* 莊子集釋. Beijing: Zhonghua shuju.

Harbsmeier, Christoph, tr. 2025. *Han Feizi: The Art of Statecraft in Early China.* Leiden & Boston: Brill.

Harris, Eirik Lang. 2011. "Is the Law in the Way? On the Source of Han Fei's Laws." *Journal of Chinese Philosophy* 38 (1): 73–87.

Harris, Eirik Lang. 2013. "Han Fei on the Problem of Morality." In *Dao Companion to the Philosophy of Han Fei*, edited by Paul R. Goldin, 107–131. Dordrecht: Springer.

Harris, Eirik Lang, tr. 2023. "Han Feizi." In *Readings in Classical Chinese Philosophy*, 3rd ed., edited by Philip J. Ivanhoe, and Bryan W. Van Norden, 323–381. Indianapolis: Hackett Publishing.

Harris, Eirik Lang. 2024. "Morality vs. Impartial Standards in the *Shenzi Fragments.*" In *Dao Companion to China's* Fa *Tradition: The Philosophy of Governance by Impartial Standards*, edited by Yuri Pines, 83–97. Cham, Switzerland: Springer.

Harris, Eirik Lang. 2025. "The *Dao* of Han Fei." In *The Oxford Handbook of Chinese Philosophy*, edited by Justin Tiwald. Oxford: Oxford University Press.

Hendrischke, Barbara. 2007. "Han Fei's Reading of *Lao Zi* 38." In *Zurück zur Freude: Studien zur chinesischen Literatur und Lebenswelt und ihrer Rezeption in Ost und West: Festschrift für Wolfgang Kubin*, edited by Marc Hermann, Christian Schwermann, and Jari Grosse-Ruyken, 127–154. London: Routledge.

Hendrischke, Barbara. 2022. "The Commentarial Strategies of 'Jie Lao' (Explaining the *Laozi*)." *Monumenta Serica* 70 (1): 71–98.

Henricks, Robert G., tr. 1989. *Lao-Tzu: Te Tao Ching.* New York: Ballantine Books.

Henricks, Robert G., tr. 2000. *Lao Tzu's* Tao Te Ching: *A Translation of the Startling New Documents Found at Guodian.* New York: Columbia University Press.

Henry, Eric, tr. 2021. *Garden of Eloquence / Shuoyuan by Liu Xiang.* Seattle: University of Washington Press.

Hightower, James Robert, tr. 1952. *Han Shih Wai Chuan: Han Ying's Illustrations of the Didactic Application of the Classic of Songs.* Cambridge, MA: Harvard University Press.

Hu, Shi 胡適. 1961. *Zhongguo gudai zhexueshi* 中國古代哲學史. Taibei: Taiwan shangwu yinshuguan.

Huang, Chun-chieh. 2001. "Mencius's Hermeneutics of Classics." *Dao* 1 (1): 15–29.

Hutton, Eric L., tr. 2014. *Xunzi: The Complete Text.* Princeton: Princeton University Press.

Ivanhoe, Philip J., tr. 2003. *The Daodejing of Laozi*. Indianapolis: Hackett Publishing.

Ivanhoe, Philip J. 2011. "Hanfeizi and Moral Self-Cultivation." *Journal of Chinese Philosophy* 38 (1): 31–45.

Johnston, Ian, tr. 2010. *The Mozi: A Complete Translation*. Hong Kong: Chinese University of Hong Kong.

Kern, Martin. 2016. "Style and Poetic Diction in the *Xunzi*." In *Dao Companion to the Philosophy of Xunzi*, edited by Eric L. Hutton, 1–33. Dordrecht: Springer.

Kim, Tae Hyun. 2010. "Other *Laozi* Parallels in the *Hanfeizi*: An Alternative Approach to the Textual History of the *Laozi* and Early Chinese Thought." *Sino-Platonic Papers* 199.

Knoblock, John, and Jeffrey Riegel, tr. 2000. *The Annals of Lü Buwei: A Complete Translation and Study*. Stanford: Stanford University Press.

Lai, Yanyuan 賴炎元, and Fu Wuguang 傅武光. 1997. *Xinyi Han Feizi* 新譯韓非子. Taibei: Sanmin Shuju.

Lao, Yueqiang 勞悅強 (Lo Yuet Keung). 2010. *Wennei wenwai: Zhongguo sixiangshi zhong de jingdian quanshi* 文內文外——中國思想史中的經典詮釋 (*Intratextual and Extratextual: The Interpretation of Classics in Chinese Intellectual History*). Taibei: Taiwan University Press.

Lau, D. C., tr. 1963. *Tao Te Ching*. Baltimore: Penguin Books.

Lau, D. C., tr. 1984 (1970). *Mencius*. Harmondsworth: Penguin Books.

Liao, W.K., tr. 1939. *The Complete Works of Han Fei Tzŭ: A Classic of Chinese Legalism*. London: A. Probsthain.

Liu, Xiaogan 劉笑敢. 2006. *Laozi gujin* 老子古今. Beijing: Zhongguo shehui kexue chubanshe.

Liu, Xiaogan 劉笑敢. 2015. "Laozi's Philosophy: Textual and Conceptual Analyses." In *Dao Companion to Daoist Philosophy*, edited by Xiaogan Liu, 71–100. Dordrecht: Springer.

Lo, Yuet Keung. 2019. "It's A Jungle Out There: Zhuangzi and the Rhetoric of Political Persuasion." In *New Life for Old Ideas: Chinese Philosophy in the Contemporary World—Festschrift in Honor of Professor Donald J. Munro*, edited by Yanmin An and Brian Bruya, 225–252. Hong Kong: The Chinese University of Hong Kong Press.

Lo, Yuet Keung. 2020a. "He Yan's *Collected Explanations on the Analects*." In *Dao Companion to Xuanxue* 玄學 (*Neo-Daoism*), edited by David Chai, 185–207. Cham, Switzerland: Springer.

Lo, Yuet Keung. 2020b. "Lone Transformation and Intergrowth: Philosophy of Self-Justification in Guo Xiang's *Commentary on the Zhuangzi*." In *Dao Companion to Xuanxue* 玄學 (*Neo-Daoism*), edited by David Chai, 367–392. Cham, Switzerland: Springer.

Loewe, Michael. 1993. *Early Chinese Texts: A Bibliographical Guide*. Berkeley: Society for the Study of Early China and Institute of East Asian Studies.

Long, Yuchun 龍宇純. 1963. "Xianqin sanwen zhong de yunwen" 先秦散文中的韻文. *The Chung Chi Journal* 2 (2): 137–168, and 3 (1): 55–87.

Lou, Yulie 樓宇烈. 1980. *Wang Bi ji jiaoshi* 王弼集校釋. Beijing: Zhonghua shuju.

Lu, Yuanjun 盧元駿, and Chen Yiyu 陳貽鈺. 1988. *Shuoyuan jinzhu jinyi* 說苑今註今譯. Taibei: Taiwan shangwu yinshuguan.

Lynn, Richard John, tr. 1999. *The Classic of the Way and Virtue: A New Translation of the Tao-Te Ching of Laozi as Interpreted by Wang Bi*. New York: Columbia University Press.

Lundahl, Bertil. 1992. *Han Fei Zi: The Man and the Work*. Stockholm: Institute of Oriental Languages Stockholm University.

Major, John S., et al., tr. 2010. *The Huainanzi*. New York: Columbia University Press.

Makeham, John. 2004. *Transmitters and Creators: Chinese Commentators and Commentaries on the Analects*. Cambridge, MA: Harvard University Asia Center.

Miller, Harry, tr. 2015. *The Gongyang Commentary on The Spring and Autumn Annals: A Full Translation*. New York: Palgrave Macmillan.

Nivison, David. 1996. *The Ways of Confucianism: Investigations in Chinese Philosophy*, edited by Bryan W. Van Norden. Chicago: Open Court.

Nylan, Michael. 2001. *The Five "Confucian" Classics*. New Haven & London: Yale University Press.

Ōta, Hō 太田方. 2014 (1783). *Kanpishi yokuzei* 韓非子翼毳. Shanghai: Zhongxi shuju.

Pines, Yuri. 2013. "Submerged by Absolute Power: The Ruler's Predicament in the *Han Feizi*." In *Dao Companion to the Philosophy of Han Fei*, edited by Paul R. Goldin, 67–86. Dordrecht: Springer.

Pines, Yuri, tr. 2017. *The Book of Lord Shang: Apologetics of State Power in Early China*. New York: Columbia University Press.

Queen, Sarah A. 2010. "Responses of the Way." In *The Huainanzi: A Guide to the Theory and Practice of Government in Early Han China*, edited and translated by John S. Major et al., 429–482. New York: Columbia University Press.

Queen, Sarah A. 2013. "Han Feizi and the Old Master: A Comparative Analysis and Translation of *Han Feizi* Chapter 20, 'Jie Lao,' and Chapter 21, 'Yu Lao.'" In *Dao Companion to the Philosophy of Han Fei*, edited by Paul R. Goldin, 197–256. Dordrecht: Springer.

Reeve, Michael Andrew Hall. 2003. "Demonstrating the World: Mind and Society in the Shuo Lin Chapters of the *Han Fei Zi*," PhD diss., Princeton University.

Reid, Dan G., tr. 2019. *The Thread of Dao: Unraveling Early Daoist Oral Tradition in Guan Zi's Purifying the Heart-Mind (Bai Xin), Art of the Heart-Mind (Xin Shu) and Internal Cultivation (Nei Ye).* Montreal: Center Ring Publications.

Rickett, W. Allyn, tr. 1985. *Guanzi: Political, Economic, and Philosophical Essays from Early China*, vol. 1. Princeton: Princeton University Press.

Rickett, W. Allyn. 1993. "Kuan tzu 管子." In *Early Chinese Texts: A Bibliographical Guide*, edited by Michael Loewe, 244–251. Berkeley: Society for the Study of Early China and Institute of East Asian Studies.

Rickett, W. Allyn, tr. 1998. *Guanzi: Political, Economic, and Philosophical Essays from Early China*, vol. 2. Princeton: Princeton University Press.

Rong, Zhaozu 容肇祖. 1972. *Han Feizi kaozheng* 韓非子考證. Taibei: Tailian guofeng chubanshe.

Roth, Harold. 2004. *Original Tao.* New York: Columbia University Press.

Sarkissian, Hagop. 2001. "*Laozi*: Re-visiting Two Early Commentaries in the *Han Feizi*." MA thesis, University of Toronto.

Sato, Masayuki. 2013. "Did Xunzi's Theory of Human Nature Provide the Foundation for the Political Thought of Han Fei?" In *Dao Companion to the Philosophy of Han Fei*, edited by Paul R. Goldin, 147–165. Dordrecht: Springer.

Shao, Zenghua 邵增樺. 1990. *Hanfeizi jinzhu jinyi* 韓非子今註今譯. Taibei: Taiwan shangwu yinshuguan.

Slingerland, Edward, tr. 2003a. *Confucius: Analects.* Indianapolis: Hackett Publishing.

Slingerland, Edward. 2003b. *Effortless Action: Wu-Wei as Conceptual Metaphor and Spiritual Ideal in Early China.* Oxford: Oxford University Press.

Tadd, Misha (邰谧侠 Tai Mixia). 2022. *Laozi yiben zongmu: quanqiu Laoxue yaolan* 《老子》译本总目：全球老学要览. Tianjin: Nankai daxue chubanshe.

Van Auken, Newell Ann. 2016. *The Commentarial Transformation of the Spring and Autumn.* Albany: SUNY Press.

Van Norden, Bryan, tr. 2008. *Mengzi: With Selections from Traditional Commentaries.* Indianapolis: Hackett Publishing.

Wagner, Rudolf. 1989. "The Wang Bi Recension of the *Laozi*." *Early China* 14: 27–54.

Waley, Arthur, tr. 1963. *The Way and Its Power.* New York: Grove Press.

Wang, Bo 王博. 2001. *Jianbo sixiang: chutu sixiang wenwu yu wenxian yanjiu congshu* 簡帛思想：出土思想文物與文獻研究叢書. Taibei: Taiwan guji.

Wang, Deyou 王德有. 2004. *Laozi zhigui yizhu* 老子指归译注. Beijing: Shangwu yinshuguan.

Wang, Hsiao-Po, and Leo S. Chang. 1986. *The Philosophical Foundations of Han Fei's Political Theory.* Honolulu: University of Hawaii Press.

Wang, Xianqian 王先謙. 1988 (1891). *Xunzi jijie* 荀子集解. Beijing: Zhonghua shuju.

Watson, Burton, tr. 2003. *Han Feizi: Basic Writings.* New York: Columbia University Press.

Watson, Burton, tr. 2013. *The Complete Works of Zhuangzi.* New York: Columbia University Press.

Wu, Yujiang 吳毓江. 2006. *Mozi jiaozhu* 墨子校注. Beijing: Zhonghua shuju.

Zhang, Jue 張覺. 1996. *Hanfeizi shiyi* 韓非子釋譯. Taibei: Taiwan guji.

Zhang, Jue 張覺. 2010. *Hanfeizi jiaoshu* 韓非子校疏. Shanghai: Shanghai guji chubanshe.

Zhao, Haijin 趙海金. 1967. *Han Feizi yanjiu* 韓非子研究. Taibei: Zhengzhong shuju.

Zheng, Chenghai 鄭成海. 1971. *Laozi Heshang Gong zhu jiaoli* 老子河上公注斠理. Taipei: Zhonghua shuju.

Zheng, Liangshu 鄭良樹. 1993. *Han Fei zhi zhushu ji sixiang* 韓非之著述及思想. Taibei: Taiwan xuesheng shuju.

Index

Due to indexing requirements for some digital versions, indexed terms that span multiple pages (e.g., 52–53) may, on occasion, appear on only one of those pages.